TOWNIES

Also by William O'Shaughnessy

AIRWAVES
A Collection of Radio Editorials from the Golden Apple

IT ALL COMES BACK TO ME NOW
Character Portraits from the Golden Apple

MORE RIFFS, RANTS, AND RAVES

VOX POPULI
The O'Shaughnessy Files

MARIO CUOMO
Remembrances of a Remarkable Man

RADIO ACTIVE

With Steve Warley and Joseph Reilly
SERVING THEIR COMMUNITIES
A History of the New York State Broadcasters Association

TOWNIES

William O'Shaughnessy

2023

WHITNEY GLOBAL MEDIA PUBLISHING GROUP

New Rochelle, New York

DEDICATION

Our father, William O'Shaughnessy, passed away in May at his home in Litchfield, Connecticut, just as this book was going to press.

The dedication was not yet written.

We would like to dedicate this to our father, who was himself one of the greatest "Townies" of all time.

Born in upstate New York and raised on the grounds of the Bedford Hills Correctional Facility for Women, he worked his way up from a golf caddy for the Westchester elite to an account executive at WVIP in Mount Kisco to chairman of Whitney Global Media.

On-air and at the podium, our dashing and debonair father interviewed, celebrated, and eulogized governors, famous writers and athletes, movie stars, designers, industrialists, presidents, cardinals, and even popes.

As much as he relished his place at the center of this "Who's Who" milieu, he also cherished the Townies, those whom he described as angels without high estate, standing, stature, or national reputation ... those who shared a passion for the wards, districts, old neighborhoods, and communities that define and enrich Westchester.

To be knighted a Townie meant you were worthy of membership in a special corps of the caring and courageous. It was a sign of respect. Our father reserved the bespoke appellations he handed out like blessings to those who were majestic in his eyes.

He loved Westchester with all its characters and cultures. He broke bread with priests, sanitation workers, cops, city councilmen, tailors, firefighters, teachers .... He loved underdogs and devoted his life to giving them a voice on the air at his beloved stations. The Townies were his "village people," magnificent and essential.

It is our hope that his legacy of generosity of spirit will live on in the communities that he worked so hard to support.

We miss our favorite Townie dearly.

Matthew, David, and Kate

CONTENTS

MASTERS OF MEDIA AND THE ARTS

CONTENTS

PREFACE

As a broadcaster I've been privileged to enjoy the podium and forums provided by WVOX and WVIP for more than five decades. And
over those many years we've written and broadcast of cardinals, governors, famous writers, disc jockeys, cabinet secretaries, athletes,
judges, movie stars, designers, industrialists, presidents, network
mandarins, and even popes.

In our seven previous books and in thousands of broadcasts, we've
thus chronicled our encounters with such luminous and historic
figures as Henry Kissinger, Rush Limbaugh, Mario Cuomo, Nel-
son Rockefeller, George H.W. and George W. Bush, Jacob K. Javits,
Fred Astaire, Daniel Patrick Moynihan, John V. Lindsay, Howard
Stern, Ossie Davis, Ruby Dee, Kitty Carlisle Hart, Nita Lowey, Don
Rickles, Malcolm Wilson, Pelé, Dan Rather, Mark Simone, Cardinal
John O'Connor, Cardinal Timothy Dolan, Toots Shor, Chris Ruddy,
Sirio Maccioni, Andrea Bocelli, Robert Merrill, Jimmy Cannon, Joe
DiMaggio, Bobby Short, John Sterling, Neal Travis, Leonard Rig-
gio, Cindy Adams, Matilda Cuomo, Jock Whitney, Walter N. Thayer,
Mel Allen, Shipwreck Kelly, Ogden Reid, Billy Bush, Jonathan Bush,
President Richard Nixon, President John F. Kennedy, Robert F. Ken-
nedy, John F. Kennedy Jr., President Gerald Ford, Governors Andrew
Cuomo and Hugh Carey, President Donald J. Trump, Chris Cuomo,
William B. Williams, Jimmy Breslin, Mary Lou Whitney, Gay Talese,
Pete Hamill, Philip Roth, and Pope Francis.

But *this* book is a long overdue and unabashed paean of acclama-
tion and admiration for those *without* high estate, standing, stature,
or national reputation. Those who were sidemen in orchestras long
dispersed.

We've also occasionally written in our previous seven volumes of
the obscure, the forgotten, and the unheralded who were important
only on their own block, in the 'hood.

A SPOTLIGHT ON "THOSE PEOPLE"

Many were legends of that old Westchester neighborhood. But not one was ever found worthy of an obit in our beloved *New York Times*. All were minor poets who lived their lives obscurely in that minor key and were beloved only of their own and their neighbors.

Each, to be sure, was an uncommonly unique character who painted color into the drab and dull lives of our neighbors in the Golden Apple. They were lifelong residents of our home heath, people with solid, unyielding roots in a community surrounded by wealth and affluence.

"Townie" is not at all a pejorative term from me. I view it as a majestic appellation and a mark of great respect. Our focus, then, in this volume is on those who cling with a fierceness to their own comfort zone and are altogether glorious but unsung, unheralded souls who exist cheek-by-jowl with the privileged in the heart of the Eastern Establishment. Mind you, we're not talking here about the "folks who live on the hill" or the landed gentry and swells of Bronxville, Bedford, Rye, Scarsdale, North Salem, Pound Ridge, or Waccabuc.

Townies exist in a world of backyard barbecues, Little League games, carnivals, parades, public parks and overcrowded swimming pools, bowling alleys, church socials, festivals, Walmart, beer kegs, the American Legion, the Lions, the Rotary, the Elks Club, the VFW, Casa Calabria, the Foresters Club, the Moose, pizza, sandlot baseball, flag football, parish priests, CYO basketball, dollar discount stores, and Italian civic dinners where the entrée does not appear until midnight and always ends with the rolling out of a grand Venetian table heavily laden with sweets and savories.

The High Holy Days in the Christian ecclesiastical calendar are accompanied by grand religious processions with statues and totems of the saint reverently borne aloft through the streets.

The Liberty Lines bus driver is their chauffeur. They are the glue, really, the underpinning and mortar, that holds our world of privilege and advantage together. They may seem like *diminuendo* and *decrescendo* in the musical world. But I've found greatness in each of them. Mario Cuomo called them "undiscovered neighborhood gems" who live out their lives with a lovely sureness in quiet anonymity.

Having been deprived by fate and circumstance of the means or wherewithal to accommodate that biblical admonition to flee to another town should they be hounded and pursued by the hard, mean, unforgiving streets of their birth, they *stay*. They stay.

Orchard Beach, Hudson Park, Jones Beach, and Coney Island are their Hamptons, San Tropez, Palm Beach, and Monte Carlo. They think ever fondly of Glen Island Casino when Angelo Badolato ran it, and they miss Freedomland just over the line in the Bronx. The Poconos and Catskills are their Sun Valley and Aspen. But they don't look forward to winter or the ski slopes. Summer is their season. Disney World is their Riviera. And most of them suffer with the hapless Mets. And the soccer pitch is not exactly where the Townies find greatness either. Sadly, they had no exposure to the magnificence of Edson Arantes do Nascimento, a.k.a. Pelé. Nor did they thrill to the artistry of Franz Beckenbauer, Giorgio Chinaglia, or Johan Cruyft gracefully dancing across the soccer pitch toward a thrilling *goal!* when they played in those Meadowlands exhibition games for the New York Cosmos.

Instead, they are drawn Sunday afternoons to the gridiron where their all-time favorite New York Giants were Andy Robustelli, Sam Huff, Joe Morrison, Charlie Conerly, Y. A. Tittle, Kyle Rote, and, of course, Frank Gifford. And the late Wellington Mara, the beloved patriarch of the Giants, is close to sainthood in these precincts. As for the hapless Jets: Most feel they should have just rung down the curtain after the great Joe Willie Namath hung up his cleats.

THE LANDED GENTRY THAT NEVER LANDED

On many kitchen walls a yellowing, faded likeness of John Fitzgerald Kennedy still appears. And, in recent years, on the peg above the coatrack is proudly placed a red "Make America Great Again" hat.

A few have tucked away in a drawer a Kennedy *PT-109* tie bar they used to clip on stained and spotted ties too short to cover their expanding waistlines. Many are hunters of deer, squirrels, and birds of the air. And the opening of hunting season is like a national holiday. On this grand occasion they scheme to visit long-lost friends upstate and when ordering in restaurants north of Poughkeepsie they need only to select "chicken parm" *or* "veal parm" ... and salad of "sprinkled bleu" *or* "plain." Bud is their drink of choice. Or Coors Light. Craft beers are for the millennials, youngsters, or "sensitive" types.

Many of their wedding receptions, otherwise spectacular, feature a cash bar ... and a $5 bill tucked discreetly in a spangled purse gets you a two-minute spin-around with the bride. And their mating rites and actual nuptials are usually accompanied by a loud guy yelling, "Put your hands together!" And not only the bridesmaids but the groomsmen too are beautifully attired in powder-blue tuxedos.

Every last one of them can tell you for certain that Sinatra's formal name is Francis Albert. But Jerry Vale, Jimmy Roselli, Neil Diamond, Barry Manilow, and Frankie Valli are their favorite singers. And Mario Puzo's *Godfather* is their favorite movie and anything with Bruce Willis or Clint Eastwood. And Dirty Harry and Tony Montana are their favorite fictional characters in the movies.

For matters of Salvation, many give a wide berth to the brainy Jesuits and opt instead for "Three Hail Mary's for a homicide," which is usually the gentle levy imposed by compassionate Franciscans.

In this predilection they actually align with a somewhat well-known Argentinian priest, a Jesuit named Jorge Bergoglio who, when he needed a name that would stand the test of time and endure down through the ecclesiastical ages, chose to be called "Francis," thus naming his entire papacy for the crazy saint who conversed with animals and the birds of the air and whispered to the wind, the sun, and even fire.

THE HEART OF THE EASTERN ESTABLISHMENT

We've written often of the famous and those of high estate covered by our radio stations in New York state and many other influential venues all over the world. Time now to give the "Townies" their due via the commentaries and radio portraits we've collected over fifty years in Westchester a.k.a. "The Golden Apple." So we went back to our archives and previous volumes for profiles of those "neighborhood gems" Mario Cuomo spoke so admiringly of. Most of them were not at all famous, but each in their own way quite unforgettable.

Here, then, are some of those glorious but unsung Townies who operated out of the glare of the public spotlight and whose lives we celebrate: ... Bill Scollon ... Alvin R. Ruskin ... Anthony Colavita ...

Arthur Geoghegan ... Teddy Greene ... Charles Valenti ... Fred Pow-
ers ... Anthony Gioffre ... Bill Luddy ... Joe Vacarella ... Alex Norton
... Nancy Q. Keefe ... Vincent Bellew ... Bert Williams ... Marty Servo
... Tony Tocci ... Joe Jackson ... Jimmy Lennon ... Napoleon Holmes
... Evie Haas ... Jenny Murdy ... J. Raymond McGovern ... Howard
DeMarco ... Rocco Bellantoni ... John Brophy ... Bob McGrath ...
Murray Fuerst ... Judge Richard Daronco ... Mario Migliucci ...
Mama Rose Migliucci ... Bob Cammann ... Judge Irving Kendall
... Edward J. Hughes ... Hugh Doyle ... Joe Candrea ... Andrew P.
O'Rourke ... Michael J. Armiento ... Bob Abplanalp ... Bill Plunkett
... Jeanine Pirro ... Phil Reisman ... Ernie Davis ... M. Paul Redd
... Monsignor Terry Attridge ... Rabbi Amiel Wohl ... Monsignor Ed
Connors ... Brother John Driscoll ... E. Virgil Conway ... Al Pirro
Jr.... Emil Paolucci ... Cindy Hall Gallagher ... Angelo Badolato ...
Marvin Goldfluss ... Charlie and Artie Librett ... Bob, David, and
Israel Streger ... Monsignor Anthony Wallace ... George Delaney ...
George Latimer ... Judge Daniel Angiolillo ... John Spicer ... Andy
Spano ... Marty Rochelle ... Bruce "The Swimmer" Merbaum ... Ken
Bialo ... Valerie Moore O'Keefe ... Augie Petrillo ... Edwin G. Mi-
chaelian ... Randall Toliver ... Ralph R. Martinelli ... Dick Gidron ...
Joe Pisani ... Dr. Richard Rocco Pisano ... Andy Albanese ... Preston
"Sandy" Scher ... Milt Hoffman ... Michael Curry Pasquale ... Father
John O'Brien ... John Branca ... Ben Mermelstein ... Irv Kendall
... Angelo Martinelli ... Elaine Unshuldt ... Samuel G. Fredman ...
Patrick J. Carroll ... I. Philip Sipser ... Paul Hutton ... Peter Mustich
... Ines Candrea ... Diane Gagliardi Collins ... Sal Generoso ... Caryl
Donnelly Plunkett ... Joe "Slick" Vitulli ... John Scully ... Alessandra
Biaggi ... Adam Bradley ... Dennis Nardone and Tony Guido ... Steve
Tenore ... Burt Cooper.

And we're also including a few spectacular individuals who, although recognized on the national scene, also repaired quite regularly to the comfort and keeping of our old neighborhood. They remind me of the wonderful description of a *true* Connecticut Yankee
as "one who always takes the midnight train home from Hartford."
So although they enjoyed a national and, in many cases, an international reputation, these Townies never lost the local connection.
In this category, we have to include the incomparable Nelson Rock-

efeller ... Ossie Davis ... Ogden Reid ... Ruby Dee ... Hugh Price ... Louis Boccardi ... John S. Pritchard ... Whitney Moore Young ... Mario Biaggi ... and Page Morton Black. We've reported on and written of them all.

They were like the appellation attached to Mario Cuomo by the great writer Gay Talese, who identified him as being descended from "village people" who liked to sleep in their own beds.

Sui generis is the word.

Unique and surely able to be defined only in their own terms.

Townies. That is what they are. All of them.

"THOSE PEOPLE" TODAY

The old neighborhood a.k.a. "The Fourth Ward" and often referred to as "The West End" of New Rochelle is changing. The Irish and Italians of which we write with affection and great respect now live cheek-by-jowl in cautious compact with Hispanics from Mexico, Guatemala, and Puerto Rico. And they communicate in a somewhat graceful parlando. These brown-skinned neighbors are referred to in certain other parts of Westchester as "those people."

Here is what "those people" do just to earn a living. They cook our meals, set our tables, wash our dishes, scrub our floors, haul away our trash and garbage, weed our gardens, plant our flowers, cut our grass in the spring, rake our leaves in the fall, shovel our sidewalks and plow our driveways in the winter, iron our shirts, wash our laundry, clean our toilets, style our hair, cut our toenails and buff our fingernails, babysit and pick up after our kids (and our pets), walk our dogs, fumigate our houses, tote our bales, shine our shoes, sell us lottery tickets, drive our school buses, sow and harvest our fields, grow our vegetables, muck our stalls, cobble our shoes, tend our vineyards, sweep our streets, paint our fences, pick up our litter, gas up and wash and fix our cars, repair our roofs, shoe our horses, carry our heavy leather golf bags across hot Westchester fairways, manicure the greens at our fancy country clubs, haul boats at our yacht clubs, hoist our banners and club burgees, move our furniture, play in our orchestras, mend our clothes, sew our buttons, empty our bedpans, push our wheelchairs, dig our graves, flip our pizzas, butter and schmear our bagels, stir our cocktails and pour our drinks, make our beds, park our cars, stack our plates, bus our tables ....

In addition to the above-mentioned "services" that they daily provide, "those people" also enrich our culture and the lives of our beloved Townies ... as well as the hilltoppers and landed gentry.

All of which brings a stunning flash of *déjà vu*.

Because we've been there. And done that ... when it was the Irish and Italians who attended to all these most necessary things.

It was not ... too ... long ... ago.

ACKNOWLEDGMENTS

This book, which has been some years in the making, owes much to many. Preeminent among them is Fred Nachbaur, the brilliant and distinguished publisher of Fordham, the great Jesuit university press in the City of New York. Fred and his legendary amanuensis Margaret Noonan conferred their blessing and imprimatur on the book from the very beginning, when we set out to do a tribute to those out of the spotlight who exist and enrich the lives of those of influence and high standing in the very heart of the Eastern Establishment.

I'm also immensely grateful to the heroic Cindy Hall Gallagher for her inspiration as we worked together on my eighth book. We also had exquisite and strategic help from Douglas Clement, a real Man of Letters who distributed his unique genius on every page.

We've also benefited from the constant assistance and dedication of my beloved compadre Gregorio Alvarez, who kept us on track and focused.

As my many friends are aware, we've encountered some health issues along the way. But I'm so fortunate I was able to confront them with the love and support of some wonderful folks to whom we dedicate *Townies*.

I'm grateful to every one. Especially my children Kate Wharton Nulty and David Tucker O'Shaughnessy and my friend Gregorio Alvarez.

Holy Mother Mary
Dr. Omar Al Assad
Michael Assaf, Esq.
Dr. and Mrs. Alphonse Altorelli
Briana Alvarez
Edward Alvarez
Erickson Alvarez
Gregorio Alvarez
Miosotis Alvarez
Judge Jeffrey and Karen Bernbach

ACKNOWLEDGMENTS

Jimmy Breslin
Michael Carnevale, OFM
Joseph Cavoto, OFM
Maggie Cervantes
Douglas P. Clement
Brian Cobb
Maria Cuomo Cole
Catherine Wilson Conroy
Governor Andrew Cuomo
Matilda Raffa Cuomo
Mario Matthew Cuomo
Timothy Cardinal Dolan
Bruno Dussin
Kevin Scott Elliott
Richard Ambrose Foreman
Pope Francis
Judy Fremont
Cindy Hall Gallagher
Rich Hendel
Scott Herman
Jacob K. Javits
John Kelly
Laura O'Shaughnessy Kowalski
Ralph Kragle
Clare Lawrence
Franco Lazzari
Mark Lerner
Rush Hudson Limbaugh III
Richard Littlejohn
Philip Lombardo
Sirio Maccioni
Archbishop Henry Mansell
Dan Mason
Tim McCarthy
Dr. James McKiernan
Renate and Thomas McKnight

ACKNOWLEDGMENTS

Col. Stavros Mellekas
Joseph Migliucci
Daniel Patrick Moynihan
Fred Nachbaur
Margaret Noonan
Amelia Jane Nulty
Flynn Thayer Nulty
Kate Wharton O'Shaughnessy Nulty
Tucker Thomas Nulty
Kate O'Brien-Nicholson
James O'Shea
Cathy and Greg Oneglia
Ellen and Ray Oneglia
Cara Ferrin O'Shaughnessy
David Tucker O'Shaughnessy
Isabel Grace O'Shaughnessy
Johnny O'Shaughnessy
Julie O'Shaughnessy
Lily Anna O'Shaughnessy
Matthew Thayer O'Shaughnessy
Dr. and Mrs. Richard Rocco Pisano
Ogden Rogers Reid
Joe Reilly
Elva Amparo Augustina Reynoso
Leonard Riggio
Maria and Constable Peter Russo
Jerry Speyer
Don Stevens
Capt. Rob Taishoff
Jim Thompson
Ann Thayer
Monsignor Robert Tucker
Chad Wackerman
Don West
Teno West

TOWNIES

The Political Power Brokers

Robert Abplanalp

Interview with William O'Shaughnessy

RA: On grandchildren: "They're delightful ... but it's always nice to see them go home. I have one—eighteen months—who moves like lightning. If you have him for about a day, you've really had a day's exercise."

On airplanes: "These days flying doesn't bother me as much as it used to when I was a white-knuckled flyer. I prefer flying some of my own planes. But, when I have to do it, I'll fly commercial. I've really decided the engineering of those jets is OK and that I'm not running much of a risk getting on one of them."

On his Catholic faith: "I don't think anybody could classify me as a religious fanatic. But I go to church. I went to Catholic schools. I support the Church. The Church is having some tough times ... but I don't know of any entity around the world that supports the Ten Commandments that isn't having a tough time. Because there seems to be so much 'semantic' interpretation of what Moses brought down from the mountain. A given word can have six different meanings these days. I think biblical interpretation is not as rigid or as traditional as I would like it. But every religion today is having its problems ... Muslim, Jewish, Protestant. There just seems to be a lot of liberalization of what we were all taught. When I went to school I was taught there were only 87 elements in the chemical tables and there would never be any more. This was out of the mouths of all the scientific professors ... the great minds of the era. Today there are 140 or some other ridiculous number! I think it goes back to the original Ten Commandments. Listen, let's get off this. I don't want to preach. I don't have a damn collar."

WO: "But do you think God has a plan for you? You're a multi-millionaire. You've got your own plane. You've got 5,000 employees. You own your own island ...."

RA: "I'm aware of that ... all the success I've had in business. I started in 1941. And I'm convinced there is just no substitute for dumb luck. If you discount that in the framework of business, you're just plain stupid ... because more things have happened to me because of luck ...."

WO: "You have been accused by my colleagues in the public press of being the best friend of a president — Richard Nixon. You miss him?"

RA: "I'll put it to you this way. I really have not been able to look at the tapes of the funeral. Not that I wouldn't like to see how I looked on the camera. I ... miss him. I recently returned from San Clemente with my family and the Nixon family. It was a little com-memoration. It's been a year ... and I don't know if it's common knowledge ... but one of the last appearances President Nixon made was at my daughter's wedding at Westchester Country Club. The wedding was on Saturday ... he called me Sunday morning to tell me what a great time he had at the wedding. On Monday afternoon he had the stroke. I ... was in the hospital every night. Bebe Rebozzo flew up from Florida ...."

WO: "Is there really a Bebe Rebozo?"

RA: "Oh, there's really a Bebe Rebozo ... he's a great guy. I mean one of the lasting things ... sort of a legacy ... President Nixon introduced me to Rebozo. And, along with my friendship with the president, that also began a relationship with Bebe Rebozo that I prize very highly. The night the president died we left the hospital two hours before he died thinking, 'Gee, he looks great. And we'll go back tomorrow to see how he is.' But at ten o'clock that night he died ...."

WO: "You're a tough guy ... was it difficult for you that you were un-able to save Nixon?"

RA: "Well, I had the realization ... I thought the doctors were crazy. His respiration was normal. The stroke had been five days before that. My own judgment of it was he looked a lot better than he did on Tuesday night. There was frustration ... I'm a good mechanic ... but there was nothing I could do about this. I'm not a miracle worker ...."

WO: "How will history treat your friend?"

RA: "Well, a strange thing ... I never really paid much attention to his books while he was alive. He sent me autographed editions every time. I've started reading them. Particularly his memoirs. I think they'll become classics ... textbooks. He will have a unique place in the history books .... The brilliance, I mean, did not ordinarily come through in a day-to-day conversation. But as I read more and more of his books ... the man was absolutely incomparable. And I highly recommend them ... I mean, I'm not selling his books ...."

WO: "What about the Nixon haters ... the dark side of your friend. Was there a dark side to him?"

RA: Not that I ever saw. There were a lot of Nixon haters. I never saw any signs in him of reciprocation of that hatred. He felt ... that people were entitled to their opinions. I never really saw anything in Nixon that aroused a reciprocal hatred. His mother was a big influence in his life ... and his father too. He came from nothing very extraordinary. They were far from wealthy. His father ran a grocery store. He worked to get himself through college. I think his parents' patience and tolerance had a great influence on his life. You know the Quaker attitude was not to hate. You turn the other cheek ...."

WO: "Is that hard for a tough guy like Bob Abplanalp?"

RA: "Well ... uh ... yeah ... from time to time, I've found it difficult. I would read things in the newspaper that I knew were absolute lies ... uh ... but Nixon's reactions were calm. I don't know if this is generally known ... but on the day he resigned, he went back to California on *Air Force One* and he was over the Mississippi River. It was about noontime and he called me to get Rebozo on the phone and meet him in San Clemente that night for dinner. I was in my office in Yonkers ... but we managed to do it. I met Rebozo in Dallas and we got to Los Angeles in time for dinner."

WO: "Was he a beaten man at that supper?"

RA: "No ... the surprising part was ... we had a drink before dinner ... uh ... well, he said: 'It's over, Bob, the presidency is over ....' And then he just went on and increased his writing and traveled a great deal. It's amazing that he was respected all over the world. I traveled with him in Russia and France and other places. He consulted with heads of state. I had the pleasure of meeting Yeltsin ... which was kind of a thrill. I remember Nixon running up the steps

[5]

and me puffing along behind him. It was just a couple of years ago. He was a valued advisor to Yeltsin."

WO: "What did you three guys—Rebozo, Nixon, and Abplanalp—talk about of an evening?"

RA: "Well, President Nixon was a great sports enthusiast. We talked about baseball, football ...."

WO: "Girls ... ?"

RA: "To the best any of us could ever recollect? Today, if the president were here and you asked about girls, Rebozo would say, 'Well, we had a very strong interest in the female gender. But my problem is ... I can't remember why!'"

RA: On Nixon: "Of all the Americans I've ever known or read about ... he is the most outstanding man. I include George Washington, Abraham Lincoln, Franklin Roosevelt. All of these men, the thread they had in common was a bloody war. Nixon inherited—not a bloody war—but a conflict ... and did his level best to stop it. In the framework of the things he prevented from happening in the future ... such as the disasters of nuclear war ... his tactical position in containing the Russians. Unbelievable! Absolutely ... genius written all over it. I've discussed this thing with Henry Kissinger many, many times. Henry was not the architect. And while I think Henry was something more, a good bit more—than the messenger boy ... I think Henry had some genius in his own right. Once he got to know Nixon he was dedicated to doing what Nixon wanted done. I don't think that during Henry's Rockefeller days he may have had the same attitude. But I like him."

WO: "Was the story true about Nixon praying on his knees [with Kissinger]?"

RA: "I don't believe a word of it. I've never asked Henry. I can picture Nixon praying in private. I mean ... I never saw him pray. I knew the man.... I mean, if he got down on his knees ... he did it in the confines of his home ... not for observation. I'm sure he prayed."

WO: "You know the story ... he called in the secretary of state ... and said, 'Henry, let's ....'"

RA: "Yes, I know ... in the Lincoln Bedroom. Actually in the Lincoln Study. It's true that was one of his favorite rooms in the house ...."

WO: "Have you ever been in the Lincoln Bedroom?"

RA: "Yes ... I slept overnight."

WO: "Is it true you and Nixon and Rebozo were closer than you were to your wives?"

RA: "Well, I guarantee you there were things the president discussed with Pat Nixon that Rebozo and I never knew anything about. And there were things discussed between Josephine Abplanalp and me that they never knew anything about. Of course Rebozo only got married ten or twelve years ago ...!"

WO: "But you were close ...."

RA: "As close as any three friends involved in their lives. I regard President Nixon as a friend. I mean ... to think I grew up in the Bronx, New York. But to picture myself as the friend of the president of the United States ...."

WO: "Tell me a Nixon story you never told anyone ...."

RA: "One day when he was vice president we were down at Walker's Cay, my place in the Bahamas. Nixon, Rebozo, and I were sitting around after dinner when the vice president requests a cigar. But the steward informs us that we were out of the kind Nixon favored. So we up and went down to the dock and took out a Boston Whaler to run across the channel to the next island where they had a general store that doubled as a restaurant. They also had cigars. And brandy. As we were about to cast off ... Leonard Garment, Nixon's counsel, came running down from his cottage to protest that the vice president was setting sail with only me and Rebozo. Nixon dismissed him with 'Go back to your briefing papers, Leonard ... we'll be fine ... we've got a flashlight and Bob knows the waters.' Garment was so upset he threatened to wake up the vice president's Secret Service agent, who had turned in early. In those days, the veep only had one or two agents. Today [Al] Gore has about 200! Anyway, by flashlight and a little moonlight we struck out into the channel. And as we crossed, the lights went on in the little village. So we sat until the wee, small hours enjoying our brandy and cigars. Now ... what no one knows ... it was the exact day the Bahamas declared independence! You can look it up! And to this day ... there are people on that remote, far-flung little island who still think the U.S. government sent the vice president of the United States to help them celebrate their independence.

In a Boston Whaler ... with two questionable shipmates! It's an absolutely true story!"

WO: "Some say the best friend ...."

RA: "Well, I have a lot of longtime friends ...."

WO: "What do you think he saw in you?"

RA: "Well, I think he saw a friend who had experience that was totally different from his. I never got involved in politics. He saw a successful blacksmith ... somebody who knew how to pound iron ... knew how to work with metalworking tools and equipment. He saw somebody who was in a field totally removed from his sphere of activity. Shortly after the election in 1968 ... I don't know whether this is public knowledge or not ... but the first place he went to on foreign soil as president-elect was he came down to Walker's Cay to see me. And while he was there he got into a discussion of what he wanted in terms of cabinet selection. He began describing the secretary of defense as 'a young man ... about forty-four to forty-eight ... somebody with broad-based industrial experience.' Well, I was forty-six at the time and had twenty-five years of 'broad-based industrial experience.' I began to get the creepy feeling that he was talking about me ...."

WO: "'Secretary of Defense Abplanalp' has a nice ring ...."

RA: "Well, it constituted a lot of other things. Number one, the company that I had built ... I would have had to get rid of it, divest myself ...."

WO: "So as Nixon went on with this ...?"

RA: "I broke into the discussion and said I think that would be a horrible mistake ... because if you're going to pull some young hotshot from the industrial world with no military background (I got out of the Army as a corporal! That gives me some distinction with two other very famous characters. One was Napoleon. And the other was Hitler!) .... My point was you're going to place this guy in a position where he's dealing with all the admirals and generals in the Pentagon who will be ten or fifteen years older than he is ...."

WO: "Did you think you could pull it off?"

RA: "Well, it wasn't a question of whether I could pull it off. Yeah ... I could have pulled it off. My point was the guy was going to have a terrible row to hoe. On the other hand, when it comes to negotiating with the Appropriations Committee in Congress, you're going to have aging senators and congressmen who all resent the youth of a guy like me. You know what he did? He appointed Melvin Laird as secretary of defense. And he got [David] Packard as assistant secretary ... which covered all the bases."

WO: "Why don't you write books?"

RA: "Well ... it's ... uh ... been suggested many times. I'm a busy man. I still go to work every day."

WO: "What do you want them to refer to you as? Friend of the president. Sportsman? Philanthropist? Industrialist? What do you want on the stone?"

RA: "Well, I hope they could just say he was a nice guy ... You know the rest of it is going to be history. As far as the history books ... I don't have to worry about it. I got 150 patents with my name in the Patent Office. That's history! Over the 45 years that I've been in this business, I have developed and filed 150 patents. You know I'm a damn good mechanic. You start as a blacksmith and you hammer iron. I was on the right street corner. I had some knowledge ...."

WO: "What of your country? They're blowing up buildings now ... it's getting bad."

RA: "I don't have any constructive ideas .... I don't know what you can do to correct the moral degradation."

WO: "You are chairman of Precision Valve. They've accused you of being the man who destroyed the ozone layer ...."

RA: "I have to tell you the element used in that aerosol manufacture has not been used for twenty years. It's referred to as CFC. At this stage it's old news that might have been true years ago. Today it's safe to use aerosol cans. You're not going to destroy the life-supporting ozone layer."

WO: "Was there ever anything to all that?"

RA: "Well, on the theory of Chicken Little, bad news travels fast. Good news is seldom ever noticed. I think Madison Avenue overblew the aspects of the ozone theory. It was sensational and so if you want to attract readers and viewers, you don't tell them the dull things that go on every day."

WO: "Do you still go to your island in the Bahamas?"

RA: "Oh yes, Walker's Cay is thriving ... with a program of deep sea fishing, scuba diving, fly fishing ....

"On fishing: I have a theory about fishing. My theory is kids who go fishing don't get into trouble. Studies have shown that most of the federal prisoners wouldn't be where they are today if they'd fished. The biggest fish I caught was a blue marlin that weighed 600 pounds. But I was like a piece of bacon when I bought it in. The percentage of prisoners who fished is so far below the normal exposure. We also have Eldred Preserve, 3,000 acres, here in upstate. Eldred is mostly to encourage young people to fish. You see a lot of fathers and sons. If you bring your kid up ... you get a fish!"

WO: "Whom do you favor among today's Republican wannabes?"

RA: "I have a strong liking for Dole. I know him ... I think he's a strong character."

WO: "Are you backing him for president ... ?"

RA: "I'm not really backing anybody ...."

WO: "Have you lost your taste for it?"

RA: "I wouldn't say that. I got involved with Nixon because I'm a Catholic and I kind of resented the way Jack Kennedy postured himself as sort of a third-generation Al Smith who was not going to make it because he was Catholic. I belong to one of the smallest minorities on Earth. I'm a Swiss Catholic!"

WO: "Mr. Chairman ... Citizen Abplanalp ... what about the current president, Bill Clinton?"

RA: "I marvel at the foibles of the American system to try to figure out how a man who got less popular votes than Mr. Dukakis could be elected president of the United States. The popular vote for Clinton was smaller! He doesn't appeal to me. It's nothing personal .... I have some problems with a Vietnam War protester who suddenly appears at all the battlefield sites in Europe. I wonder how does he suddenly adjust himself. Here is a guy who protested the draft bitterly. How does he make the switch to commander-in-chief?"

WO: "What about Governor Pataki?"

RA: "Again, I don't know about the breadth of his experience. But I think his intentions are in the framework of what his mandate is: less government. I think he's trying to do something. And I'm for it."

Andy Albanese

"AN ICON PROPERLY RESTORED"

(with a little help from four governors!)

Remarks of William O'Shaughnessy
Italian-American Citizen Club Dinner-Dance
Alex & Henry's
Eastchester, New York
October 13, 1995

County Executive O'Rourke; Assemblywoman Hochberg; Supervisor Cavanaugh; Legislator Delfino; Commissioner Ray Albanese; Supervisor Doody; Council members Ford, Pinto, and Vaccaro; Judge Porco; President John, and President Tony. And Anthony J. Colavita Jr., who is his father's son. Also my pal Dave DiRubba ....

This is a very strong Republican group. And so I won't remind anyone of the night in 1982 when I came home from Andy's restaurant with a pizza and a check for a thousand dollars for Mario Cuomo's campaign! (*laughter*)

Ladies and gentlemen ... that you would allow an O'Shaughnessy to present himself on the occasion of your Columbus Day dinner-dance speaks volumes as to your legendary forbearance, understanding, and generosity. I won't take advantage of the privilege by intruding for very long on your evening.

I come for a friend. An old and valued friend of many years. You have left your hearth and home on this perfectly splendid Indian Summer night in Westchester to honor one of your own.

It is fitting that you have appropriated this brilliant day to pay tribute to Andy Albanese. For he is a child of your neighborhood. He is of you and yours. It is more than appropriate that we are here. Some would say it is a miracle, Andy! (*laughter*)

I can tell you nothing you don't already know of him. A Supreme Court judge—Alvin Richard Ruskin—once told me that as a youngster in this fabled town, there were none poorer, but none richer, I suppose, in terms of dedication, fortitude, devotion to this town, to this community . . . and to the Board of Legislators he once served as chairman.

Today the Albanese family is synonymous with this town whence came Francis X. O'Rourke, Tony Colavita, Nick Colabella, and Vincent Bellew.

Everyone who loves Andy is here tonight. His incomparable Linda. And Ray and John and Greg and their wives and their children who are now Andy's children. (Forget grand . . . children!)

We honor them all as we pay tribute to one of New York state's most endearing and enduring public servants. Milton Hoffman calls him "venerable." We call him "ours."

In White Plains, the county seat, in the corridors of power, he is known as "Legislator Albanese" or "Mr. Chairman." In his family restaurant he is the gracious, colorful, outgoing impresario who feeds Frank Gifford, Y. A. Tittle, Robert Merrill, Larry Tisch, and a whole host of failed priests, monsignors, and not a few rabbis and rogue cops! (*laughter*) And all of us.

In everything he is a vivid, zestful, beguiling presence. Even in adversity . . . when confronted with not one, but three, life-threatening illnesses. And Andy, you didn't have to put us through all this for the last two years! All that wheelchair stuff with the jet propulsion! And the Kojak look! We'd have given you the damn "Man of the Year" Award anyway! (*applause*)

But through it all you never changed. I remember the race for governor last fall. A friend whose words we will hear shortly flew into the Westchester County Airport. And when my colleagues in the press started piling on the governor . . . someone from the crowd, a man in a wheelchair bellowed: "Mario . . . why don't you just tell them to go to hell!" (*laughter*)

Nancy and I attend a lot of tributes and testimonials. I can remember so many right here at Mario Faustini's Alex & Henry's. And at the Rye Town Hilton, the Waldorf and other venues, other ballrooms, across so many nights and years.

But I cannot remember an occasion when four governors of the Empire State felt compelled to express themselves about an honoree.

You have heard the sentiments of His Excellency Governor George

Pataki. Governor Pataki spoke of Andy's "immeasurable" contributions to our state. And we thank the governor for his gracious gesture and for his citation, which will receive a place of great honor in Andy's den.

Now Governor Pataki's three living predecessors would also be heard this night.

First, the graceful and articulate fiftieth governor of New York, Malcolm Wilson, who is so beloved in these precincts:

> We have shared countless evenings at political and civic dinners—many of them at Alex & Henry's in the town which you have distinguished for so long.
>
> It is fitting and proper then that you are receiving the Eastchester Italian-American Club's "Man of the Year" Award at this particular venue in your home heath.
>
> The award, which is given for service to your community, speaks volumes of your dedication as well as your longevity. Please know also that a neighbor and friend who was privileged to serve as the 50th Governor of New York has valued your counsel as I treasure your friendship.
>
> My daughter Kathy and I both salute you and wish you years of health and happiness as you continue your exemplary career.
>
> You are truly *sui generis*.

Thank you, Governor Wilson. Now a note from Governor Hugh Leo Carey:

> I join with all your Westchester neighbors in saluting one of New York state's best-known public servants.
>
> The Italian-American Club's designation as "Man of the Year" is a fitting tribute to your many years of service to your beloved town of Eastchester and to all of Westchester.
>
> As you gather this night with your family and friends ... please know that all of us are grateful for your public service and inspired by your dedication and perseverance. You truly are one of New York's most vivid and respected figures.
>
> Forgive me only for using a rogue like O'Shaughnessy to

convey my very best wishes to you, Linda, your children and grandchildren.

Thank you, Governor Carey. Except for the last line! There is one more message from a former chief executive ... dispatched this day from Willkie, Farr & Gallagher, a law firm in New York:

> Your designation as "Man of the Year," Andy, by this great charitable and civic organization pleases all your many admirers throughout New York state. And Matilda and I are among them. We will never forget your wise counsel and your friendship. You taught us something about courage too.
>
> There has never been any question about where Andy Albanese stood on the great issues of the day, whether his position was popular or not. You are one of New York's treasures.
>
> Matilda and I continue to receive good reports on your remarkable progress. We send prayers, our congratulations, and our love to you and your beloved Linda.
>
> Signed: Mario (*applause*)

Thank you, ladies and gentlemen. As I look out across the room, I see my beautiful Nancy Curry ... and a man who served yet another governor. Joseph Wood Canzeri came here this evening with some wonderful stories of you, Andy, and our marvelous, zestful neighbor Nelson Rockefeller.

You were always the only one entitled to call him "Rocky" on all those occasions over at Pocantico. (*laughter*) He loved you, Andy.

And I remember Nelson's memorial service at Riverside Church when you and your spectacular Linda strode right up to the front to pray, cheek-by-jowl, with all the Rockefellers, for your friend and neighbor. You were in the third row. (*laughter*)

I felt privileged to be seated in row ninety-three with Perry Dur-yea, our candidate for governor that year. And Barry Goldwater sat— alone—in the last row of the great church. But there was our shy, modest, retiring Andy in the third row. (*applause*) I think Canzeri had to "dislodge" the Spanish ambassador!

But it was right and proper that you were there to honor Nelson. And it is right that we are here to honor you.

We love you, Andy. We are so grateful you're back among us. An icon is properly restored. And, frankly (and somewhat selfishly), we could not imagine Westchester without you.

And so we are accompanied this evening with feelings of love and admiration. And also great relief that you have prevailed in all your recent travails and struggles.

The old Jesuits used to say the finite is the strongest word in any language.

In Latin, it's *esse*. To be.

Andy ... you are.

And we are all so damn glad.

Judge Richard Daronco
ONE OF THE NEIGHBORS' CHILDREN

*Richard Daronco was a U.S. federal judge who was
murdered in his back yard in Pelham, New York.*

The television networks, all of them, had it on, and Louis Boccardi's Associated Press satellites moved the terrible bulletin across the skies to damn near every newspaper and radio station all over the face of the Earth. "United States Federal District Judge Richard Daronco has been assassinated in the Village of Pelham, in Westchester County, New York."

But here it was quite different. Some son-of-a-bitch had shot Dick Daronco, who was one of the neighborhood. We saw him in the drugstore and on the golf course. We saw him on his knees at St. Catherine's on Second Street, and we heard him play his horn in a Dixieland band.

Daronco once had a weekly radio show on WVOX. Someone from this radio station introduced him to Senator Alfonse D'Amato, who recommended him for the federal bench. We watched him stand among the great, gray eminences of the federal judiciary to raise his hand and take an oath in a packed federal courthouse in Foley Square after Ronald Reagan had called him to say he wanted him on the bench—for life.

I feel dreadful telling you about what happened to Dick Daronco, how some poor, tortured man with a scrambled-egg mind, a gun, and a heart filled with hate came all the way up from Pennsylvania to find Corona Avenue so he could walk through the bushes at number 207 and go right into the back yard to empty a gun into Dick Daronco as he tended his garden. The man, Koster, didn't just murder a federal judge; he took one of the neighbors' children, one of great gifts and charm and brightness.

I will only tell you a few of the many things I know about Daronco. He laughed a lot. A man of great, spontaneous wit, Daronco would kid the other judges in the courthouse in White Plains, reserving his best lines for Justice Alvin Richard Ruskin, who came to work with a tuna fish sandwich in a brown bag and who called here on Saturday with an awful sadness in his voice to find out if Dick Daronco was going to make it.

I liked this man. He always found discreet ways to inquire of Samuel Fredman, Esquire, and of me, when I was going through a divorce up in the 9th Judicial District courthouse. I made Daronco miss a flight to sit down for coffee one day at Le Cirque restaurant so that a U.S. Senator could meet him. I told Senator D'Amato that Daronco was one of our very brightest and would surely make a splendid candidate for a federal judgeship.

I made speeches for Daronco back in the '70s, when everyone around here thought he could go all the way in this state, maybe even to the governor's mansion. Daronco was much more than the "able, gifted" judge they had been calling him. And I was not alone. He was like a son to Joseph Gagliardi, the former chief judge in Westchester, who wanted Daronco to succeed him. But on the streets of Westchester and in the neighborhood, he never carried himself like a judge. Rather, he was friendly and outgoing, laughed a lot, and told wonderful stories.

There is thus a terrible heaviness here in the neighborhood after the events of this weekend and what happened in the back yard of 207 Corona Avenue. There is shock and grief. There is no laughter.

As I sit here in front of the microphone at his hometown radio station, my mind drifts back to a story I once heard from Judge Daronco. It is a small story, a personal one.

It seems Joan and Dick Daronco were out in the Hamptons for a family holiday just a few summers ago. In the weeks before starting his vacation, the judge had quietly visited a doctor, a cancer specialist, who had called him back several times with those dreadful words: "Let's take more tests."

The Daroncos had rented a modest house from a very religious woman, and when they arrived, Dick and Joan Daronco stayed away from the beach and close to the telephone, waiting for the verdict from the cancer doctor. For several days, nothing—no word came. And then, as Dick told it, one morning as the sun was burning through the clouds, he went out to inspect the owner's back yard. In a corner of the garden, he noticed a statue of the Virgin with gentle flowers growing up around it. After looking around to make sure his fashionable Hamptons neighbors couldn't observe him, the young judge knelt down and said a prayer to the Blessed Mother. At the precise moment he said the words "Holy Mary, Mother of God, pray for us sinners, now, and at the hour of our death," the phone rang in the cottage. It was his law clerk relaying a message from the cancer specialist: "All clear. Everything negative." And Joan and Dick Daronco went off to the beach to sit in the summer sun.

That is just one story I know about the federal judge who was murdered in his own garden over the weekend. All I can really tell you is that Dick Daronco was a bright star in the neighborhood—and he laughed a lot.

May 24, 1988

Bill Luddy

THE DEMOCRAT

*Westchester was, for years, a bastion and safe haven
for the Republican Party. There were few Democrats in
those days—but Bill Luddy was their leader.*

"The man," said Jonathan Swift, "who can make two ears of corn,
or two blades of grass, grow on the spot where only one grew before
would deserve better of mankind and render more essential service
to the country than the whole race of politicians put together." But he
never knew William Luddy, who announced yesterday that he would
retire as Democratic chairman of Westchester.

William Luddy of White Plains, County of Westchester, is a politician the way our fathers imagined them to be. He is of the party
of Franklin Roosevelt, Adlai Stevenson, John Kennedy, and Hubert
Humphrey—and he helped all of them.

It's not easy for a man to be a Democrat in affluent Westchester,
but Luddy made it a calling and gave it his own dignity and grace. He
led his broken, demoralized party out of the defeat and confusion.
With perseverance, guts, wit, candor, and charm, he made the two-
party system in Westchester. That would be reason enough to mourn
his decision to step down, but he also kept it going. He hung in there.
The big bankers, the utilities, and the contractors did not help with
the money—but he used ideas, words, and passion in place of dollars.

You remember Luddy back in the 1950s when he would welcome
young men and women into his small, unpopular political party. The
Republican Party was run by lawyers in White Plains and by discreet
telephone calls between Harrison, Yonkers, and Eastchester. But the
young moved toward Luddy for ideas in those days. And you watched
Luddy keep it going when the bucks got scarce. He gave it his own
standing and stature the year he had to install Democratic headquarters next to a pizza stand in the urban renewal section across from
where the Davega discount store used to be.

He was candid and honest with the press, which is why Milton

Hoffman went out of his way in yesterday's papers to be nice to him. You could get a straight appraisal from Luddy on any of his candidates, even if they were less than stellar. And if you wrote a piece murdering one of them, Luddy would call you up after the broadcast to talk to you as if you were an errant son who just didn't understand what he was trying to do.

His finest moment came a few years ago at the Tarrytown Hilton. Luddy was one of three bigshots chosen to receive an award from the National Conference of Christians and Jews. The speeches were long, and Luddy did not get a chance to speak until almost 11:00. By that time most of the well-heeled crowd had departed anyway, the better to tee off at Winged Foot or Blind Brook the next morning. But Mr. Luddy got up and talked about brotherhood in a way those remaining in his audience had never heard—and it wasn't done in platitudes but was one-on-one, and he had you living next door to a Jew and across from a Black family.

It was the finest speech on the subject of bigotry and hatred I've ever encountered. Luddy did not use a note. And because he delivered his comments to an almost empty room, there are not many people who will remember what he said that night. But we will never forget the speech—or the man, William Luddy.

Our reporters would see him, year after year, at the Roger Smith Hotel—in a wretched banquet room of that shabby, run-down hotel—as the results from Republican Westchester came pouring in to defeat him. As Michaelian, MacCullum, and the victorious Republicans celebrated in proper fashion at a posh venue across town, I usually found Luddy working on a Scotch, talking about his Democratic Party, the two-party system, democracy, and America, which had much to learn about these things in 1971.

And there he was making a speech in the dreary Roger Smith at 2:30 in the morning with only one single college student and his sleepy, bored girlfriend hanging in to listen to this glorious man. We edged out of the ballroom at 3:00 a.m., and Luddy was still going strong. And I remember feeling very secure that night about this whole democracy thing as it came off his lips.

Soon Luddy will retire. The one consolation is that Max Berking will replace him. But when Luddy goes, he takes a big chunk of our past with him. His was the Westchester of Ed Hughes, Bill Fanning, Ted Hill, Charley Mortimer, Tex Cooke, Bill Butcher, Fred Powers, Ralph Tyner, Frank O'Rourke, Edwin Gilbert Michaelian himself, Arthur Geoghegan, and Malcolm Wilson. But they were the Establishment, while Luddy stood off and sang his song for the young, the poor, the Townies. Your father and the people of the old neighborhood would have understood about William Luddy.

January 19, 1971

J. Raymond McGovern

"BUY THEM A DRINK!"

J. Raymond McGovern was a powerful lawyer with a statewide reputation. He was comptroller of New York state.

J. Raymond McGovern, who will be buried at mid-day, when the sun is overhead in our Westchester skies, was a great man. He was also a friend, champion, advocate of WVOX radio. Thus, we will allow the other media to tell you of his illustrious feats and legendary deeds on the state level. We knew him better as a wonderful friend who simply could not resist helping if it was in his power to help.

Tall, courtly, well-dressed, and beautifully tailored, his mind keen and alert, J. Raymond McGovern, a senator and comptroller of the Empire State, did more for this city and county than we perhaps realize. When he died, they put his obituary on page 10, but J. Ray McGovern and his kindness, thoughtfulness, and generosity will outlive any of those world figures mentioned on page 1.

Often we would stop in at his law offices on Huguenot Street, and he would be dictating to his secretary in the open just off the lobby. We would try not to disturb him. But McGovern's rich, strong voice would call out, "Come in here, my boy." We would talk about politics and about his state and about the city. He would always mention Malcolm Wilson and what a fine, decent man the governor is. And he would always inquire after this radio station: "How is it doing? Is this fellow helping you? Can I do anything?"

He was that kind of man. He helped his community station get started—and he helped keep us going. But McGovern helped a lot of causes and a lot of people. Sometimes, he would call and say: "Listen, O'Shaughnessy, I want you to try to help so-and-so. He's a good fellow." That was the highest tribute Ray McGovern could give you.

He was a very successful lawyer and a man of "probity," as Monsignor Thomas Moriarty will put it when he preaches over him at Holy Family today. McGovern would sit at the old Schrafft's on Main Street with Arthur Geoghegan, the bank chairman, and Bill Scott, the realtor, and Owen Mandeville of Larchmont. And while other men of their times and station sat at country clubs, they would discuss great issues over the ninety-cent special Monte Cristo sandwich with cranberries on the side.

And then these men would walk, or saunter, down Main Street, and give it some style and brightness and kindness. McGovern was the spiffiest and most debonair. He talked to everybody.

And when his beloved wife, Elsie, died three weeks ago, and you asked how Ray was taking it, Arthur Geoghegan and Bill Scott told you: "Don't worry about Ray. He's a real pro."

It's like another old friend said: "McGovern would walk into a bar in the old days and, when the bartender would point out some individuals who had been working to defeat him right in his own city, McGovern would give a wave of the hand, smile, and say, 'What the hell. Buy them a drink.'"

Just three weeks ago, McGovern walked down the middle aisle of Holy Family, behind his wife, as Governor Malcolm Wilson and his wife, Katherine, watched. This morning, as he goes down the center aisle for the last time, we will remember his great style—and so much more.

March 16, 1974

A Farewell Tribute to
Andrew P. O'Rourke

There will be other tributes and many honors in the coming months for you, Admiral O'Rourke ... with proclamations filled with encomiums. And they might even designate a building, a road, a park, or a bridge in your name. You'd probably rather have a battleship!

We know not what beckons Andy O'Rourke ... judicial robes, academia, a prestigious law firm, or the *New York Times* bestseller list. But Andy ... you have to get this straight ... if you forget everything else said tonight ... know only this: We go with you wherever you go. We ... go ... with ... you.

But all of that will be dealt with another time, in another venue. Tonight this is a "family" party, a bittersweet occasion, to be sure. You have reluctantly endorsed it, Mr. County Executive, so as not to disappoint the devoted staff that planned it and summoned us to honor you. And we want to recall, briefly, the uniqueness of your administration, the uniqueness of you. So this is a tribute and an appreciation for your thirty-two years of public service, which, combined with your eight years of active military duty, totals forty years!

Here tonight in Westchester, the "Golden" Apple, and for the privilege of presenting Admiral O'Rourke ... they chose a private! I didn't even make PFC ... but I had the three best jobs, Admiral, on the post. I served "overseas" during my entire tenure in the army ... in Staten Island! At Fort Wadsworth. And I had the three best jobs ... the post commander's driver, editor of the newspaper ... and I tended bar in the officers' club! So, clearly, you didn't check my background before you allowed me up here tonight!

The story of Andrew O'Rourke is well known to all here assembled. You know all of the details ... raised by an Irish mother after his father passed away when he was only one. But I spent a good part of the weekend studying the archives, and I noticed that his official biography curiously didn't mention a few things.

"He is a model of public service," said Andrew Cuomo.

And in 1986 you helped Governor Cuomo prove that you don't have to be as tall ... as good-looking, as smart, or as experienced as the other guy ... if you have enough money! At least that's what Cuomo says!

You have been "a superb public servant ... effective, committed, high-minded, principled, but not ideologically obsessed," says Governor Cuomo. "Andy O'Rourke served with a graciousness and warmth that the political world will miss."

Your commitment to taxpayers, the improvement of government services during your stewardship, and the reforms of our bureaucratic systems will be remembered forever ....

But nowhere does it mention, Admiral O'Rourke, that because you did such a good job as county executive, the elders of the state Republican Party bestowed on you the unique privilege ... and I'm not sure if it was a task, an honor ... or a privilege ... but you ran for governor of New York state. You did it without money, without support from even your own tribe. It was underfinanced and against long odds. It was an implausible pursuit. But they said, as so many others have over the years, "Send me an Andy O'Rourke." And so you did it, armed only with your wits, your intelligence, your decency, and your charm. You joined the battle; you carried the banner ... and also that damn cardboard cutout of Mario Cuomo all across the state!

Andy's bio doesn't tell us these things, ladies and gentlemen, or a lot of other things. That he was a Quiz Kid on the coast-to-coast radio program. Nowhere does it say that he served in the Persian Gulf, as the general told us tonight ... "when our country needed his wisdom and judgment in the Judge Advocate staff." He'll never admit it, but he's also a very successful author. Many politicians don't even know how to read books. He writes them!

So tonight you've come to honor a Quiz Kid, a city official, a county legislator, a chairman of the board, a lawyer, a law professor, a teacher, a writer, a published author, a military officer of flag rank and now an admiral of very high standing, a navigator, a judge advocate general, and a civic leader. But you'd never hear it from him. So tonight, hear it from us. I'm very happy to be your surrogate to help you remember some of it.

There's no mention in your bio or résumé, Admiral O'Rourke, of the housing you built with Andrew Cuomo that became a national model for transitional housing duplicated all across America. And Workfare! Some midwestern governors took credit for it and a mayor of Newburgh fiddled around with it ... but Andy O'Rourke started it here and perfected it and made it work.

There have been disappointments in the story of Andy O'Rourke, which is a work in progress ... the run for governor perhaps. But a banker said at cocktails this evening that if you did nothing else you won the respect and support of investors and kept Westchester's bond rating high as a result of your splendid stewardship. And for that alone we owe you, Andy.

And you brought to all of it a wonderful good nature and a kindly spirit. You are simply the nicest man any of us have encountered in public life.

We thank you, Admiral ... Mr. County Executive. We're proud of you. We're proud to be your friends. We are glad you are of us and ours.

January 2013

Bill Plunkett

Interview with William O'Shaughnessy

WO: "He's a great Westchester civic leader, senior partner, and founder of Plunkett and Jaffe. If I were buying stock in a law firm I'd buy stock in that one ... ask Mario Cuomo, he'll tell you. He's an advisor and counselor to governors ... the previous one *and* the current one. The press calls him the number one F.O.G., as in friend of George, as in George Elmer Pataki. He's been very busy working on matters of state to get his friend and former law protégé up and running as our new governor. He is also president of his beloved alma mater, Stepinac High School. He does so much for them and so many other organizations. He is the husband of a woman of dazzling presence and great intelligence, Caryl Plunkett. William Plunkett, Esquire.

"I still can't believe Pataki beat Cuomo."

BP: "I know you can't. A lot of people can't. You've known George Pataki for a long time, as I have, Bill. You know what a terrific person he is ... what an able man he is. And I think we're going to see that come through as he proceeds into his first gubernatorial year. Strong, forceful, committed ... an excellent leader ... a great campaigner and a fellow of real substance. As the people of this state get to know him you'll be watching the evolution of somebody who I believe will be one of the greatest governors in the history of this state."

WO: "I believe everything you tell me, Bill Plunkett. Pataki has the equipment to be a great governor. Is that what you're saying?"

BP: "There's no question at all. Columbia Law School, Yale undergraduate ... worked his way through both. He's a lawyer. He's a farmer. He has the common touch. He also has the intellect. Governor Pataki is what many of us used to call a natural for this business. He has a great rapport with the people. When he is engaged ... for instance the other day up at Reader's Digest, he insisted upon getting out in the audience to meet the people, not just the business leaders but the ordinary people. That's George Pataki. He's a regular guy and a great guy."

WO: "He was your junior partner."

BP: "Many people said *I* worked for George Pataki! George was with our firm for about fourteen years, yes. He was outstanding. He's a very able guy in anything he does. Except, he's not a good shooter with the basketball. He's a rebounder."

WO: "Do you play ball with him?"

BP: "We've played together in the past. I'm getting too old for this."

WO: "Be careful with this. There are those abroad in the land who say ... and I say this not to flatter you but they say it: They should've run Plunkett for governor."

BP: "They're confused. Why should I run for governor? George Pataki had the courage to run for governor. He made the sacrifices necessary to run, and he won. He's now the governor. You can't get any better than him and you certainly can't argue with the results."

WO: "You've been around Westchester for years. Nelson Rockefeller Jr., now thirty, working for Senator Dole in Washington. He called yesterday and he said, 'You've got Bill Plunkett on the show. He's a great man. He could have been county executive.' You could've had a judgeship ten years ago. Why didn't you do any of it?"

BP: "I have different priorities. First of all, I have tremendous respect and admiration for anyone who runs for public office and who serves. It's a demanding, challenging, twenty-four-hours-a-day, seven-days-a-week job. For those who serve, I say thank you ... no matter what party you're in. Particularly today ... in this world ... it is a tremendous sacrifice and we all owe them a debt of gratitude. I don't care what you think about them. We have a tendency to nay-say people in this world, which I find unfortunate. My priorities are different. My priorities are family, church, my law practice."

WO: "But you and Caryl Plunkett are on every dinner committee for every cause. You're always giving speeches. Why don't you just leap in?"

BP: "It's not a twenty-four-hours, seven-days-a-week thing that I do or that you do for that matter, O'Shaughnessy. I'm able to pick and choose my spots. A political person cannot. You're not in control of your life when you're in politics. Again, I respect them tremendously, but it's not my calling."

WO: "I hear that you're working pretty hard on the governor's budget and on advising and counseling him. I feel good that you're whispering in his ear, but who else is?"

BP: "I'm just one of many. I have no special connection at all other than that the governor and I are very good friends. George Pataki is one of the best listeners you'll ever want to see. He genuinely cares about what you have to say. That will be one of his great strengths. He listens ... he assimilates very well. He's one of the quickest studies. So when you talk about an issue, as complicated as it might be, he gets the point very quickly. He also has assembled, and I give him enormous credit for this, one of the great executive chambers that will serve in this state. His secretary is our longtime friend Brad Race, who is a very successful lawyer who has made a great sacrifice to take this job ... in the best traditions of public service, really. It's costing him mega-bucks to take this job."

WO: "Who else is in the court?"

BP: "Mike Finnegan, who was with our firm for many years, is a favorite of mine. He is counsel to the governor. Those are the two top positions. And he has two or three other people. I regard them all highly. They're terrific. One of the really distinguishing characteristics is the fact that George Pataki delegates. He's not a man who keeps everything to himself. He has as his deputy secretary in charge of public authorities and agencies a fellow named Lou Thomson, who is a special friend of mine ... a partner for years ... but he's really one of the most able guys in the state. You're already seeing his abilities in some of the things that are starting to evolve with these public authorities."

WO: "My colleagues in the public press are worried about the D'Amato influence on these guys."

BP: "Your colleagues in the public press are often confused, as you know, particularly about Governor Pataki! Senator D'Amato is a United States senator from New York. He is the ranking Republican. When it came time to select a gubernatorial candidate, obviously, the ranking Republican in the state is going to have something to say about it. D'Amato did not ordain Pataki. It was the "Governor of the Week" club there for a while. They kept floating all these names. Throughout it all, George Pataki persisted. George Pataki said, 'I'm going to run for governor. I want to put my candidacy first before the leaders and then the public.' He never deviated from that. I know the governor to be a man of great principle and substance, and he's been absolutely consistent all along. When Senator D'Amato finally realized what a great candidate he had here, then he embraced George Pataki's candidacy. Of course, he supported him ... and of course the governor owes Senator D'Amato a great debt of gratitude, as do we all."

wo: "One more question on Pataki. There's a story going around that on election night you and George Pataki had supper ... a steak dinner .... Do you remember what he asked you?"

BP: "We did have dinner, yes, along with Mr. Race and Mr. Conway."

wo: "Didn't he ask you, 'Are we going to win this thing?'"

BP: "He did ask that question, and my answer was, 'I hope so.' Anybody who could have said with complete authority an hour before the polls closed that Governor Pataki was going to win ... I wouldn't know on what basis that statement could be made. We *thought* Governor Pataki would win. We *hoped* he would win. There was no empirical data to suggest that was an absolute certainty. It was a toss-up going in."

wo: "Mario Cuomo ... you enjoy the friendship of both governors. You hired one of Mario Cuomo's youngsters, Madeline, and gave her a job right out of law school. Mario Cuomo regards you highly even though you beat him. You're now competing, aren't you?"

BP: "Because he just became a lawyer? I don't think anyone is competition for Mario Cuomo. I mean that. He's one of the most extraordinary persons and public figures that's ever been seen in this state ... a man of enormous talent and intellect. I don't know of a finer speaker that I've ever seen with the possible exception of Sister Bridgette Driscoll, my friend at Marymount. Mario Cuomo is ... a class by himself as a public figure. It's a wonderful family. The Cuomos have a great sense of family ... something that is particularly important to me and I know to you, Bill. Mario Cuomo ...

I wish he hadn't run. Twelve years was enough. He had an uphill fight because of that and I happen to be in favor of term limits."

WO: "Even for Pataki?"

BP: "No question about it. I think Pataki should get out after eight years."

WO: "You have another endeavor, I've learned. Your law school roommate wants to be president of the United States. It must have been something in the water."

BP: "My law school roommate, Lamar Alexander."

WO: "Do you think he can possibly be president?"

BP: "He has the same chance to be president that Governor Pataki had to be governor."

WO: "That's a great line. Do you really believe it?"

BP: "I really believe it."

WO: "He looks like kind of a dull guy."

BP: "He's a great guy. How many honky-tonk piano players do you know in the United States? How many guys have appeared at the Grand Ole Opry on a regular basis and can play any type of piano! He was a two-time governor of Tennessee, a White House fellow, a Circuit Court law clerk to a very prominent judge in New Orleans, Judge Minor Wisdom. He comes from East Tennessee, which was one of the few places in the South that remained loyal to the Union during the Civil War. He's a great family guy, a religious man without wearing it on his sleeve. He's very strongly rooted in values and, really, a first-class guy ... a man of enormous intellect."

WO: "What about Colin Powell?"

BP: "What about Colin Powell? Who knows? Is he a Republican? Is he a Democrat? Does he want to run? Will he run? There can always be speculation about new candidates. Again, I go back to what I said a few minutes ago about Governor Pataki. There was a new candidate every week floating around. Politics is based upon, as you well know, those who are persistent ... those who have a goal ... those who stick with it such as Governor Pataki did. Those are the people who eventually prevail in politics. You can't be in and out. You're either in or you're out. Lamar Alexander and Phil Gramm and Bob Dole apparently are the three top contenders right now, and Lamar is perfectly situated. He's got money. He has excellent advisors. He's very well situated in New Hampshire and Iowa. Obviously, I'm hopelessly biased."

wo: "And obviously, you're persuaded Clinton has got to go."

BP: "I believe he does. But I must say, a man who is persistent, who takes a challenge and is focused on his objective. I respect that."

wo: "He's like Lazarus. You can't kill him."

BP: "I don't know that he's been dead and buried yet, but I admire those characteristics and I think the American people admire them. I'm not a person who says this is a sure-shot Republican win in '96 at all. I believe it will be a real contest."

wo: "Tell us about our home heath, Westchester. There's a terrible battle going on between Tony Colavita, who is your friend and my friend, and the Spanos of Yonkers. I only know what I hear in the public press, so it must be true."

BP: "That's your first mistake, but you know that, Bill."

wo: "Don't you believe what you read?"

BP: "It depends who is writing it!"

wo: "Tell us what's going on. We both know we like Tony Colavita."

BP: "All that said, it's time for a change in Westchester. It's no secret that our good friend Tony did not enthusiastically back George Pataki, and it's no secret many of Governor Pataki's people think that the chairman should move on."

wo: "To the victor belongs the spoils."

BP: "That's partly true. Tony has been a chairman here for a long time and he's done an excellent job. He's a dear friend of mine and I make no bones about it. Tony Colavita deserves to be treated with dignity and respect. He's been a great chairman. I'd like to see him voluntarily step down."

wo: "Maybe we can do a deal right here. Put a little 'dignity and respect' on the table."

BP: "It is not for me to say or to do. If you're asking me a personal opinion, that's what I'd like to see."

wo: "But it's unseemly, what they're doing."

BP: "And unfortunate. It's always unfortunate when such good friends like Tony and Nick Spano are at loggerheads. Nobody likes to see that, and I hope that it will end soon."

WO: "Can we disagree on this as we do so often? I'm for Colavita."

BP: "I'm not against Colavita. It's time for Tony to step down. I have talked to Tony about this. We are very good friends. We serve on the Stepinac board together. I had the privilege of conferring the Hall of Fame honor on him last year. I think the world of Tony."

WO: "In Westchester ... I know you're very active in the County Association with Larry Dwyer and George Delaney. There used to be the Bill Butchers, Fred Sundermans, Harold Marshalls, Fred Powerses, and the Ed Michaelians."

BP: "You're older than I am. You remember all these guys?"

WO: "Where once giants walked the land. These guys ... they weren't so great, but we thought they were. They were active in everything and they built the county. Where are the builders of tomorrow?"

BP: "The county has changed a little bit. We used to get those bright, attractive young men and women out of the banks and the business establishments in the county. The days of the strong personal banker, the Jim Hands or your friend Tom Langan, for instance, who knew everybody ... and went to the wakes and funerals ... are gone. I'm also reminded of Malcolm Wilson who, to me, is in a class by himself. But it has changed. You're not seeing the same leadership that you would normally see coming out of the corporate businesses. Probably the thing that strikes me most is I think you're going to see significant leadership coming from women in this county. There are a tremendous number of able women across the board who will begin to step up here. You're also going to see leadership from law firms ... there are a lot of competent people in Westchester law firms."

WO: "A lot of them take, but don't want to put back."

BP: "There are some people who give of themselves. I think of B. J. Harrington, who gives so much to the 52 Association. Joe Carlucci, Frank McCulloch ... my own brother Kevin Plunkett is a rising star ...."

WO: "You mentioned the fiftieth governor of New York. He's now eighty years old and practices law to this day in White Plains ... Malcolm Wilson. You were his advance man, weren't you?"

BP: "George Pataki, Brad Race, and I were his advance men. We were his upstate coordinators in 1974, and there is no greater man that has walked this Earth than Malcolm Wilson, as far as I'm concerned. He's great in every respect. We both know his compassion for people. We know his intellect. We know all the people he has helped ... all the things he has done. We know his outreach, his decency, his family values, and his dedication to the church. You don't find that package very often in one human being. God bless Malcolm Wilson is all I can say."

WO: "Give me ten seconds on the Cardinal Archbishop. You're a Knight of Malta, which is very high in the church, higher than I will ever get. John Cardinal O'Connor ...."

BP: "He is an absolutely great leader. A man of principle. A man of courage. He understands that you don't have to bend with the wind. He knows what he believes in and he represents that belief better than anybody I know."

WO: "Andy O'Rourke, the county executive ...."

BP: "A great county executive who will go down in history as the county executive who has done as much as anybody, if not more, to make this a truly great county."

WO: "Caryl Plunkett ..."

BP: "She's a great lady ... the mother of six spectacular kids. I love her."

WO: "Thank you for coming on the show."

BP: "You're one of my idols. Even though we were on opposite sides of the last race for governor!"

1994

Frederic B. Powers

THE TOWNIE

*Frederic B. Powers was an industrialist and philanthropist
who dabbled in politics as chairman of the Westchester Republican
Party. I once heard him admonish Nelson Rockefeller, "Nelson,
you're acting like a damn jackass!" This occurred in Rockefeller's
own living room. Fred Powers was wonderful to me and
mine for many years.*

I do not possess the talent or toughness—or the desire, for that
matter—to separate myself personally from this morning's editorial,
which is about a man named Frederic Powers.

Industrialist, civic leader, politician, philanthropist: Powers was
all of these things. He was also my friend and a great patron and
champion of this, your own community radio station.

As we attempt this broadcast of what Fred Powers did for Westchester and try to recall the kind of man he was, I feel like a prize-
fighter who has gone to the well once too often over these airwaves
and on this microphone. Nothing I could say would do him justice.
He was the mother lode when it came to an awareness of his fellow
man. The clergymen use that wonderful phrase "a sense of community." Powers owned it. He wrote the book.

Although he would ride around in that big Cadillac with the famous FBP plates, Powers was basically a "townie." Now, don't get
me wrong. Perhaps I should not use that word, because not everyone has the same respect and affection for it as I have. By "townie" I
mean someone who has roots in his community, someone who loves
his neighbors. For all his directorships and foundations and the Supreme Court judges he made and appointed as Republican leader,
Powers was basically a townie. This was his town, and you were his
neighbors.

He was a man of elegance and eloquence and style and great wit.
He could hobnob with Nelson Rockefeller, whom he admired and
loved and once accused of acting "rather like an ass," and at the same

time be genuine, dignified, and as down-to-earth as any man who ever lived in our county. When he was Republican county chairman he would sit at those political dinners surrounded by ward heelers from Yonkers, winking and laughing and waving his right hand through the air with the ever-present Marlboro. Waiters, bellhops, cab drivers, paperboys, and garbage men all loved him. And it was fitting yesterday that one of the first callers at George Davis Funeral Home was a cab driver.

Powers had, in abundance, that wonderful and becoming trait of older men who go out of their way to help younger men. And every time I'm tempted to give short shrift to someone seeking my own poor advice, or not take the time to see a youngster trying to break into radio, I try to recall Powers and his splendid example.

By the thousands, they came over the years to his office on Petersville Road, some after his money for a favorite cause, but most for his judgment and advice. He was where you started for ideas or development projects—or radio stations. Although Powers rarely gave you straight-out advice, you would ride home after a session with him, and it would come to you—and the whole thing would be clearer.

Jean Ensign, WVOX's wise and prescient executive vice president who has known Powers a long time, said yesterday that Westchester is losing a lot of giants. "I hope you have young men coming up," she said.

Well, I'm an optimist about this, and I have to assume that we *are* developing future leaders with the style of Fred Powers. But it's going to be a lot tougher, because they won't have this marvelous and extraordinary man to help them start the climb toward splendid projects and great accomplishments.

Powers had been in and out of the cardiac-care unit six times in the care of the world-famous specialist Ira Gelb. We knew he was slipping and in trouble last weekend when his wife, Irene, and son, Fred Powers Jr., came out the side door of the hospital. Neither looked good. And so you urged them to try a long shot and retain some wonderful Irish nurse like an Ann Kenny to go in there to check on him just once more.

But it was asking too much of that heart, which had done so much and been so busy in our lifetime. It was too much for even a jolly Irish nurse with a twinkle in her eye, or even the legendary Dr. Gelb.

I really loved this flamboyant, colorful, warm man. So many take and put nothing back. But every once in a while, central casting sends you a Fred Powers to even things up.

September 12, 1975

Hugh Price

Interview with William O'Shaughnessy

WO: "Tonight, ladies and gentlemen, a national figure who is one of our neighbors. He's lived in Westchester for many years. He was a member of the editorial board of the *New York Times* ... a senior executive at Channel 13 and a vice president of The Rockefeller Foundation ... but he is now taking on his greatest and most important national assignment. Please welcome the new president of the National Urban League, Hugh Price. We're so proud of you, Mr. Price. You've been all over the country making speeches ...."

HP: "I've essentially made one speech that has been covered all over the country. That's very efficient."

WO: "You sit where once a man named Whitney Moore Young sat. Remember Whitney Young? He was our New Rochelle neighbor."

HP: "I live right next to him. As a matter of fact, when my wife and I go walking we pass right by Whitney and Margaret's house. Several of the past presidents of the National Urban League have been Westchester residents. Vernon Jordan lived in Hartsdale. John Jacob, my immediate predecessor, lived in Hartsdale."

WO: "What's John Jacob doing now?"

HP: "John has just become executive vice president of Anheuser-Busch. He's got a major position overseeing all their communications and public service operations."

WO: "And Vernon Jordan?"

HP: "Vernon is, of course, a force in Washington, D.C. He's a partner in a law firm and I think he's categorized as President Clinton's best buddy."

WO: "I won't hold that against him or you. Are you political ... Democrat or Republican?"

HP: "I'm a Democrat by nature. I was once very active in Democratic politics in New Haven when we were there. I've been a little less active in partisan politics since we moved to the New York area ... but I'm a Democrat."

WO: "Back in the '60s and in the '70s your predecessor, the late Whitney Moore Young's heart stopped beating on a beach in Africa."

HP: "There are many interpretations of what happened. He may have been caught in an undertow or something ... he was swimming. I've read accounts and there is a little bit of dispute about it. But he was swimming in some very difficult currents and it's not clear if it was undertow or a heart attack. He was a very strong swimmer and he was in very good shape. People wonder ... but the fact is he died in Africa."

WO: "I still have a framed card that Margaret Young, his widow, sent out. It had a black angel and a white angel talking to each other in Heaven with wings and it said, 'Lord, Whitney Young is here.'"

HP: "Margaret is a very special person. She is a very dear friend."

WO: "Whitney Young was different and some people think you're quite different. You have to spot the players for us in civil rights. First of all, are you a civil rights leader?"

HP: "I'm uncomfortable with that characterization. I have become that, I suppose. I oversee an organization concerned not just about civil rights, but also social and economic justice. So our mission is economic, social, and racial equity in this country. The Urban League historically has been concerned with trying to help people move from poverty into the economic mainstream. It was Whitney who actually brought the Urban League foursquare into the civil rights movement in the early '60s in conjunction with the March on Washington in 1963. The League essentially added that to its portfolio and is now concerned with all of these issues."

WO: "But while many civil right leaders ... I have to use the term ... were out on the street picketing, Whitney Moore Young was in the boardroom saying, 'I want fifty jobs.'"

HP: "There are people who work inside the mainstream ... building bridges and helping folks across. There are people who straddle the mainstream and the outside and say, 'God damn it, somebody has to build some bridges.' And there are some people who say, 'Even if they build bridges ... I'm not going to cross, because I don't believe that the grass is greener on the other side.' The Urban League operates inside the mainstream ... building the bridges. There are advocacy organizations and sister organizations like the NAACP, which stands and says, 'Somebody has got to build bridges. God damn it, build bridges.' And then, of course, there are others who are more separatist in nature who are dubious about whether or not the bridges are strong enough and whether the grass is greener and that's a crude way of dividing up the roles that we all play."

WO: "Help me spot the players now. You mentioned the NAACP. They've had tough times. They deposed their president Ben Chavez. Do you know him?"

HP: "I don't know him. I have just taken office. I'm in my seventh week. It is a difficult time, but I have no doubt the NAACP will bounce back. It's a resilient organization and it has a very important role to play. Its chapters have got to be there when strident advocacy is absolutely necessary . . . strident, yet constructive, advocacy."

WO: "Tell me about the Rainbow Coalition and Jesse Jackson."

HP: "Jesse Jackson is an historic figure in the African-American community. He's a great and remarkable man. Jesse established our bonafides as candidates for prominent national office. He has played a historical role in our movement. The Rainbow Coalition is an attempt, as the name implies, to build bridges across communities and to try to affect a multiracial coalition for economic, racial, and social justice in this country."

WO: "But is Jesse Jackson legit?"

HP: "Oh sure, he's legit. Jesse is a brilliant man. He has dedicated his life to our work. With the kind of smarts and charisma that he has, he could've done anything he wanted to do. He has devoted himself to our cause."

WO: "He's not in it for himself?"

HP: "You have to be internally driven in order to do this work. Anybody that runs for elective office has to be internally driven. You have to have some ego to keep overcoming the obstacles. But I think Jesse is in it for people. I don't have any doubt."

WO: "You mentioned those who don't want to go over the bridge. Are you talking about Farrakhan?"

HP: "I think . . . throughout the history of the African-American community . . . there have been people who have been skeptical that the mainstream was really open to us. Marcus Garvey ... Malcolm X, in his time ... that skepticism is bred of a reality that over our history ... whether we're talking about slavery or the kinds of economic changes that are occurring now ... there is a reality basis for that skepticism that in fact there will be room for all African-Americans in the economic mainstream. There is a reality based on the perpetuation of racial discrimination in this country and the attitudes that whites have toward blacks. My view is that you can't let those obstacles stymie you from trying to cross into the mainstream because I don't think there is any future in separation. Skepticism about whether or not the economic mainstream will ever admit us, whether white America will ever be comfortable with us, provides the fodder for those who aren't willing to cross the bridge."

wo: "You were on the editorial board of the mighty *New York Times*. You ran a television station and served at the Rockefeller Foundation .... Have you seen a reluctance against Hugh Price?"

hp: "I have encountered it, sure. I wasn't president of the station. I made a run for the presidency of the station and my candidacy wasn't taken seriously, in my judgment. That was quite instructive to me that the station and that selection committee wasn't 'ready.' It wasn't a question of not having been chosen president. I can deal with not having been chosen president. What was difficult was not being taken seriously as a candidate."

wo: "Why didn't they take you seriously?"

hp: "I don't know. That's one to talk to the search committee about, but I know that I wasn't. Those are the experiences that you encounter when you smack your head against the glass ceiling and it smarts and you don't forget it. But the fact is that many Blacks are breaking through. We have a neighbor of mine in New Rochelle, Ken Chenault, who runs American Express."

wo: "I've heard he lives in New Rochelle. Is he a good fellow?"

hp: "Oh yeah. A very good fellow. Dick Parsons, who is a resident of Tarrytown, is head of the seventh- or eighth-largest financial institution in this country, Dime and Anchor Savings. African-Americans are breaking through, because, as I said, there is no future in isolation. The glass ceiling does break, but you have to have people who are willing to pound against it and take the mallets and even crack it with their head."

WO: "They're talking about Parsons for governor!"

HP: "Dick Parsons can do anything that he wants to do."

WO: "He's also a lawyer. Do you know who he represents? Happy Rockefeller ...."

HP: "I don't know that he does now ... but I knew that he once represented the Rockefeller family. His grandfather ... if I'm not mistaken ... had worked as a groundskeeper on the Rockefeller estate."

WO: "How about Carl McCall, sir?"

HP: Terrific. A terrific human being. I've known Carl for many years. He's very capable; also can do anything that he wants. Carl is very dedicated to public service. He preceded me at Channel 13. He worked in government affairs for Citibank. He was chairman of the Board of Education in New York City. He too is the kind of fellow that could go off into the private sector and do a terrific job, but Carl has decided to dedicate his life to public service. That's what makes him tick."

WO: "What about Hugh Price? Do you have the political bug?"

HP: "Not really. I thought about that a number of years ago when I was in New Haven. There was an opportunity to run for a state Senate seat. There would have been a three-way primary ... and the name of the fellow that went on to win the primary was Joe Lieberman ... now a U.S. senator. But I stared then at the possibility of running and decided I didn't want to because I didn't want my life to be so public. I didn't want to be in the public eye that much ...."

WO: "Well, you're in it now."

HP: "I'm in it now. I feel like I'm ready. But also at the time I would have had to work for a company and I felt I would have been a 'kept' politician. There was no way to practice law and develop an independent source of income. And I didn't want to work for a major corporation and be an elected representative because I don't think I could've been free in the judgments that I would have had to make. But I am in the public eye now. It's an interesting experience to have people dissect every word that you say and interpret it. I've been in public life before. I was a city administrator in Connecticut."

WO: "Who supports the Urban League? Who sustains you?"

HP: "We receive support from a variety of sources. We get government grants from agencies like the U.S. Department of Aging and the U.S. Department of Labor. We have support from corporations and foundations. To a much lesser extent we get support from individuals. It's a mix of that kind of support. We get support from mainstream institutions to do the kind of work that we do inside the social and economic mainstream."

WO: "Is it fair, then, to ask you ... as you acknowledge where the support comes from ... what you think of some of the players on the national scene? You're a national leader. What do you think of Bill Clinton?"

HP: "I think Bill Clinton is a remarkable man. I like his politics. By and large I think he understands the issues we care about and he cares about the issues we care about. He's obviously having a tough time and I hope that Bill Clinton will get back out into the countryside and talk to people about what is on their minds. I think his instincts and his policies are by and large compatible with my own personally and are comparable with the kinds of things that we care about. The expansion of the earned income tax credit to provide more income for low-income working people, the expansion of Head Start—the new education legislation that establishes higher goals for young people—the effort to extend health care to working families that don't now have it ... those are initiatives that are very difficult, and he's been brave in pursuing those initiatives ... and I wish him well."

WO: "What do you think of Clinton as an individual? When you and Mrs. Price sit around your New Rochelle home ... do you really like him?"

HP: "Yeah, I like him. He's had his problems. He is a human being. We don't spend a lot of time talking about his troubles. We hope that he can navigate them and we hope the American people can place them in perspective because for me what he stands for and what he's trying to do is vastly more important."

WO: "What about in this state ... there's a big battle for governor.

Mario Cuomo running again ... and George Pataki. How do you see that?"

HP: "I believe very strongly in Mario Cuomo and what he stands for."

WO: "They're just trying to kill each other."

HP: "That's to be expected. I don't know George Pataki at all. I haven't really followed his policies, but I think Mario Cuomo and his views are more consistent with my own and I essentially know where I personally am coming out in that race so I haven't had to track it closely. That race has coincided with my assuming the presidency of the National Urban League, which I started on July 1st. I've been pretty much consumed with the obligations of that position."

WO: "As you move around this country ... what's the politically correct way ... is it 'Black-American' or 'African-American' ... ?"

HP: "I'm going to be cavalier about this. That's an issue that doesn't interest me. I'm fifty-two years old ... and I've been called five different things in my lifetime ... and I'm waiting for my sixth now that I'm in my sixth decade. I've been Negro, colored, Afro-American, African-American, and Black. I don't expend a lot of energy thinking about that. I guess the two words we tend to use now are Black and African-American."

WO: "Why did I ask you that question?"

HP: "It's something that we can get tangled up in. In fact, the curiosity didn't occur to me until several years ago when I was listening to a Latina colleague of mine stumble over whether she was Mexican-American, Chicano, or Latina ... and she was about thirty. It occurred to me that she has wrestled with three labels in her thirty years, while I've wrestled with five in my fifty ... and it's not something I lose much sleep over."

WO: "Will we get to the point where we don't do labels?"

HP: "I'm not sure we will. We seem to be in a period where that's very important, and I think a sense of self and people is critically important. Again, that's not something that I expend a great deal of intellectual energy wondering about. The big transition for me and for people of African-American descent was essentially in the '60s when we crossed over from thinking of ourselves as Negroes or coloreds to Blacks, which obviously had color connotation. That was a big deal and I had thought that we put the labeling to bed at that juncture, but obviously we haven't. To be perfectly frank, it's kind of an uninteresting question."

WO: "In your speeches you worry about the children of America, you worry about cities …. Moynihan has some ideas about this. Where are you? I'm going to give you a lot of power. You can do anything you want with cities, our own included; what would you do?"

HP: "I think I would try to make our schools work for youngsters so that they all … not just a select few … but all have the kinds of schools that they need in order to be successful in the twenty-first century. If you look at what has happened to the economy of cities, many of the jobs that required only blue-collar skills, but none-theless enabled people to participate in the economic mainstream and to earn enough to buy a home and a car, those jobs have essentially vanished from the cities."

WO: "What kind of jobs?"

HP: "Factory workers … the kind of work my uncle did. My uncle lived in the center of New Haven and walked to his factory job. The factory he worked for is gone. He was not a college man. He was essentially a factory worker. If you have low education and low skills, then you can only earn lousy wages … so I think that we have to make sure that all of our children have much higher skills that enable them to participate in that part of the economy. The Information Age economy. The Service economy that is growing and providing decent wages. That's concern number one. The second concern is that many parents are not there for their children. A lot of that is dictated by economic reasons. I'm part of a group in Westchester called the Westchester Clubmen, and we support a program up at the White Plains YMCA for young African-American males at the middle school. Many of their mothers are out stringing together several jobs that don't pay terrific wages and they can't be home at 3:00 o'clock when their youngsters come home. So we have to make sure that there are constructive activities and caring adults in the lives of all of our youngsters when they're done with school and over the summer while their mothers and fathers are out working. I think we have to rebuild what I call the 'developmental infrastructure' for youngsters. That is an infrastructure that is now being fulfilled by gangs. And that is why we have this upsurge in gang activity and violence because essentially there is nobody home for our young people once school is out. I think we also have to look at the economic condition and economic self-sufficiency of families. Somehow, even as we work in preparing our youngsters to participate in the economy, we've got to do a much better job of helping their parents, who are living in inner-city areas, gain access to the mainstream economy. I think that means focusing even harder on job training. But preparing people for jobs that are in the sectors that are paying decent wages. I think we have to work with public-sector and private-sector employers and say, 'You have got to include people who live in the inner cities in your work force.' We can't have a society that walls off significant sections of the population from economic opportunity, because if we have that then we end up with the kinds of struggles and tensions within societies now and we end up with the erosion of the economic base of communities, the erosion of families and the exacerbation of the kinds of social tensions and crime that we have."

WO: "Is that an intelligent way of saying that the rich are getting richer?"

HP: "That's exactly what has happened. It used to be that the rich grew richer and folks that weren't rich nonetheless progressed. They weren't moving at the same pace, but everybody was moving forward. But now if you are well educated and highly skilled you have enjoyed a tremendous growth surge in the last couple of decades. If you are low skilled and not well educated, your purchasing power has declined by 20 percent or so in the last couple of decades. That is feeding a lot of the social tension, and it's feeding the impulse on the part of those who want to separate who say there is nothing in this mainstream for me."

WO: "There are people watching who are thinking about people who don't want to get off of welfare. People that are on SSI now ... they can't read or write ... they don't do welfare ... they do SSI. Everybody is on the dole, it seems."

HP: "Everybody is not on the dole. Most people that are on welfare are only on it temporarily. They're passing through because of some family situation ... because they've lost their job due to a shutdown of a plant or whatever. But it's also a fact that some number of people are on welfare for a longer haul. Some people may like it that way, but I don't think most people want to be on public assistance. I think, as they run the numbers and look at their economic opportunities, the numbers don't add up if they don't have insured health care where they work and if the only jobs they have access to pay poverty-level wages. If they look at the alternative of public assistance with insured health care and the ability to be home with their children compared to working and earning poverty-level wages, no health care, and no child care ... the calculus doesn't make any sense. That's the problem now. Economically, people in some parts of the country are better off financially being on public assistance than they are working. We've got to do something about that, and that's why the press by the president to greatly expand healthcare coverage for low-income workers and the press to expand child care and Head Start and the press to expand the income supplement of people who are earning low wages are all very important because, if we expect people to work, work must be worthwhile financially."

WO: "But there are people watching attractive, intelligent, articulate, and bright Hugh Price ... and they're thinking that he wants more government doles."

HP: "I don't want more government doles. I want the African-American community ... and everybody, frankly, to do a much better job of making sure that their children are prepared for the twenty-first-century economy. That's our responsibility as parents, in the first instance ... and that's the responsibility of each of our communities and each of our ethnic groups in the second instance, not just to make our public school systems work better but the responsibility of ensuring that your children are equipped for the twenty-first century. And that rests with us who are parents. I think that the responsibility of ensuring that the developmental infrastructure is there for children is essentially a public responsibility."

WO: "You mentioned that before. You mean gangs. What do you put in there in place of gangs?"

HP: "The schools that once had a vast array of extracurricular programs and no longer do ... that used to be a public responsibility. We now say that government shouldn't do that. The park and rec departments that had all of those clubs and youth workers and teens ... that used to be paid for by taxpayers. They don't anymore ... and we need that now. The YMCAs and the boys' clubs and all of those programs that provided all of those father figures who are no longer there ... that was all a part of the community's responsibility to its children. They've all walked away from that responsibility as parents and taxpayers. That's not government. That's not dole. That's community responsibility for kids. If the economy doesn't work, then society has to look at that question. If there aren't enough jobs that pay decent wages, that is not a problem that individuals can solve. That is a society problem."

WO: "I don't think you walk away from anything ...."

HP: "I try not to."

Bill Scollon

HELP ME WITH THIS KENNEDY THING

*This is not an editorial. It's just plain personal, because that's
what this whole thing is to each one of us, especially if you are Irish.
I suppose it's for a political gadfly named Bill Scollon, who lives in
New Rochelle, but it's really about John Kennedy, who was killed on
us in Dallas, Texas, a little more than a thousand days ago.*

Bill Scollon is the only one who can help me handle this thing about
President Kennedy, which is at me a lot these days. It creeps up
whenever I hear someone talk about Texas. I remember that dreadful day whenever I drive through an underpass, and I can't help the
funny feeling I get when I pick up a book in a barbershop and see all
the ads for guns.

Scollon helps because he's Irish, too. And John Kennedy belongs
to all people, but you have a special claim on him if you were raised
by a father who told you Al Smith was the greatest man who ever
lived, followed closely by Jimmy Walker and Jim Farley.

Scollon is an advertising man who works in New York, but he
hangs around New Rochelle a lot, too. And I think of Bill Scollon
when I try to figure what this thing about John Kennedy has done to
all of us. Scollon may be the brightest kid who ever came out of New
Rochelle schools, because he went right to college at Oxford, which
is in England. He's a little guy, and he looks Irish in that his eyes
twinkle and he can get excited about things in the blasé world. He
makes his money in advertising, and to relax, he designs crossword
puzzles for the Gannett newspapers. His soul, however, is committed
to politics, and he talks a lot about John Kennedy.

Scollon thinks, for example, that all Democrats are good and that
all Republics are bad. I'm not as sure as Scollon that all those who
claim to have inherited John Kennedy's mantle really deserve it, even
if their name is Kennedy. I do agree, though, that a lot of those who
will tell you they hate Bobby, his brother, were the same ones who
hated John Fitzgerald Kennedy.

[49]

Maybe Jimmy Cannon said it for all the Irish in a column in the *Trib* over the weekend. Cannon is a sportswriter who writes about the games men play. Raised on the mean streets of the Lower West Side, he was trying out a lovely deception on his readers by suggesting that the Irish really don't require a great team like Notre Dame any more, because they have John Kennedy and they have what he means.

Scollon would understand this, and I hope you do. John Kennedy is all the kids who never went to Deerfield, and even though he went to Harvard and had a lot of money, he happened for all the kids growing up today on mean streets everywhere.

They talk about this thing that is still at us, which is personal everywhere. And they were talking about it at Patrick J. O'Neill's saloon, on Lawton Street, last Friday night. There was an old retired cop saying he hated the Kennedys, because he knew Honey Fitz, John Kennedy's grandfather—and according to this old Irish cop from New Rochelle, the line stopped with Honey Fitz. He was saying that he hated the Kennedys, and this cop's name starts with an "O."

But for most of us, when Jack made it to the White House, we weren't Micks anymore.

1966

Kirby

The cell phone rang as I sat at P. J. Clarke's bar talking to four Catholic priests who work by day as hospital chaplains. They know about death even on this particular Easter Sunday night. Richard Littlejohn, our veteran overnight and weekend manager, only calls with bad news. "I'm sorry to ruin your Easter, Mr. O'."

"Who is it, Rich?"

"Bill Scollon, they found him on the floor in his apartment."

That's how I learned William Kirby Scollon died alone a few days before Easter. He was a slight, elfin little guy with dancing eyes and a stunning intellect who came to our station on Tuesdays to preside over his own radio program.

The New Rochelle police officers who found him at 6:00 p.m. on Easter informed us he had been gone "for a few days." According to Frank Ippolito, his radio sidekick, Scollon was preoccupied as recently as Friday afternoon preparing remarks on immigrants and Iraqi war veterans for this week's show. It was vintage Scollon to the end.

A bit stooped and hunched over from a full life, he spoke in a croak. But Scollon was one of the brightest guys I ever met, an opinion shared by Jack Kennedy, who would call him to discuss the great issues of the day at the Carlyle Hotel—before and after he became president of the United States. Bobby Kennedy also sought Scollon's advice, and Scollon proudly wore the legendary PT-109 tie clip, a staple for Kennedy staffers and admirers.

Scollon became the gray eminence of the Democratic Party in these parts and cranked out thousands of speeches and position papers for local, regional, and national candidates on a wide range of issues. He hung around Miriam Jackson, the Democrats' mother hen who became chair of the Westchester County Democratic Committee, and John DeRario, the Little League czar and a powerful voice on the County Board of Legislators during the '70s.

He was married for a brief time but for the last several decades reverted to life as a confirmed bachelor. He spent his time over the years at a lonely flat in downtown New Rochelle and would celebrate Easter and Christmas with Bill Mullen, a Verizon executive, and his wife. Thanksgiving was reserved for the elderly councilwoman Ruth Kitchen; and he regularly shared the Sabbath with our own Larry Goldstein.

In his spare time, William Kirby Scollon *designed* crossword puzzles for the *New York Times* and Gannett. A great wordsmith, he insisted on clarity and precision in both written and spoken English and would often lecture me on my poor syntax.

A confirmed Democrat, Scollon vigorously objected to wvox's Republican endorsements and opposed our presence in Vietnam and Iraq.

For many years, Scollon skimmed along the periphery of Democratic politics as chief of staff for Max Berking, the courtly, graceful state senator who later became chair of the Westchester County Democratic Committee. They were a formidable team at the ballot box and in Albany, and they also ran an ad agency on Madison Avenue.

When he wasn't at the Carlyle with the Kennedys, Scollon would hold court at Paddy O'Neill's saloon on Lawton Street. During lunch hour, the bankers and merchant princes of the town would inhabit the place. And at night, it became a little less hectic when Hughie Doyle, Tommy O'Toole, and Bill Sullivan came to debate with the little Irishman with the facile mind. And one night, Ken Auletta, the great *New Yorker* writer, came by for advice on Howard Samuels's campaign for governor of New York.

Some people called him "Kirby," because he was related to the Kirbys of Rye, a prominent local family. I just called him Bill. By any name, he emanated a bright aura in every season of his life.

He died alone in an apartment in downtown New Rochelle, and he never made it to Easter dinner at Mullen's house.

wvox lost a talk-show host. But all of Westchester and New York state lost a marvelous, endearing character.

Original broadcast, April 17, 2006

Walter Nelson Thayer
GRAY EMINENCE OF THE EASTERN
ESTABLISHMENT

Walter Nelson Thayer was a New York publisher and investor whose partnership with the legendary John Hay "Jock" Whitney made him one of the most influential members of the Eastern Republican Establishment, those monied brahmins sometimes known as "limousine liberals" or "Rockefeller Republicans" who made up the progressive-liberal wing of the GOP.

From his office suite on the forty-sixth floor of the Time-Life building in midtown Manhattan, Thayer, also widely known as "WNT," helped launch the political careers of John V. Lindsay, Jacob K. Javits, Ogden Rogers Reid, Nelson A. Rockefeller, William Warren Scranton of Pennsylvania, Kenneth Keating (even Bobby Kennedy paid an off-the-record courtesy call on Thayer when RFK had designs on Keating's New York Senate seat), and John Connally of Texas. As a young man, he helped persuade General Dwight D. Eisenhower to run for president and helped the war hero wrestle the Republican nomination from Senator Robert Taft of Ohio. Thayer also tried mightily to get Nelson Rockefeller into the White House, most notably at the Republican National Convention in Miami Beach in 1968, when Mr. Whitney, Thayer and their friend William S. Paley had to sit by in helpless splendor in penthouse suite 1A of the Eden Roc Hotel and watch, on one of Bill Paley's multi-screen television sets, as Richard Nixon and Spiro Agnew won all the marbles.

Fortified by his own shrewd business acumen and Jock Whitney's ample purse, Walter Thayer also tried to breathe new life into the venerable *New York Herald Tribune*, a highly respected but fading national daily purchased from the Reid family. Together they battled the recalcitrant, unyielding newspaper unions of the day. But the *Trib* was hemorrhaging badly and went under on August 15, 1966. (I've written about the sad day Whitney and Thayer sounded the death knell for this once-glorious newspaper in my first book, *Airwaves*.)

For one brief, shining moment in New York journalism, the *Trib* was home to a great stable of writers including Murray Kempton, Jimmy Breslin, Tom Wolfe, Stanley W. Woodward, Seymour Krim, Dick Schaap, Eugenia Sheppard, Clay Felker, and Red Smith.

Many think the *Herald Tribune*'s finest moment came in 1964 when that bastion of Republican views and persuasion endorsed Lyndon B. Johnson over Barry Goldwater, the conservative GOP standard-bearer. It was a monumental—and courageous—decision, for which John Hay Whitney, the paper's principal owner, received accolades ... and more than a few vitriolic denunciations for being a traitor to his party and his class. Most observers believe it was Thayer who helped push the patrician Whitney and his beloved *Trib* over to the Democrats and Johnson for the first time since the paper's founding by Horace Greeley.

After the newspaper gave up the ghost, Thayer helped cobble to-gether the remnants of the *World-Telegram*, the *Journal-American*, and the *Trib* to produce the short-lived *World Journal Tribune*. Thayer was also publishing director of the *Trib*'s sole surviving sister publication, the Paris-based *International Herald Tribune*, which wielded enormous worldwide influence among foreign lead-ers, American expatriates, and tourists traveling abroad who relied on it as the only English-language paper available overseas. WNT, again representing Jock Whitney's interests, managed to keep peace among the *IHT*'s other investors, the Sulzberger family of the *New York Times* and Katharine Graham of the *Washington Post*. (The paper lived on and is now owned exclusively by the *New York Times*.)

The Whitney interests, at about this time, also acquired *Parade*, the Sunday magazine supplement headed by the colorful super-salesman Arthur H. "Red" Motley (who later became head of the U.S. Chamber of Commerce).

Although Mr. Thayer was perhaps best known in newspaper and print circles, he also provided the financing for the first suburban radio network. The New York state–based network stations were WVIP, Mount Kisco; WGHQ, Kingston; WFYI, Mineola; and our own WVOX and WRTN in Westchester.

There were many other fiefdoms in the Whitney empire, among them J. H. Whitney & Co., made up of old-money partners and investors who went way back with Ambassador Whitney (he had once been ambassador to the Court of St. James's). These included Sam Parks, Benno Schmidt, and the elegant, affable Walter J.P. Curley, who was himself later ambassador to France and Ireland. And there was Corinthian Broadcasting, a group of five CBS television stations, headed by C. Wrede Petersmeyer and a brilliant, rising young executive, Philip Lombardo. Dan Rather got his start at their Houston station. But none of these other corporate entities held the spotlight, the cachet, or the political juice of Thayer's Whitcom.

Thayer shrewdly also steered Whitcom investment partners and Whitney Communications into a chain of regional newspapers in Maryland. And he was one of the first investors in Mary Kay Cosmetics, having been greatly taken by its glamorous founder, Mary Kay Rodgers, and her sons. Plymouth Rock Publishing and Waterways Guide were other ventures. And Thayer and Whitney were among the first to take advantage of government programs to encourage "minorities" by investing in the broadcasting ventures of Eskimos!

Thayer was also a wise mentor to and patron of many of the rising young men of his day, many of whom went on to excel in finance, communications, and public service. The *New York Times* printed WNT's observation, "New York is littered with guys whose only goal is to make money ... they almost never do." Among the cadre of bright, young executives who gravitated to Thayer were Lee Heubner, Archibald Gilles, John Roche, George Gilder, Bruce Chapman, Edward Barlow, Robert Blank, James Mott Clark Jr., who had been a protégé of Milton Eisenhower, and Raymond Price, the Nixon speechwriter. Also a young Bill O'Shaughnessy.

For many years Thayer provided the funding to sustain the Ripon Society, a liberal Republican study group and think tank. And earlier, when he first came to New York as a very young man, he also founded a remarkable charitable endeavor, Vocational Foundation, an employment agency of "last resort" for those thought to be unemployable. VFI survives to this day.

He also had enormous influence with the television networks—especially CBS. And, although he once told someone that CBS Chairman William S. Paley was his "best friend," the austere, reserved Thayer always called the legendary CBS founder "Mr. Paley." During the waning days of Paley's reign, in the '60s and '70s, network insiders often cited Thayer's extraordinary influence on Chairman Paley. In fact—and this has never been told or reported—Mr. Paley, on several occasions, invited Thayer to become president of CBS and take over "the Tiffany network."

He also resisted the importunings of Presidents Eisenhower and Nixon to come out from behind the scenes and take a more visible role in the affairs of the nation. He had, in every telling, a very distant, complicated relationship with Richard Nixon, who nonetheless offered Mr. Thayer ambassadorships to France and Denmark as well as several cabinet posts. It was widely reported that one night in the White House Nixon called Walter Thayer "the brightest, toughest son of a bitch in this country."

Although he held his distance from Nixon right to the end, WNT was persuaded to head a blue-ribbon national commission to take on the daunting task of reorganizing the government of the United States.

A man of great personal charm and charisma, Thayer was a two-handicap golfer at Blind Brook in Purchase, New York—where his clubs were stored for years in the locker next to President Eisenhower's. He was also "captain" of the *Cherokee*, a sixty-five-foot Hatteras motor yacht based at Lyford Cay in the Bahamas during the winter and in Long Island Sound every summer.

Elegantly attired in understated Davies & Son suits from London, WNT would often stop in of an afternoon and unwind with Pete Kreindler, Jerry Berns, Walter Weiss, Bruce Snyder, Sheldon Tannen, and Terry Dinan at "21." He would also stop in next door for a decidedly non-alcoholic visit with Bernard "Toots" Shor, who once bodily lifted up—in mid-bite—a prominent record company executive, removing him from a corner banquette to accommodate "a great man," as the incomparable Toots called WNT. (Thayer apologized to the fellow and bought him lunch when Toots wasn't looking.)

Footnote: Several thousand New Yorkers and national political figures (including President Nixon) filled St. Thomas Episcopal Church in 1989 to bid farewell to this extraordinary man. Here are the highlights of that tribute to Walter Nelson Thayer.

Walter Thayer's personal papers and voluminous correspondence reside in the Permanent Collection and Archives of the Herbert Hoover Library at the University of Iowa in West Branch, Iowa.

On a personal note: For all his vaunted reputation for toughness (his nickname was "Wily Walter"), Thayer doted on his grandchildren, who included Matthew Thayer O'Shaughnessy, David Tucker O'Shaughnessy, and Kate O'Shaughnessy-Nulty.

Eminence gris.

August, 2003

Whitney Moore Young Jr.
NATIONAL LEADER, MORTAL MAN, NEIGHBOR

*Whitney Young, the national civil rights leader,
lived in New Rochelle.*

Whitney Moore Young Jr. always believed in what his friend Senator Jacob Javits called "the genius of the free enterprise system."

Young was an extraordinary resident of our city and county, who plowed right into the conscience of the Establishment—and may have done more for Black men and women in our nation than anyone else. We are not forgetting Martin Luther King Jr. and John Kennedy. But Whitney Young had a different approach, a different style. History may yet show us that he accomplished more in the boardroom than other civil rights leaders did in the streets. He did not come on, this man, like a Sherman tank or like gangbusters. Instead, he won to his side the big men in our country—and then enlisted them in his cause.

He would inspire men like Nelson Rockefeller and persuade corporate heads like DeWitt Wallace of *Reader's Digest* and Donald Kendall of PepsiCo to appoint African-Americans to executive positions of their companies. Other civil rights leaders of his day started at the bottom—in the streets—and worked up, often to the accompaniment of unrest and tumult. Young started right at the top, and he never used his powerful and high-level contacts to his own advantage.

The articulate and soft-spoken man from Oxford Road, whose heart stopped beating on a beach yesterday in Nigeria, was a splendid model and an inspiration to all Americans. "Hang in," he said. "Trust in this country. Work hard and believe in the sometimes elusive magic of the free enterprise system."

The world was his stage. And yet, at a dinner party a few years ago attended by William Paley, President Nixon, Henry Cabot Lodge, John Hay Whitney, and others of high estate, he bombarded his dinner companion with questions about Westchester schools and the city government in New Rochelle.

And last year, at the opening of the world headquarters of PepsiCo, we asked him how the giant bottler was doing in hiring minorities. He said they were doing better than most. And then, when he saw Donald Kendall coming, he winked at us and said, "I'm still selling." And then he put his arm around Kendall and walked him out into the sunshine to do a "little selling," as he called it.

The cause of free enterprise as well as the cause of civil rights has lost an eloquent and graceful champion. And Westchester has lost one of its most illustrious citizens.

Young was a classy man. His contributions in terms of self-confidence for his own people were immeasurable. He got his message across to all Americans, but he never stooped to conquer. He was a national leader, but he was also a mortal man and our neighbor. As such, Young leaves a special family on Oxford Road, which has lost a husband and a father.

March 8, 1971

Westchester Guiding Lights

Rocco Bellantoni:
"You . . . the Best!"

Rocco Bellantoni served briefly as a councilman. He was a "Runyon-esque" character who operated out of a delicatessen in the West End of New Rochelle.

It's Friday, the sixteenth of March, I will be glad for spring. First, however, I have to tell you about yesterday and about what happened to our city.

The Honorable Rocco Bellantoni Jr., a.k.a. Rocky Bal or just plain Bellantoni Junior, stood me and the city manager up for lunch yesterday. The former New Rochelle councilman and West End political leader was somehow unavoidably detained, you see, by a massive heart attack, which slammed against him and killed him as he lay alone yesterday morning in George Vecchione's New Rochelle Hospital.

We've told you before how important the man was to his town. He was out of Damon Runyon, Ring Lardner, and Jimmy Cannon. He was just as colorful and, if you'll allow me, just about as heroic as any character created in their minds over a typewriter. He was, for a while, the hardest-working city councilman—and this takes nothing away from Alvin Ruskin, Hugh Doyle, Donny Zack, or Joe Pisani. He was also the most compassionate councilman New Rochelle ever had.

Rocco had an enormous capacity and talent for friendship. And all afternoon and late into the night they were recalling stories about the man in the saloons and in the neighborhoods of the city. Generoso, the haberdasher from downtown, and Armiento, the born and bred police commissioner, and Donny Zack, the junior high school principal, and DeJulio, the politician and greeter: They all walked around in the Westchester sunshine with this terrible, sinking feeling deep inside them when they heard about Rocco Bellantoni.

Frank Garito, the former mayor, was coming down from Boston. And Sam Kissinger, the city manager, was on the phone. Over in

Mount Vernon at the headquarters of J. A. Valenti Electric, a man named Napoleon Holmes, who made quite a stir during the civil rights battles, was in the office of Jerome Valenti, the president of this big firm, and tears appeared on the cheeks of both of them.

Former state senator Anthony Gioffre canceled appointments with some paying clients of his law firm to go over to a club in Rye where they sat and drank and talked about their marvelous, appealing friend, Rocco.

Alvin R. Ruskin, a justice of the New York State Supreme Court, was presiding at a divorce trial in the Westchester County Courthouse, a place where husbands and wives go to kill each other—legally and all according to the law. Ruskin was watching all this when Edward Storck, his law clerk, motioned for him to come down off the bench so he could hear that Rocco had died alone in a hospital at the age of forty-nine.

Leonard Paduano, the decent and gentle man who is the current mayor of the city, broke down and cried in his office at City Hall.

At the *Standard-Star*, our newspaper, June Shetterer, the sensitive reporter who writes lovingly about the ones we lose, leaned into her typewriter yet another time. The words appeared across the top of the front page in last night's paper. And a bright young reporter named Fjordalisi was on the phone, asking around about this Bellantoni for a piece in tonight's paper. Nothing Shetterer or the young reporter or any of us, including O'Shaughnessy, can produce will capture for you what Bellantoni meant and who he was.

He was, straight out and simply, the most generous and extravagant man any of us have ever met. He earned his keep in a lot of ways—at a deli on Second Street where the Portuguese and Mexicans have moved in with the Italians. He had a piece of a small trucking company, and he would fix up old houses and rent them. In his salad days, he drove around in a big white Seville that had the license plate "ROCKY" on the back.

But when he was on the city council, he almost went broke by working at the people's business full-time and ignoring the wishes of his neighbors, who elected him to only a part-time position. He never learned how to be smart about politics, and, as a result, his business suffered. They say he tended bar and helped out in a place called Giovanni's, but I'm glad I never saw him there. And none of us saw him the night last month when he collapsed from heart tremors on his way to the mayor's inaugural ball at Nick Auletta's Glen Island Casino. He would not have wanted us to see this either, and so he checked himself quietly into a hospital.

When it was going good, he loved limousines, and he could throw around money. I think he probably knew just how to get to *jai alai* up in Bridgeport of an evening. And he surely dazzled more than one lady at those ornate roadside clubs down in Fort Lee by the George Washington Bridge, where he would go to relax and have fun and dance.

I once sat with him in Nelson Rockefeller's box at Saratoga, and I sat with him in an old dusty pickup truck as I listened to his latest scheme for repairing a busted marriage. I also saw him ride a bulldozer, but I was afraid to climb up on it with him.

There were lots of girls, but his mother was the only woman in his life. And when Mama Bellantoni died, Rocco went into a long period of mourning from which he never fully recovered. After his defeat in the 1980 election, he spent his days just being Rocco Bellantoni. He passed the time helping people; trying to reconcile husbands and wives; straightening out young, street-smart, tough Townie kids in the Fourth Ward; and feeding hungry people. Even if he didn't like you, he would look at you and say, "You … the best!" He risked his political career to help Mario Cuomo, who was not of his political tribe, but, somehow, you knew these two heard the same music.

Back in the early '70s, some women went to him (we called them girls in those days) to start a softball team in the city. Rocco, the big, dumb "feminist," found the dough and admonished them to be careful when sliding into home plate, and to be alert at all times to the possibility of a bean ball.

A few weeks ago at Giancarlo Ferro's restaurant in Bedford, Rocco got good and mad at me for telling Lynne Ames of the *New York Times* about the time the city marshal hired Rocco's trucking company to help evict a family. When Bellantoni arrived on the scene and saw what was happening, he reached into the pocket of his work pants and peeled off thirteen $100 bills to square the family's back rent.

Rocco took sides and helped his friends, and he could probably be tough in a proposition. But yesterday, the city manager and the police commissioner were saying that Bellantoni was a "pushover ... a soft touch ... and a sucker for a sentimental song." But we knew all this, and more.

A few years ago, while sitting as a member of the high council of the city, this child of the streets of the West End, this big, spectacular, generous man, decided he wanted to pray—in a church. However, inasmuch as he was not exactly a familiar face at St. Joseph's, his neighborhood parish, he hesitated lest someone think he was "getting religion" just to garner votes. You will recall we have a few politicians in this town who fish. So the Honorable Rocco Bellantoni Jr., for the last several years, met his Maker, secretly and stealthily, at out-of-the-way churches where he was not known. This is a pretty personal thing I know about him, and I wasn't sure I should tell you about it on the radio this morning—about this marvelous character who had to sneak into church so as not to ruin his reputation.

That reputation, I think—nay, I'm sure—is pretty secure around here. Even through the last few lean years, when some of his friends fled and some of his turned against him, the wonderful things he did kept coming back to remind you about him.

And yesterday, Jerome Valenti, the big, rich businessman, was saying that they should name something for Rocky Bal. You will be hearing more about it on this station, where we will remember him for a long time. And every time I get down on this damn town, I will remember it was Bellantoni Junior's town—at least for forty-nine years.

Rocco. You ... the best!

March 16, 1984

The beautiful chapel at Sound Shore Medical Center
was later dedicated to Rocco Bellantoni Jr.

Remarks of William O'Shaughnessy

Memorial Service for Page Morton Black at Frank E. Campbell Chapel, New York City (September 12, 2013)

I won't intrude for very long on your September afternoon.

Thank you, Robin Elliott, for gathering so many influential friends of an extraordinary woman.

Many of you knew her as a great philanthropist of national renown for her leadership of the Parkinson's Disease Foundation, which was founded by her beloved husband, William Black. Others remember Page as a gifted artist who could play and sing achingly romantic songs like an angel.

She lived for decades in a grand house in what the *Times* referred to as an "enclave" off the coast of New Rochelle. It was aptly named as Premium Point.

It was from this redoubt that she conducted her own personal philanthropy and raised millions for national charitable causes.

And among her enthusiasms, I'm proud to recall, was wvox, New Rochelle's community radio station. She would dispatch missives, suggestions (actually "directives") to me and mine, often about the great issues of the day. She backed the more enlightened politicians (when such existed) and she put her money where her heart was.

Like, for instance, during the broadcast celebrating the fiftieth anniversary of the natal day of wvox. It was a very big day for us. And as I went into the studio, settled in behind the mike, and strapped on my earphones, I inquired of the engineer who the "sponsors" were. There was just one: Page Morton Black.

When I later asked why she was so nice to our little 500-watt flamethrower of a radio station, Page said, "Many years ago the *Herald Tribune* gave me a flattering review. That was long before I met William Black. And you married the boss's daughter ... didn't you marry Jock Whitney's daughter?"

I replied: "Not exactly, Mrs. Black. I married a wonderful girl named Ann Thayer, whose father, Walter Nelson Thayer, was president of the *Trib* ...."

And she said: "Well, it was a great review anyway!"

Truth to tell, I'm not sure that speaks well of the station. But it does speak well of those qualities of loyalty, generosity, and friendship—as well as a long memory—that others have identified.

Her iconic red dress has also been mentioned. The first time I saw it was many years ago when a big limo pulled up to the station and a lady in red, the Lady in Red, got out and handed an envelope to our receptionist. "Here, Mr. O'Shaughnessy will know what to do with this ...." It was a political contribution for a young aspiring Italian fellow—actually a failed baseball player with too many vowels in his name—Mario Cuomo.

I hope I don't do damage to her reputation by telling this story in front of all you Republicans. I'm a "Rockefeller-Catsimatidis Republican" myself. And it's nice to see John and Margo here. As well as Len Berman. And the legendary Sy Presten ... great New Yorkers, as Page was.

And so we are here today to remember a lady who touched so many for ninety-seven years. I will mercifully yield now with just one more small story about Page.

Several of her friends here assembled and all the obits mentioned the "Chock full o' Nuts" song. And every year on her birthday, we would play that damn jingle. And one year, after we had played it three times ... she called up and asked if we had played it yet. The engineer said, "Yes, ma'am ... three times." She said, "Well, I missed it this year ... do you think you could indulge an old dame and play it just one more time?"

You can be sure we did.

So people will remember Page and that damn jingle for years to come.

And you'll remember her great philanthropy.

Have it as you will ... I'll remember her as a neighbor.

Please don't hold it against her then ... that she had a soft spot for failed baseball players ... or Irish broadcasters.

She was a hell of a dame.

And her lovely music lingers. In every key. A generous, engaged, and thoughtful neighbor. In every chord. In every tempo.

And, like I said, in the neighborhood.

John Branca

A Whitney Radio Commentary:
W VOX 1460/AM, W VIP 93.5 FM

John Branca, who died this week in Florida at eighty-six, was a beloved Mount Vernon icon. Many knew him as the brother of the legendary Brooklyn Dodger Ralph Branca. But John Branca put up a lot
of numbers on the scoreboard of life all on his very own. And for all
his laurels and high estate in the world of politics and sports, Johnny
Branca was a Westchester Townie.

Although he spent his last years in Florida pushing a market basket
through Walgreen's and flirting with the silver-haired widows in the
Piggly Wiggly supermarket, John Branca will long be remembered
around here as a New York state assemblyman and Commissioner of
Recreation in Mount Vernon, the landlocked, struggling Westchester
city. He was a celebrated high school coach, and Mario Cuomo even
made him chairman of the New York State Athletic Commission,
where he cleaned up the brutal, violent sport called boxing. And, always, he was one damn good friend of this community radio station.

Back in the '6os and into the '7os, "Commissioner" Branca, as everyone called him, would preside and hold daily court on the benches
at Hartley Park and listen to the pleadings and importunings of the
old men of the neighborhood who would bring him their problems
laden with heavy dialects grown in the hills of Calabria, Guardia
Lombardi, and Bari. Branca listened to and savored all of it. And
tried to assist.

He was a most agreeable figure and a class act in every season. Although he never became mayor of Mount Vernon, John Branca was
a powerful political force, and you needed him on your side in every
proposition.

He was of a Mount Vernon when giants walked the land in that
city ... larger-than-life personalities like Joe Vacarella, Augie Petrillo,
the banker Walter Moore, Sal Quaranta, Tommy Sharpe, Judge Ir-

ving Kendall, Reggie Lafayette, Tom Delaney, David Ford, Frank Connelly Sr., M. Paul Redd, Frank LaSorsa, and a struggling theater kid named Denzel Washington. Also young rising stars like Gary Pretlow, Jimmy Finch, Roberta Apuzzo, Clinton Young, David Alpert, and Ernie Davis. The great preacher W. Franklyn Richardson, soon to become a revered national figure, would climb up in the pulpit at Grace Baptist Church on Sundays. And Ossie Davis visited his mother every weekend.

For a good, long time, Branca sat before the wvox microphone, presiding over our Pepsi High School "Game of the Week" as a play-by-play announcer and color commentator. He had a wife named Millie, and she was part of it too, a very big part.

John Branca spent the last two decades in Florida, where he never saw his beloved Westchester overrun by insufferable Yuppies in their bmws and Mercedes. These people, who send their kids to Hackley and Rye Country Day School, do not know of Hartley Park, where he sat on warm summer nights.

He was a politician the way the men of our fathers' time imagined them to be.

This is a Whitney Media commentary. This is Bill O'Shaughnessy.

August 2, 2010

John Brophy

LEADING THE PARADE

John Brophy led every parade in southern Westchester for twenty-five years. I can still hear the music coming up the street behind him.

John Brophy never studied Latin or went to the university, and, thus, he would take no offense if you called him *sui generis*. For John Brophy of New Rochelle is truly unique unto himself. He has a face that might have belonged to a sergeant in the old Irish Republican Army, when they used to ambush British troops moving down through Glen Maloor or Glendalough. But our John Brophy is not blowing up any statues of Lord Nelson. He's too busy worrying about the people of the city of New Rochelle.

Brophy has fun doing for others. He's not too big on the fancy charities we have in this county, where you have to be born into the right family in order to help your fellow man via the very social and most phony charities. Rather, Brophy is a bread-and-butter man. He's a tireless worker for the Salvation Army, because they give people food for their stomachs and clothing for their backs rather than cocktails and lawn parties attended by a lot of wealthy stiffs in black ties. That's the route John Brophy goes—and that's why we like him.

Brophy runs every parade in this town, except when we marched to choke the city's economic vein. And John doesn't buy the anti-Vietnam stuff. He flies with the American Legion. We remember a parade that John ran last year, around Thanksgiving. Somebody got the bright idea of having another wonderful old man, Jim Grady, sing the "City Alive" song while perched on top of a trailer truck. They even had a band. But the band was on a different truck, which was supposed to stop in front of the reviewing stand. Now the cold air got in Jim Grady's tonsils, and he was about as far out of key as you can go—and the mobile orchestra was hitting clinkers, too. John Brophy almost said some very bad things, which a grand marshal of a parade is not supposed to say, especially with a lot of kids around.

Brophy is the world's champion sucker for lost causes. When someone has a good cause and they get turned down by everyone else, they go to John Brophy. He gets on the phone and calls a few friends, which means he might call about a thousand people, and Brophy pulls it out of the fire.

He's fiercely loyal, and when somebody asked him why he was such a big Teddy Greene fan, John said, "Teddy is a man of his word," which is a very good reason to like a politician in this day. He's a glorious old gent, John Brophy, and now he's wound up about Flag Day, which is today—this very day.

We hope John Brophy sees a lot of flags flying today. He'll be very happy about that. And, as for us, we can't resist telling you that every time we see a flag, we think of John Brophy, who always shows up in the cold, mean, early hours at the Draft Board in the Pershing Square Building to send our kids off to Fort Dix and Vietnam. They go early, very early, but John Brophy has never missed a "sendoff," as he calls it. He actually gives these kids comb-and-brush sets and prayer books and a handshake. He also gives them something to fight for—and something to come back to.

What a beautiful coincidence that Flag Day just happens to fall on the birthday of John Brophy, who always seems to be coming up the street at the head of a parade.

June 14, 1967

William Butcher

A STAND-UP GUY

For several decades, Bill Butcher was chairman of the old County Trust Company and Westchester's most powerful banker. He was responsible for many of those big corporate buildings on either side of the Cross-Westchester Expressway (I-287). A bridge named for Mr. Butcher crosses over that busy road.

The Establishment of Westchester will meet in high council this very night in the pristine town of Eastchester. The big landowners, developers, industrialists, corporate executives, movers, bankers, and tycoons who populate the Westchester County Association will come together to honor William Butcher, the former chairman of the County Trust Bank.

William Butcher is a special man who has had an enormous influence on your life. You may not know this modest, decent, witty man when you pass him on the street, but he had a lot to do with how we live in the Golden Apple. Thus, more people will turn out tonight for this William Butcher than for any big-name guest the Westchester Association ever presented—and they have presented Richard Nixon, James Buckley, Donald Kendall of PepsiCo, Art Larkin of General Foods, and Thomas Watson of IBM. Bill Butcher will outdraw all these guys—and he deserves to. Because no one around the county now comes close to him in terms of service and devotion to Westchester.

The others are accomplished men, one and all, faithful, loyal, and true. But Bill Butcher, the son of a social worker from Newark, by way of Cincinnati, has had more of an impact on the quality of suburban life than any of them. And so the clan will gather tonight, and the captains of industry will assemble over Scotch and beef and try to thank him, as will Nelson Aldrich Rockefeller, who will rush back from a meeting with Richard Nixon to talk about this William Butcher.

But hell, all these are bigshots. It's just too bad Dan O'Brien, the able guy who is running the dinner, doesn't let some working stiff get up and tell how we all owe Butcher because he was the one who got a lot of firms to relocate here and thousands of jobs over the last twenty-five years.

He performed his public service and worked his magic as chief drumbeater-poet of our charms in his own easy style over the years. And as everybody else was wasting five hours on a golf course, Butcher got Continental Banking and Dictaphone on a tennis court. It is a brisk game that everyone is taking up today, but if you want to mix it up with sixty-five-year-old William Butcher on a tennis court, you'd better be prepared to do something great for Westchester— because Bill Butcher has retired from his bank, but he'll never retire from Westchester.

This is a poor tribute this morning to Mr. Butcher, because you can't get him to talk about himself. We tried all of yesterday morning. He is, as you know, a member of the board of the MTA, and when you mention that, he will tell you he considers Nelson Rockefeller the country's leading statesman because the governor is a "stand-up guy," which is the highest compliment Bill Butcher knows. And he will next spend half an hour discussing the responsibility we all have to "nourish" our environment. You can ask Bill Butcher about those friends who are trying to make him county executive and he will hit you with a line like: "I feel sorry for a political party that's so bankrupt it has to dredge up a sixty-five-year-old guy like me to run."

But if you listen closely to William Butcher and don't let him put you off, you will get the picture of a man who doesn't look back much because he is just beginning life at that magic age of sixty-five, when other men are ready to cash in their chips and live the sweet life. Of his years as a banker he will say only: "Hell, there are a dozen guys at the County Trust who will make me look sick in a few years." You really have to poke around and get it from his friends that he is a director of Pace College, Dictaphone, White Plains Hospital, the School for the Deaf, and the Burke Foundation.

William Butcher has had a greater influence than any man at the Westchester County Association, but he will steer you around and away from himself and tell you about a man named Joe Hughes, his predecessor at County Trust, and how Hughes and *Reader's Digest* and the old Westchester Lighting Company (now Con Ed) and the Macy's chain started the organization he distinguished and that will honor him tonight. He will dart and weave and advise you to keep an eye on Ed Weidlein, the head of the Union Carbide complex in our county, who, he feels, is starting to emerge as a "real stand-up guy." Also a William Plunkett, Esquire.

"We've got to broaden; there is still a lot of parochial thinking around here. We've got to recognize that New York City exists—we're part of a region," says Bill Butcher. "My game plan is to do something about the mobility of the region—how people are going to move around in a few years." He signed out as chairman of the board of the County Trust Bank, and he turned around and opened an office to continue his volunteer work on his "projects." And his talk in that office is of the future. Incredibly, he doesn't dwell much on those days of drama and growth as he moved one of Westchester's leading banks to the $1 billion mark. And he has almost forgotten how he helped finesse IBM into an Armonk apple orchard right past the narrow objections of yesterday. Tomorrow is clearly bad.

The big companies he lured to our area help pay a lot of our taxes. And fashionable as it is to rap the MTA, we all might just think once in a while about this sturdy and warm and wonderful man who left the chairmanship of a billion-dollar bank to worry about those trains and roads that take us to work and home again.

William Butcher has already done enough to be called "Mr. Westchester." But this amazing man is still at it and, as they rain down accolades on this fine, bright man, you can look up at him on the dais and be sure that this B tennis player from Fox Meadow will be using that natural way of his to disguise more exciting and daring dreams that he intends for our future. As one of Westchester's promotional brochures might put it, William Butcher is one of our county's greatest natural resources.

1972

The Townie Soapbox Orators

A WVOX Commentary by
William O'Shaughnessy, President

Word came this morning of the passing of Ines Candrea. You will not read of her life in the *New York Times*. Around these parts she was known as the widow of the late Joe Candrea and mother-in-law of one Anthony Galletta. Mrs. Candrea was eighty, and I speak of her on this radio station because for so many of those eighty years she used WVOX as her own personal soapbox, as did her late husband.

And as we mourn Mrs. Candrea this day, our mind drifts back to her shy, modest, retiring husband, who was cut from the same outspoken cloth. And when he went to what Malcolm Wilson would call "another and, we are sure, a better world" on December 21, 1999, we went into this studio and said these very words about the man:

> Joe Candrea was a Runyonesque figure. But instead of Broadway or The Great White Way, his canvas was our home heath. It was here in New Rochelle that Joe Candrea lived most of his years with great conviction.
>
> He confronted every proposition and civic issue with a relentless passion. Although his résumé said "newspaper delivery man," Joe Candrea could put power and energy into words, which usually became majestic proclamations. His podium was behind this microphone, or on any street corner he could find.
>
> He possessed what most of us search for all our lives. There was a sureness to Joe Candrea's proposals and observations. He was the great articulator, the undiminished champion of the forgotten neighborhoods in the West End of our city.
>
> The politicians used to call it the old Fourth Ward. It is where Rocco Bellantoni once lived. And Tony and Sal Tocci and the Fosinas came from there. But in recent years there

was only Joe Candrea to rage against injustices as they might be committed against his neighbors in the West End.

New Rochelle was his mistress. And also his fortress. He felt about our city the way some men of his generation look upon the United States Marine Corps or the Notre Dame football team. Other callers and radio talk show hosts discuss with great erudition the cosmic issues of the day. Theirs is an international curiosity or a national inclination, but Joe Candrea's enthusiasms and passions extended only as far as the city limits. ZIP code 10801 was his territory, baby, and don't you forget it.

He ran flat out and went straight for everything. There was no halfway station ... no middle ground with the man ... and never, ever a doubt about where he stood on civic issues, politicians, bureaucrats, and other disreputable types.

He was all about building up the damn neighborhood.

Have I got it right, Joe?

That was spoken for Joe Candrea, who, like I said, was the husband of one Ines Candrea, who left us early this morning at eighty.

There were other vivid townie orators who used this WVOX broadcasting station over the years as their own personal soapbox. Back in the '60s there was a brilliant, cerebral David Kendig who drove them nuts at city hall. And Lorraine Trotta, whose son Frank is now a big-time lawyer in Greenwich and works with Lewis Lehrman, who spent millions trying to become governor. Our roster of townie callers in those days also included Bob Schaeffer, who called himself "The Neighborhood Watchdog" or was it "Junkyard Dog"? Memory fails. Bob weighed in on everything and everyone. So did Ken from Pelham and Frank from Connecticut who used to be Frank from Mount Vernon.

Every day on our "Open Line" programs they were there opining, arguing, debating, raging, cajoling, attacking, occasionally even flattering, and, on rare occasion, actually saying something nice about one of our neighbors.

Mario Cuomo once told me he prays for "sureness." Our callers never had that problem. They brought a rock-solid, unshakeable sureness to most of their pronouncements.

Other stations had Scott Shannon, Imus, or Howard Stern. We had Mitch from the North End and Bruce the Swimmer, a Libertarian who ... lived ... his ... life ... the ... way ... he ... damn ... well ... pleased. And there was always, it seems, Mr. Cam, who demanded to be addressed just so. But I'll not leave this planet until I find out his regular, normal, human, given first name. He's gotta have one.

Day after day here on the radio there was Ann Witkowski, Peggy Godfrey, Mary Tedesco, and a brilliant William Kirby Scollon, who was descended from the Kirbys of Rye but became a New Rochelle "townie" in good standing. He was a friend of Bill Mullen, no blushing violet he, who could also climb up on our soapbox. Right out here with Mullen would be Dave from Mamaroneck, Joanne, Alex from Greenburgh, and Michael Brown. They could all talk.

Some of our regular callers were possessed of great insight and a few were even accompanied by a stunning intelligence concerning matters political. One of the most brilliant was—and still is—Angela Scarano, who reveled in the moniker ... "Nudge." She was. And is. In the best possible way.

Also we recall Anthony Galletta, the Candrea son-in-law; Charlie from the West End; Lorraine Pierce; and don't forget Bob, her husband. And the late, great "Woody." That's all ... just "Woody." There was a Rae Rega and an Isabel. And I have gone this far without mentioning the incomparable Carmine Saracino. And Mrs. Green.

Actually, some of these "frequent" callers were so good (and so frequent) we couldn't resist giving them their very own weekly shows: Colonel Marty Rochelle, the Yonkers legend who never met a judge he doesn't like. Or a district attorney. And Mike Scully, the world traveler, who gets better every week. But I wish he'd let me "enlighten" him on the great issues. I'll bring him around. Like when Andrew Cuomo is sworn in ... and Scully jumps off our 190-foot radio tower! And Lou Felicione, who opines about everything New Rochelle when he's not posting on Facebook. He has his very own show too. And Sam Spady.

Sometimes I've felt like taking a page from my friend—and mentor to us all—Bob Grant, who, when he couldn't abide it any more, would just scream into the microphone: "Get off my phone!" It was tempting, I should tell you. But then the advice we received so many years ago from Alvin Richard Ruskin would break through all the cacophony, noise, dialogue, and often disagreeable chatter.

Alvin Ruskin was mayor of New Rochelle back in the '60s before Nelson Rockefeller made him a judge. And one day he took me aside: "Your damn station is gaining a national reputation . . . . The *Wall Street Journal* called you 'the quintessential community station in America' . . . and so on. And all that is well and good, O'Shaughnessy. But don't let it go to your head. And don't forget the Townies. They made you. They're the strength of your station . . . people with opinions."

Judge Ruskin was a wise man then. And he is to this day—retired, in his nineties, and living in Stamford, Connecticut.

Like I said . . . other stations had Imus, Scott Shannon, and Howard Stern.

We had Ines Candrea and Joe and all those other marvelous soapbox orators.

And with it all . . . there really was never a dull moment.

Have I got it right, Anthony . . . ?

Broadcast August 2, 2012

Joe Candrea

Joe Candrea was a Runyonesque figure. He might also have been imagined in the mind of Ring Lardner. But instead of Broadway, the Big Apple, or the Great White Way, his canvas was our home heath. It was here in New Rochelle that Joe Candrea lived most of his sixty-seven years with great conviction.

He confronted every proposition and every civic issue with a relentless passion. Although his résumé said "newspaper delivery man" and "truck driver," Joe Candrea could put power and energy into words, which usually became majestic proclamations. His podium was behind this microphone, down at city hall or on any street corner he could find.

He possessed what most of us search for all our lives. There was a sureness to Joe Candrea's proposals and observations. He was the great articulator, the undiminished champion of the forgotten neighborhoods in the West End of our city. The politicians used to call it the old Fourth Ward. It is where Rocco Bellantoni once lived ... and Tony and Sal Tocci and the Fosinas came from there. But in recent years there was only Joe Candrea to rage against injustices of every kind as they might be committed against his neighbors in the West End.

I expect the greatest appellation I can apply to Joe Candrea, this morning, is to remind our listeners that he was, ultimately and essentially, a "townie." The way Evie Haas, she also of sainted memory, was a "Townie."

New Rochelle was his mistress. And also his fortress. He felt about our city the way some men of his generation felt about the United States Marine Corps or the Notre Dame football teams. Other callers and radio talk show hosts often discuss, with great erudition, the cosmic issues of the day. Theirs is an international curiosity or a national inclination, but Joe Candrea's enthusiasms and passions extended only as far as the city limits. ZIP code 10801 was his territory, baby, and don't you forget it.

He could murder you one day on the radio and a few hours later encounter you at a civic meeting with a warm embrace and even a kiss on the cheek. He ran flat-out and went straight for everything. There was no halfway station ... there was no middle ground with the man ... and never, ever a doubt about where he stood on civic issues or politicians, bureaucrats, and other disreputable types.

His loss, then, is a very significant one, I think, for our city. For, you see, we have thousands of residents who use the place as a bedroom, who take and put nothing back, who never have an opinion about anything, who live out their days without ever trying to make things better.

Speaking of which: Mario Cuomo talks often these days about the admonitions of a Hebrew God, with these two marvelous phrases, *Tikkun Olam* and *Tzedakah*, which mean: "You are all children of one God. You are all separate and entitled to dignity and respect for one another. And your mission is to repair the universe and build up the neighborhood."

And then, according to the great Cuomo, the Christians stole it whole from the Jews with the outrageous suggestion, given to them by a carpenter's son in the temple one day, that we should love our neighbor as we love ourselves.

So, you know, as we reflect on all of this, I think ... that's what Joe Candrea ... was all about. He was all about building up the damn neighborhood. But as Mayor Idoni and legislator Maisano said on the radio yesterday ... that work is not ... quite ... finished.

Have I got it right, Joe?

Hugh Doyle

THE COUNCILMAN EMERITUS

It is the morning after Election Day. But we are thinking about a man named Hugh Aloyisius Doyle. He was the councilman emeritus of our city.

There was so much he loved: the Coast Guard, the little Saint Gabriel's Catholic parish, the Elks, the Kennedys, the Democratic Party, the city council on which he served.

And for three days at Lloyd Maxcy's funeral home, they came to pay respects to old Hugh Doyle. They came out of the wet streets of the South Side of town. And they came from way outside our city—from the Bronx, Brooklyn, and from as far away as California. They came to New Rochelle all this week with their stories, holding on to their love for this good, decent man.

The organizations he loved were represented: the Rowing Club, the Coast Guard, the Elks, the Knights of Columbus, the Holy Name Society. The people also came to wake old Hughie—the Italians, the Irish, and the Jews came, townspeople and neighbors, rich and poor, from all walks of life—their only credentials, the appellation they all carried with considerable pride: friends of Hugh Doyle.

As the old gentleman lay there surrounded by grand floral tributes and guarded by the regal-looking Knights of Columbus in full dress with their flowing red satin-lined capes and golden swords, Hugh Doyle's cousin, Betty Gordon, was saying: "His friends were his jewels ... but he didn't think of them like a collection." The Irish are the only ones left on the planet who would say something as lyrical and graceful about this old man who had just died. And then a Black man came up to Betty Gordon to tell her how Hughie Doyle got him an apartment in 1929.

He was out of the time of Al Smith, Jim Farley, Jimmy Walker, Francis Cardinal Spellman, and pitching horseshoes on lazy Sunday afternoons. And he knew about such quaint things as camaraderie and patriotism, of joining and belonging.

It was a fine wake. And Hughie Doyle would approve, said Alvin Ruskin, the former mayor—because Hughie made more condolence calls than anyone in history during his seventy-eight years. And Father George Homell, the popular priest from Blessed Sacrament, once said he saw Hugh Doyle at so many funerals he thought Doyle was the funeral director Maxcy.

And because this old man with his brogue and white hair touched so many lives, just about everyone in this sad city has his own story about Hugh Doyle.

Mine started the very first week I ever set foot in New Rochelle. It was twelve years ago, when there was a very big "do" indeed at Temple Israel, an anniversary or something. And as everyone who was really important at the time was to attend, I made it my business to crash the affair to drum up support for this community radio station.

The only name or face I recognized was that of the legendary Stanley Church, who was surrounded by hale fellows, well met, in one corner. And then I spotted a man who used to be a car dealer in this town. He was wearing a blue blazer, this car dealer, and his name was Peter Griffin. And when I tried, awkwardly, to introduce myself as "the new guy in at the radio station," he quickly disengaged my hand, to put it mildly, and drifted off. (There had been a lot of "new guys" at the radio station.)

And then I remember that a kindly white-haired man came over to my side and said his name was Hugh Doyle and "Who would you like to meet, young man?" And so for the next several hours Hugh Doyle introduced me to every person in the place. The names and the faces have blurred along with their rank and station title. But I remember Hugh Doyle, who rescued me in an alien sea of strangers twelve years ago.

And so after his wake at Lloyd Maxcy's I went with Judge Alvin Ruskin and his wife, Sylvia Bessen, to have an ice cream soda. We came out of the cold rain and sat in this ice cream parlor and told each other Hugh Doyle stories. And most of them made us laugh.

And as we sat in this ice cream parlor feeling good with our memories about Hugh Doyle, Alvin Ruskin said: "Bill ... do a good piece on the radio for Hughie."

But I can't think of any greater tribute to the man, ladies and gentlemen, than to report to you that we were sitting there and smiling and feeling warm and friendly and very good on this night after he had just died.

There are a lot of wealthy and powerful men in this county. But when they go, how many people will sit in an ice cream parlor feeling about them the way Alvin Ruskin and I felt about Hugh A. Doyle?

Broadcast November 8, 1977

Dr. Richard Fraser

Interview with William O'Shaughnessy

wo: "Tonight we're going to talk about doctors, healthcare, and mortality. The old Jesuits used to say you don't really mature until you deal with that word ... mortality. The man we are about to meet knows a lot about that. For our doctor we've chosen a clear-eyed, jut-jawed, central casting handsome man who is a great sportsman ... a sailor at the American Yacht Club ... a relentless tennis player. Now, nobody has ever accused me of being a rocket scientist or a brain surgeon. He is a brain surgeon ... a neurosurgeon. Perhaps the finest in the nation: Dr. Richard Fraser of Rye, New York. Let me see those hands. How much are those hands worth?"

RF: "My mother thinks a lot. They are not insured."

wo: "They're not?"

RF: "It's an odd question that you asked. As I tell my patients and my residents, you don't operate with your hands, you operate with your brain. It's judgment, not manual dexterity. You can teach almost anybody to do an operation ... even a technically difficult one. What you can't always teach is when you should operate and perhaps even more important when you shouldn't operate."

wo: "I want to talk to you about that. My father-in-law, B. F. Curry the auto magnate, first discovered you. You don't just do brains ... you also do other stuff."

RF: "That is correct. Spinal surgery as well."

wo: "You threw Mr. Curry out of the office."

RF: "That would be true of most spine patients that are sent to me. Spine surgery is certainly, by my standards, the most abused surgical procedure ... either back or neck ... in neurosurgery. The vast majority of spine surgery that is done in this country, by my standards, is not indicated. That's a pretty terrible statistic."

wo: "Why do your colleagues do it?"

RF: "Money! Well, that's unfair. I was too quick to say that. Money is certainly a big motive. I think a lot of surgeons honestly think they can make a patient better by operating on their neck or spine when most of those people, if they did an exercise program and a physical therapy program, would get completely better as did your father-in-law."

WO: "I want to talk to you about doctors. Do you like being a doctor? Do you want your kids to grow up and become doctors?"

RF: "I would love it if one of my four daughters would grow up and become a doctor. I think it's a wonderful profession. I think it's fascinating and very gratifying, but also very burdensome. I went into medicine for all the wrong reasons. My girlfriend at the time had a father who was a doctor, and I decided to emulate him and it's the luckiest decision I ever made. I've been a doctor since 1962."

WO: "Dr. Fraser ... you let a guy operate on your brain and open up your head ... that's a sign of trust. You really have to trust a guy."

RF: "It is truly a transfer of trust. Just yesterday I was taking a brain tumor out of a young mother of four and the tumor was right next to her speech area. The big risk is that she's going to wake up and be unable to speak and perhaps paralyzed on the right side. She said that she was terrified and I said to her that she had every reason to be. Here I am a stranger and I'm going to open up her head and take out this brain tumor. As I explain to people, I'm just an instrument. I am a trained instrument who will try to do the best job possible. I strongly believe that a lot of what we do is luck if it turns out well or I like to say that God's guidance came in there."

WO: "Do you operate on your friends?"

RF: "Occasionally."

WO: "Is that tough to do?"

RF: "Believe it or not, once you've made the decision to operate and you're actually in an operation, you've forgotten who this person is. It's a task that you must carry out. Personalities are totally gone. The truth of the matter is that most of one's patients become your friends. The difficult burden in neurosurgery ... for me, because mostly what I do is take out brain tumors ... and half of those people have malignant brain tumors and they'll all be dead and I'll see the tears ... that's very difficult to deal with."

WO: "Do you know that up front? Do you tell them?"

RF: "I tell somebody. Somebody in the family has got to know. You've got to tell the truth. You have to be candid ... candid without re-moving all hope. I don't tell you, 'Look, Mr. O'Shaughnessy, your tumor is malignant and you're going to be dead in a year to two and much of your last few months you're going to be paralyzed or have lost your conscious human traits.' I don't say that sort of thing. I tell a patient generally, if their tumor is malignant, that we will control it for a period of time. Most people don't ask how long they have to live. Very few people ask that ...."

wo: "Do you think they sort of know?"

RF: "I'm sure they know. It's extremely rare for a person to ask me if I can cure their tumor. And if they do ask ... then I say that I don't think so."

wo: "You say it's a combination of luck and God. What are you say-ing ... that God is smiling on certain people?"

RF: "I don't know if I can explain this ... but I certainly believe that we take individual responsibility for what we do ... but there's a lot of guidance that comes in there and I can't tell you where it comes from in neurosurgery. After one has practiced this craft ... after a certain period of time ... there's a lot of nonverbal learning that goes in there that some people would call intuition and judgment. It doesn't come out of a textbook. You can't teach it to somebody. It's experience. Any pilot will tell you the same thing, as would anyone who has practiced a technical craft for years. I don't know if you're getting my message. I'm not sure what my message is."

wo: "Are you ever operating and say, 'God, this is a tough one'?"

RF: "I do that all beforehand."

wo: "I got some pictures from your office at New York Hospital Cor-nell Medical College. Is this you doing an operation?"

RF: "Yes, it is."

wo: "Which one are you?"

RF: "I'm the fellow in the center holding his hand out for an instrument."

wo: "How many people are in the room with you there?"

RF: "Generally me and one or two assistants who are young doctors in training to become neurosurgeons and an operating nurse and a circulating nurse."

WO: "We have another shot of Dr. Richard Fraser ... neurosurgeon. There he is."

RF: "That's a picture of me taking on a brain tumor in a young girl."

WO: "How young?"

RF: "At the time I think she was nine. Now she's a young mother."

WO: "How long do these operations last? How long are you standing there?"

RF: "The longest brain operation I was ever involved in took about twenty-four hours."

WO: "What?"

RF: "That was when I was a resident. That operation today would take me about four hours. That was an unnecessarily long procedure performed by a very deliberate neurosurgeon. All neurosurgery should be performed with deliberateness, but this was excessively so. For me the average brain tumor takes probably two to three hours, and we generally do two or three of those in a day."

WO: "Are you exhausted when you come home to Rye?"

RF: "No. I used to be when I started out in this business. If you're taking a brain tumor out I would have to put my feet up for the rest of the day because I would be emotionally drained and just tired beyond belief. It's a matter of doing so many now I don't find it fatiguing at all."

WO: "You are a leader. You've risen to the top of your field ... neurosurgery. We read in the public press today that your whole profession is in chaos. First of all on the national level ... what about this healthcare problem? Hillary Clinton is working on it. I would be astonished if you thought that was a good idea."

RF: "I don't think it is a good idea. I don't know that Hillary Clinton has any special training to arrive at the appropriate decisions of what is proper for healthcare in the United States. I come from Canada, which has a long history of free medical care. Of course there's no such thing as free anything ... but it's taxation-provided healthcare ... so that no individual pays for any individual costs."

WO: "Is the Canadian system better?"

RF: "I have a daughter who lives in British Columbia, in Vancouver, who was recently desperately ill. She came through a major op-

eration and lengthy hospitalization and that cost me nothing ...
not one cent. I am grateful for that. I contrast that with my wife's
being a tennis player of great reputation since she was a child ....."

WO: "Ann Fraser ... she's the bionic tennis player."

RF: "She's the bionic tennis player. She recently had a wrist fusion
... because of all these years ... causing a dislocation of her wrist.
The total bill I received for that you could buy a new car with. I
didn't pay for that. My insurance did, but it was a huge, huge cost.
To address your problem ... the central problem of all Americans
... is that healthcare costs in this country are absolutely through
the roof."

WO: "Who's making the money? Is it the doctors who are packing it
in?"

RF: "There are some doctors who are excessively rewarded, there
is no question about that. If you take the total healthcare bill of
roughly $900 billion this year ... that will be $2 trillion by the year
2000 ... 20 per cent of the GDP. That's a totally uneconomic cost
to the nation."

WO: "Should the government try to fix it, doctor?"

RF: "No question. But to try and fix it and go after doctors' salaries is
going after the tail on the mouse because total doctors' remuneration in this country represents less than 10 percent of that total
bill. So are you going to go after 10 percent? That doesn't seem to
be intelligent, to me. I'd rather think ... doctors represent less than
1 percent of the total population in the nation."

WO: "But haven't doctors gotten away from that hometown country
doctor in the horse and buggy who makes house calls? I'm going
to tell you something bad I know about you. You make house calls.
Somebody told me a woman, not of standing or high estate, had
a problem with her son who wasn't moving ... a five-year-old kid.
You told her what to do over the phone and you showed up at the
door unannounced and wanted to look at the kid."

RF: "That's true."

WO: "I also understand your phone number is listed, which puts you
in the great minority."

RF: "I don't know if it does put me in the minority, but I'm not going
to unlist it."

WO: "Why? Don't you get a lot of cuckoo calls?"

RF: "We get a few and my six-year-old daughter handles them pretty well. To answer your first question ... I think doctors have gotten away from the type of doctor my grandfather was and, unfortunately in many ways, it's impossible to turn back. My grandfather didn't even have X-rays. They'd been invented, but he didn't have them. Today I have the gold standard of computerized imaging, which is an MRI scan. It allows me to perform surgery that couldn't be dreamed of even ten years ago. So, in many ways, medicine today, and certainly neurosurgery, is totally different from what it was twenty years ago. I think that doctors, in the main, still go into medicine because they're interested in helping people and they are interested in biology."

WO: "Is there still a Hippocratic Oath? Do you guys still take it?"

RF: "Yes, we do."

WO: "What is that all about?"

RF: "That Hippocratic Oath, which at Cornell at least, is recited by every medical student at their graduation ceremony, promises to care for patients; to provide free care for patients who cannot pay; to teach one's craft to others for no remuneration and not to disclose the details or illnesses of patients to others. It covers it all."

WO: "But would you not agree, sir, that a lot of doctors are like conglomerates? You have to work your way through about twenty-three nurses to get to the doctor. Big business. They have 'PC' after their names ... professional corporations."

RF: "It's true, and I hate it. There are many doctors who believe in revenue enhancement and trying to make as much money as possible."

WO: "That's a nice way of saying money grubbing."

RF: "That is there. It's funny you bring this up because ... I don't want to sound self-serving and I'm certainly one of the better-remunerated specialists and we have three cars in the driveway and all that .... I'm pleased to be able to say that at least for myself and for some of my colleagues ... about one-third of what I do is for free. Typically it is some kid who is sent over from Israel or from Greece and their parents have sucked up their last shekel to get them here ... they have no insurance. Typically it is a brain tumor ... and I take it out for free and I have an anesthesiologist who gives a free anesthesia. New York hospitals had a long tradition of giving free medical care. For instance you may have heard about that girl in Sarajevo, yesterday it was in the *New York Times*, who had a terrible shrapnel injury from a firefight in which her mother was killed. We were organizing to bring her over here to New York to give her free medical care. Fortunately, she went to England and she is being taken care of there."

WO: "I hear you almost have an office in Armenia or some exotic place. What the hell are you doing poking around there?"

RF: "I don't have a drop of Armenian blood in my veins as far as I know, but shortly after the earthquake in Armenia, which was in 1989, within twelve hours of the earthquake Dr. Edgar Hasepian, who is a very prominent neurosurgeon at Columbia Presbyterian, asked me to go to Armenia and lead a medical relief team. And for reasons that I really can't identify ... I said yes. I have to say that was the most searing experience I have ever seen. I have not lived through a world war. I have seen pictures of what our bombs did to Berlin in 1945 and it was almost an exact replica of that. Modern buildings totally shattered. Stairwells, which is apparently a very efficient way to kill the Armenians ... people would run into the stairwell during the earthquake and the stairwells would collapse with a bunch of concrete stairs falling down! The dead were dead ... and most of the dying were dead by the time we got there. There was very little we could do. We're going back again. But now it's for a different reason and that's because Azerbaijan and the Armenians are having a little quarrel and there are a lot of people shot up and we're going to go and provide healthcare for them. I've got a Cornell team going ...."

WO: "With all of this ratcheting around the globe helping people ... somebody told me that money follows you. Somebody told me the other day that a lot of people just throw money at you and your institutions."

RF: "I have to say that I have never actively solicited a cent from anybody ... and I've got a lot of New York's wealthiest people as patients. I would also say that they have been among the most generous people that I have run into. Typically, at Christmas time, checks will come in ... and this is unsolicited money that we use for research purposes at Cornell Medical School. I am very grateful to them all."

WO: "Is there any hope in your bosom that the whole healthcare field is going to sort out and get some balance and equilibrium to it?"

RF: "I think that is going to come, for sure, but I think that there are going to be some major battles on the horizon. Doctors are very resistant to change. The American Medical Association was a very reactionary group for many, many years. That's no longer the case. I think they represented doctors. Doctors like to think of themselves as the last bastion of the individual entrepreneur who makes his own rules and runs his own business and is not told how to do it. That's not going to happen anymore. It costs too much. There are too many different standards of care. There are too many people who don't have health insurance and don't get the care they should get. Doctors have lost that tradition of giving free care. Everyone used to do it. Now if you don't have a card that shows you're able to pay the cost you can't get through the door. That's wrong. I think this is all going to be corrected at cost to everybody ... in terms of you may not be able to choose a doctor of your choice. Doctors are not going to make decisions about what they are going to do without other people questioning whether the decision is an appropriate one. That in many ways is going to be good. It will eliminate a lot of unnecessary surgery."

WO: "How about the community hospital? Is United going to survive? Is New Rochelle going to survive? St. Vincent's?"

RF: "I don't think any of these hospitals are going to survive unless they are aligned with a major medical center. United Hospital is in the process ... and I hope this comes to fruition ... of joining New York Hospital. Westchester County has a lot of hospitals in big trouble. If they don't align themselves with major medical centers or big healthcare providers they are going to have financial difficulties. United Hospital happens to be the one that I know in our community and I think that it is a terrific institution. Of course a hospital is not the bricks ... it's the people. All the doctors that I know at United Hospital ... in every specialty ... are of a very high caliber."

[93]

Hon. Salvatore T. Generoso

"THE LAST LEGEND"

Remarks of William O'Shaughnessy, Saint Joseph's Church,
New Rochelle, New York

May it please you, Father O'Halloran, pastor and shepherd of Saint Joseph's ... still to this day a special and influential parish.

I will be mercifully brief. That instruction comes, mind you, not from Father O'Halloran ... but from a Higher Power—Lindsay Generoso!

How wonderful that the elders of the town—past and present—turned out this morning to celebrate Sal Generoso's life. I see bank presidents ... police commissioners ... judges ... academics ....

So many of standing and stature and high estate in our home heath are here assembled with his friends from the West End of our city ... the neighborhood that he never left and to which he always returned from all his postings in public service and his exalted positions in civic affairs and municipal government.

He was a legend, perhaps the last to carry that appellation, and greatly respected at city hall and in the world of politics. But he was beloved on these streets where he lived and loved with Jean ... whom he now joins.

I won't intrude for very long on your morning ... because there is actually very little I can add to your knowledge of the body of his work over ninety years ... or to the canon of his exploits and successes in matters political and charitable.

We're here for Sal. And for Jimmy. And for Lindsay. And we're here for ourselves ... because we need to be.

He was a politician the way the men of our fathers' time imagined them to be.

And as we pray for Sal and savor his marvelous life ... our minds drift back to different times. Times when we were all young. And we can't remember Sal without summoning up warm reminiscences of those who enjoyed his favor:

Frank Garito ... Joseph Raymond Pisani ... Rocco Bellantoni Jr. ("Rocky Bal" or "Junior") ... Alvin Richard Ruskin (the mayor and judge) ... State Senator Tony Gioffre ... Ogden Rogers Reid (a wonderful congressman and First Amendment champion who, incidentally, is ninety years old on this very day) ... Tommy Faso ... Nelson Rockefeller ... Dick Daronco of sainted memory (after whom our courthouse in White Plains is named) ... Carl Vergari ... Malcolm Wilson ... Lenny Paduano ....

The Republican chairman even liked a few Democrats: Tim Idoni ... and Mayor and Judge Vinny Rippa most certainly enjoyed his blessing and imprimatur.

His influence and benevolence were everywhere apparent. And all around us. I found something in the station's archives I once wrote about Sal, the political leader:

> I didn't always support the candidates who enjoyed his
> favor. But I can't think of any individual ever put forward
> during his stewardship who was not qualified for the position.
> Indeed, he often bravely stood alone against negative,
> reactionary elements to try to keep the party moving forward
> in a progressive, enlightened direction.

That was from 1991, twenty-four years ago. That's what we thought of him then. And that's what we think of him now at the end of an altogether exemplary life.

In Sal's ninety years he taught us so much, so many lessons ... about friendship ... about loyalty ... about service .... about being ... in ... the ... arena.

I will always be grateful that among his enthusiasms was a struggling radio station in the basement of the Pershing Square Building. But I quickly learned the town was really being run from down the street on North Avenue from a haberdashery, a men's clothing store—called The Mannerly Shop. (I'm talking here of real influence. This was even before Dominic Procopio or Jimmy Generoso hit their stride!)

You've read of Sal's charitable work in the public press. His dynamism and generosity are the stuff of legend in this neighborhood and in our city. Like I said, they were part of those lessons he taught us.

These are just a few of the many memories I wanted to share. Others of far more articulation and grace than I possess ... like Steve Tenore, devoted Harriet, his caregiver ... and, of course, his beloved Lindsay—they can tell you better, more intimate, sweeter stories of a life well lived by a really generous man, as Father O'Halloran called him. The last few years, we know, were not easy for Sal. The great Dr. Pisano, I'm told, actually gave Sal the biblical name "Lazarus" as he fought his battles against infirmity in recent years.

And so as I mercifully yield ... I just want to say one thing to the son and heir with whom Sal was so well pleased.

Jimmy ... we loved him too.

Thank you for sharing Sal with us. And thank you for carrying on his instruction and example which really was to all of us: To assist ... to assist ... to assist.

June 24, 2015

Arthur Geoghegan

THE TOWNIE BANKER

Arthur Geoghegan was New Rochelle's preeminent banker for a number of years. He ran one of the last independent banks in the county.

Commodore William Gibbons, a great icon of the sailing world, who is himself of a certain age, was surveying the winter coastline in Rye earlier this week. Mr. Gibbons is a marvelous, witty, zestful character who has been somewhat successful in life. Among his holdings are downtown Rye.

Gibbons's enthusiasms are legendary, and I have been the beneficiary of his generosity. For every time Bill Gibbons sees me at his beloved American Yacht Club, where he is the most popular member and probably the most knowledgeable concerning things nautical, the former commodore marches right up to my table and hands me a crisp $1 bill, "to get a haircut!"

But on this recent winter day, Mr. Gibbons came up and told me: "New Rochelle lost a friend, O'Shaughnessy. You and I lost a friend." And then he told me that Arthur Geoghegan died the week between Christmas and New Year's. Now, since I read six newspapers every morning, I could not believe I had missed the sad news of Arthur Geoghegan's passing at the age of ninety-one.

But it was indeed confirmed that very afternoon by lawyer Jack Geoghegan, who remembers when his father was the most powerful and influential man in New Rochelle.

Arthur Geoghegan was president and chairman of the old First Westchester National Bank, and he controlled the town from his office in the big building at Lawton and Main. In the days when giants walked the landscape of finance and populated the civic life of Westchester, White Plains and William Butcher, John Kley, and Tom Langan of the County Trust Company; and Harold Marshall, Fred Sunderman, and Jim Hand of the National Bank of Westchester. And over in the land of Sleepy Hollow, a young realtor turned banker named Bill Olson would soon make the move in the stratosphere of influence. Mamaroneck had Leo Heithaus; Mount Vernon had Walter Moore.

But New Rochelle had only Geoghegan, who was our townie banker. And each day, in every season of the year, Arthur Geoghegan would walk four or five miles, right down North Avenue to his office. It is also known that "Red" Geoghegan, while strolling this big, broad boulevard through the heart of town, made himself and his bank very important in the lives of countless working men and women and families.

Arthur Geoghegan was a member of the Winged Foot Club and the New York A.C. But he was most at home at Paddy O'Neill's saloon on Lawton Street, where he would eat off paper plates and talk to everybody about the city he loved. The only time he left the glorious informality of Paddy O'Neill's was for his weekly lemon squeeze, at the old Schrafft's on Main Street, with Owen Mandeville, the realtor; J. Ray McGovern, the legendary barrister; and William Scott, a handsome man who drove a gold Cadillac. Here at these high councils, over ninety-cent cranberry sandwiches, the business of the town would get done.

Most of the bankers of today would not understand about all this. For they—with few shining exceptions—are much too busy maintaining their high estate and standing on the corporate hierarchy of remote holding companies, while hiding behind their marvelous technology, ATMs, recorded messages, and unlisted telephone. But Arthur Geoghegan was a real, live, breathing, caring, concerned, available community banker. If you were good for his town, he would back you. It was as simple and easy—and smart—as that.

This was all very long ago. In recent years, Mr. Geoghegan moved up county and rode horses and told stories to his grandchildren. But, every once in a while, his mind would drift back to Paddy O'Neill's and lunches with Manny and McGovern and Scott. They're all gone now, and so is Arthur Geoghegan's way of doing business.

Memo to our news department: He was a lot more than a "retired banker."

January 11, 1997

Theodore R. Greene
MR. NEW ROCHELLE

Teddy Greene was a controversial, charming, irresistible rogue and a master politician in the Queen City. Many did—but I couldn't hate the guy.

GREENE: THE TOWNIE POLITICIAN

No one was ever neutral about Teddy Greene. There is no *maybe* in his dictionary, no halfway station, no neutral ground where he has ever walked. If you don't like politicians, you won't like Teddy. And if you dislike politicians, then you really don't understand this country and the way it works—and you surely will never figure out the extraordinary city in which we live.

Politics and Teddy Greene run together. And you can't understand the Honorable Theodore R. Greene unless you acknowledge that he is, first and foremost, a townie politician. Whatever else he is, whatever he has accomplished, it is subordinate to his love of politics, plain and simple. In the mind of Teddy Greene, politics, plain and simple. In the mind of Teddy Greene, politics means helping, talking to them, communicating with them. And you can't do any of these things well unless you first love them. Teddy loved in great abundance.

In his time, in this city, we have had our political superstars, our legends. In our brawling, sprawling past, though, none were as colorful as Teddy. None stirred our passions and emotions as did Teddy. We had some great ones in our day—in both parties. They were fabulous. Teddy was fabulous—and unique. No one brought more energy and enthusiasm to the political calling. He could be a firm, fast friend, and, if you were his friend, he never faltered. And he could be a relentless adversary.

But there is something I want you to know about him: Teddy was never mean, never bitter, never vicious, never vindictive. Yet, he was a scrapper. Many of us have been on both sides with Teddy over the years. It's no secret that we prefer to be on his side in any proposition, rather than in opposition.

But Teddy never held a grudge. You could run a primary or give a talk or broadcast an editorial murdering Teddy, and in retaliation, he would merely give you an appealing grin, that slight, sly smile that always made him look as if he had stolen the cookie jar—or at least the key to city hall.

Many politicians took from their calling. They feigned an interest in the people in the wards, deceived them, and then got out—with an appointment to a no-show job or a state commission. But Teddy kept coming back. Politics was like a mistress whose charms he couldn't shake. The people on the mean streets of his city knew they could go to Teddy with a request. Politicians are different today.

Often Teddy was a lonely runner. He stood alone when he advocated a controversial north–south arterial for New Rochelle, known as the Pinebrook Boulevard–Potter Avenue Extension. That meant you wouldn't have to fight your way downtown via North Avenue, the boulevard of traffic lights.

Hundreds of people came one dark, desperate night to the Henry Barnard School to hear this upstart councilman and to denounce his "wild, reckless" proposals. As Teddy stood before them, there was an overflow crowd outside. He held them at bay with his charm and rhetoric, until the grand moment when he unveiled the giant street maps for their perusal. As he did, a tremendous wind blew through the jammed auditorium, knocking down Teddy's easels and blowing his maps and plans right off the stage. Teddy looked around and said, "I know everyone else is on your side. It looks like God is, too!"

His greatest contribution, perhaps, was his patronage and advocacy of the New Rochelle Outdoor Arts festivals, which, in the 1960s, brought thousands of people to our city.

He was a patron of the arts but not in a tony, high-class, establishment way. Teddy helped and encouraged more grubby, rag-tag artists, sculptors, and assorted creative types than anyone in our city. Many of them had talent that existed only in Teddy's eye—but he helped them, encouraged them, challenged them, and championed them.

He couldn't see the beauty, however, in the cupola. Who remembers the cupola?

The late Hughie Doyle and Joe Pisani wanted to preserve this great work that once adorned the top of the old city hall. They suggested erecting a grand tower at the corner of Main Street and Memorial Highway, on top of which they would display the cupola. Doyle and Pisani had some powerful allies in this sentimental scheme: Jack Dowling, the banker, for example. I even pitched in with a stem-winding, impassioned editorial.

Teddy, however, had a different idea. He politely suggested installing the cupola on a buoy in the middle of the Sound as an inspiration to passing ships in the night. When someone asked how he proposed to get it out to the site, Teddy thought it would be a fine idea if Doyle, Pisani, Dowling, and O'Shaughnessy climbed up on the damn thing and rowed it right out there!

Teddy was a great conservationist and nature lover. He tried to establish a twenty-four-hour, around-the-clock, live-in, female guard to keep an eye on the chipmunks at Ward Acres.

He improved our international relations and became a great favorite of the French. When the delegation from La Rochelle came on their official visit, and our welcoming committee scheduled a thrilling tour of local Huguenot cemeteries, historical markers, and statues, Teddy said, "We'll have none of that!" And he promptly arranged for our visitors to see several Broadway shows and eat at some good local restaurants. When Teddy later visited La Rochelle, it was the greatest landing since D-Day. The mayor kissed Teddy a grand total of ninety-three times at the airport—on the cheek!

Teddy was always running—running art fairs, Chamber of Commerce dinners, class reunions for New Rochelle High School. And it seems he was always running for office.

He was the Harold Stassen of New Rochelle politics—only, Teddy won a few times. In fact, he won most of the time. He served a total of sixteen years on the high council of our city. He was elected first in 1953, when he and Tom Nolan ran a primary against the organization. And then in 1957 he won again. Then, in 1961, he stepped aside on the advice of his longtime friend Burt Cooper.

But everyone knew Teddy would come back—and he almost did in 1963, when he lost by a heartbreaking thirty-seven votes to Hughie Doyle.

And then in 1965, like Lazarus, Teddy won again.

He won again in 1969. Who compared him to Harold Stassen anyway?

And he ran for mayor so many times, we've lost count. Though he never became mayor, he was Mr. New Rochelle in the minds of thousands.

People outside our city—in Albany, in New York City, and in neighboring states—when they heard you were from New Rochelle, would always ask affectionately and respectfully: "Is Teddy Greene still raising hell down there?" And I can tell you a certain vice president of the United States and former governor asked me once or twice if Teddy Greene was still "raising hell down there!"

One night, we came to honor him "for the many years he has served our city," as the press release put it. It was really because his friends came as surrogates for the people of this city—all the people he helped over so many years, all those people on whose behalf he interceded at city hall, all those people he persuaded Alex Norton to find room for in the hospital, all those cops he fought to keep on the force, all those people he found jobs for, all those kids he got into Iona College, all the people he did favors for, all the people he tried to help.

Teddy, we know you as a politician—but above all we know you as a friend.

And so this comes not alone from us, but from the entire city: We're glad you're our friend.

December 3, 1979

Napoleon Holmes

THE ADVOCATE

*Nap Holmes drove the politicians and cops crazy,
always sticking up for someone in trouble. He also spent a lot of
time at our radio station, pleading for his cause du jour.*

If Napoleon Holmes did not exist, our community would have invented him. He was—and continues to be— a champion and advocate for the poor of our city, the forgotten, the misunderstood, the despised, the friendless, the hurting, the afflicted—and especially and always, those in trouble. Like a heat-seeking missile, he is drawn relentlessly, inexorably, and surely to the side of those who have no defender, those who are without hope, those in this city who have no standing or high estate. This man sings for the little people, on the street corners, in our neighborhoods—and I cannot imagine this town without him.

First of all, he is aptly named: NAPOLEON! Napoleon Holmes: a strong, vivid name for a strong, vivid leader! Could you imagine if his father, in a moment of fancy, had named him "Timothy" (no disrespect, Mr. Mayor!) or "Sandy" (or to you, Judge!) or "Fred" or "Bill"? No, "Napoleon" is just fine for this warrior, this advocate, this windmill-tilter, this troublemaker. Napoleon will do quite well, thank you.

I inquired of Hugh Price, our neighbor who is of the National Urban League, what the proper, respectful "designation *du jour*" might be for a Black man or woman these days. He said it's all "irrelevant" now anyway, because he has been called six different things in his lifetime, which is our lifetime. From "colored" to "Negro" to "Black" to "African American," and now to just "American," which is how it was meant to be and how it should always have been.

I don't know about the national "politics" and nuances and rivalries and fiefdoms of the civil rights movement. I only know that during my time on Earth, in my city, the NAACP was the most active, the most intelligent, the most effective instrument for change, for fairness, for equality. While the NAACP—nationally—helped push open the doors to integration and led the way to the passage of the Civil Rights Act of 1964, the Voting Rights Act of 1965, the Fair Housing Act of 1968—while all this was going on in Washington or Albany or some other place—Nap Holmes was here, out on our streets, advocating, preaching, encouraging, pushing, nudging, suggesting, pleading, stirring things up and calming them down.

For example, he was down at city hall in the corridors of power (and, more often than not, on the sidewalks outside city hall), marching, picketing, screaming for change and simple fairness. He was in our courthouse, at the side of our young, those who could not afford the big lawyers in the Pershing Square office building or down from White Plains. He was at the newspaper, with Elmer Miller and Walter Anderson and Phil Reisman and Bill Cary, demanding coverage—and at WVOX, the radio station, insisting that his point of view be heard. Our editors and executives have had countless calls and visits from Holmes, always about someone else—never for himself or his own family. His "projects"? "Get this fellow in a nursing home." "Get this woman, a widow, in a hospital." "Get this youngster in college—or in the civil service or in the police department or into church."

What Napoleon Holmes was, ladies and gentlemen, and what he is to this day, is an advocate—an advocate whose legacy of fighting for unpopular causes will shine over this city like the Northern Star, giving direction and guidance to civil rights leaders—and civil servants—well into the next century.

On Friday, just a few days ago, in the rain of New York City, I went, alone and unannounced, to a campaign appearance of the governor, just to see how well he was doing. He was doing fine, but in that rain last Friday, Mario Cuomo, another fighter of conscience I greatly admire, said these words: "Everything I know of value or worth started as something unpopular. We believe in grand aspirations. And we don't believe in pulling up the gangplank."

If we need any more inspiration we should keep in mind one of the marvelous descriptions of the man you honor, Napoleon Holmes:

"The NAACP's quiet, effective struggle is like the power of the sun. True power never makes any noise. The sun is powerful. It doesn't argue with the nighttime. It just smacks the nighttime right out of the sky!"

1991

Edwin G. Michaelian

My first two books did not do justice to Westchester's legendary Edwin Gilbert Michaelian.

The man who served as county executive from 1958 to 1973 was, by any account and in every telling, the Father of modern-day Westchester.

It was Michaelian's genius and sophistication that caused all those corporate headquarters to be built along the Interstate 287 corridor.

First as mayor of White Plains, and then as county executive, Michaelian was "Mr. Westchester" during a period of explosive growth in the Golden Apple. While other municipalities and suburban venues greeted developers and investors with red tape and bewildering, often outdated ordinances, Michaelian "coaxed" the hostile bureaucracy into a mode of cooperation and often dynamism.

During all his years in public service, Mr. Michaelian's endeavors enjoyed the imprimatur of the Macy–Westchester Newspapers (now Gannett), whose elders William Fanning, George Helm, Joe Shannon, Edward Hughes, and Milton Hoffman backed his every thoughtful move. The gifted county executive was also able to count on the support of the local Establishment, which included the fabled William Butcher, who ran the old County Trust Company (now Bank of New York), and Harold Marshall, Frederick Sundemann, and James Hand of the National Bank of Westchester (now JP Morgan Chase).

Michaelian, who held himself at the remove from party politics, was nonetheless a shrewd politician who managed his portfolio as Westchester's chief executive without any opposition or interference from Nelson Rockefeller or Malcolm Wilson, who, although focused on Albany and Washington, used Westchester as a power base.

Michaelian was too bright, too decent, and too popular for anyone to seriously threaten or interfere with his enlightened stewardship. He ran his fiefdom of a million subjects in the Heart of the Eastern Establishment in a low-key, solid, thoughtful fashion, assisted by a loyal cadre of top-flight advisors who included the diminutive Leonard Berman, a former dentist from Mount Vernon and Nils Hansen, a wealthy bachelor from Mamaroneck who, as Michaelian's Karl Rove, devoted every working hour to the county executive's fortunes. Two other able deputies were the scholarly Sal Prezioso, who, after his time in local government, headed up the Michaelian Institute for Governance at Pace University ... and Henry Barrett, the young scion of the Barrett political dynasty of Katonah in northern Westchester. Barrett was Michaelian's protégé and point man on the Westchester Board of Supervisors.

Even though he enjoyed almost universal support from all the established power centers of the day, Mr. Michaelian also took an extraordinary interest in the two local radio stations we were trying to develop in the southern tier of the county. Perhaps aware that most of the population resided south of 287, the county executive did everything he could to encourage our efforts.

Every month or so ... the call would come to meet him for a "lemon squeeze" lunch at Westchester Hills Country Club. And at the appointed hour, the county executive would appear behind the wheel of his big white Cadillac, which was his only affectation. He always drove himself, quite in contrast to many of his successors who were preceded by bodyguards and heralded by "advance men." Michaelian always came alone.

After some fascinating conversation about the great issues of the day, Mr. Michaelian always inquired about the health and welfare of wvox and wrtn.

"Is Bill Butcher helping you?"

"Tell Bob Greene to give you some business."

"Go and see Fred Powers about this account."

He asked nothing for his blessing. And when I asked him why he was so inclined toward my faltering, erratic efforts, Ed Michaelian said, "I sense that you're trying to do the right thing with your stations, William."

The big county office building up at the county seat is named the Edwin Michaelian Building.

Few of the citizens who go there each day to petition their local county government remember the man whose name is on the façade.

He was a gentleman–public servant of his time. And he gave us everything we have today.

EDITORIAL OF THE AIR, MARCH 27, 1969

Last night the Westchester Republican County Committee convened in high council at the County Center. Delegates came from all over our broad county to select candidates who will confront you on the ballot this fall.

Most people think Republicans are only from Pound Ridge or Bedford or Bronxville, but last night we saw men who actually work for a living. They are devoted to the party of Abraham Lincoln and to Dwight David Eisenhower, who lay dying this night in a hospital bed.

They were men who have deep lines cut in weather-beaten faces— men who work with their backs and their hands. Oh, there were names like J. Rockhill Gray and Charles Darlington the Third. But most of all the Republicans who showed up last night were solid, middle-class, hardworking and with too much hair tonic. They came up from the streets of Mount Vernon, Yonkers, New Rochelle, and Port Chester to support a man named Edwin Gilbert Michaelian, an elegant, cerebral man who sells rugs for a living. They, the delegates, can relate to that.

The big story last night was who was going to be chosen to run for supervisor, but for us the big story was Edwin Michaelian—a Phi Beta Kappa from Yale who has been our county executive since 1958 and thus sets the tone not only for the Republican Party but also for the County of Westchester itself. Michaelian sets the style, the pace. And whatever Westchester is today, he must get the credit—or blame.

He got up there last night to accept the nomination of the Republican Party and Michaelian stood there in the bright lights wearing a blue blazer with his hand in his pocket. They called him a "brilliant administrator." And Edwin Gilbert Michaelian talked about good government and leadership and imagination, and he spoke movingly and eloquently about Westchester, calling it "The Capital of Suburbia, USA," which would sound cornball coming from anyone else but Michaelian, who truly believes we live in the "Wonderful World of Westchester."

Eugene Nickerson of Nassau County gets in the *New York Times* more. But we'll put Michaelian up against Nickerson any day and spot you five yards.

EDITORIAL OF THE AIR, OCTOBER 27, 1969

We admire and support Edwin Michaelian.

His brilliance, virtue, and dedication are among the great natural assets of our Wonderful World of Westchester. His talent and achievements are obvious to all the many residents he has served so well for so many years.

If excellence, commitment, and devotion in the public arena are to be rewarded, Edwin Michaelian will be re-elected by an overwhelming majority. He is the solid and strong leader who stands out in a time of flash and tinsel, devoid of substance or meaning.

The person who is county executive can influence the way you live. And so we present Michaelian and recommend him after a good deal of reflection. It's clearly a tribute to this exceptional man from White Plains that this campaign has been wanting for any meaningful or substantial issues. Day after day Mr. Michaelian's opponent, Max Berking, the Democrat, holds up Nassau County as some sort of ideal when it comes to governance.

Mr. Berking obviously admires Eugene Nickerson. But the Democratic candidate's enthusiasm is not shared by the people of Westchester. Or by WVOX. In his only other brush with anything that resembles an issue, Mr. Berking has suggested that our community college lacks the same accreditation as Yale or Williams. Westchester Community College serves the sons and daughters of those truck drivers from Yonkers who pay $300 a year so they can have a fighting chance in competition with the progeny of millionaires who go to Yale and Williams and who pay thousands of dollars for accreditation by the Middle States Association.

We believe Westchester Community College has no place in the political arena and that Mr. Berking may have done a disservice to the dedicated faculty—as well as to the earnest students—of our growing local college. Having spoken on this one point, we'll not countenance any criticism of Mr. Berking, who is a real gentleman and truly a fine individual. We have supported Senator Berking in the past and we hope we'll have the opportunity to do so again. But not against so eminently qualified a public servant as Edwin Michaelian.

Royall Tyler, a young man from Boston who later became chief justice of the Supreme Court of Vermont, once wrote, "Why should our thoughts to distant countries roam, when each refinement may be found at home." Westchester is infinitely superior to any other county in the state. Edwin Michaelian helped make it so. Let us then look to him for any refinement in our government.

This is a race between two real gentlemen.

But for Westchester County Executive, we warmly endorse the candidate of the Republican Party, the incumbent, Edwin Gilbert Michaelian.

Peter Mustich, Townie

A WVOX and WVIP Commentary
by William O'Shaughnessy

It was right there in the *Journal News* daily newspaper that Peter Mustich of New Rochelle, New York, had died. The key phrase being "of New Rochelle."

That said it all about the man. All other details of his life and passing are meaningless and irrelevant. For this Mustich was a Townie, and any achievements, accomplishments, and milestones of his eighty-eight years must yield to his relationship with his home heath.

Peter Mustich was "of New Rochelle" in every season of his long life. But the venue of his days is not to be confused with the New Rochelle of E. L. Doctorow, Cynthia Ozick, Teresa Brewer, Ossie Davis, Robert Merrill, Page Morton Black, Frances Sternhagen, John Kluge, Mariano Rivera, Dick Van Dyke, or Ken Chenault, boss of American Express. We're not talking here about Overlook Road or Premium Point either. Or about the Joyces or the Powers family.

Nor would you put him in Scarsdale, Bronxville, Bedford, or Rye. 10801 and 10804 were the ZIP codes where he got up each morning. And among his enthusiasms were the Chamber of Commerce, the Elks Club, the Lions, Holy Name Church, the Police Foundation, and this local community radio station where he would appear in our lobby almost weekly with some importuning or pleading.

Peter Mustich was a Catholic, but he carried instincts taught by the ancient Hebrews. He probably didn't even know the words *Tzedakah* or *Tikkun Olam*. But it came most naturally to him as he set about to build up the community, to make it stronger, better ... sweeter. He didn't need some old rabbi to tell him, "God created the universe, but didn't complete it ... that's your job." It was in him, a part of the man.

It seemed like he was around these parts forever. But Mustich did not go back as far as Lou Gehrig, Norman Rockwell, Frankie Frisch, or Eddie Foy and the Seven Little Foys, New Rochelle residents of fable and myth.

But he could absolutely tell you all about Teddy Greene, Alvin Ruskin, Alex Norton, Sam Kissinger, Hughie Doyle, Bob Cammann, Jack Kornsweet, Murray Fuerst, John Fosina, Darby Ruane, Sid Mudd, Jim Bishop, Jack Driscoll, Jack Dowling, Marty Traugott the handsome plumber, Dominick Procopio, Frank Connelly, Bill Scollon, Art Geoghegan, Bill Sullivan, Amiel Wohl, Ben Mermelstein, Vinny Rippa, Ruth Kitchen, Lenny Paduano, Frank Garito, Arnie Klugman, I. B. Cohen, the Libretts, Harry and Bob Colwell, Dorothy Ann Kelly, Jim Maisano, Ogden Reid, Tommy O'Toole, George Vergara, Tim Idoni, Nick DeJulio, Rosemary McLaughlin, Evie Haas, Doc Kiernan, Rocco Bellantoni Jr., Joe Evans, Nick Donofrio, Stanley W. Church, Elmer Miller, Donny Zack, Mike Armiento, and P. J. O'Neill, keeper of the most glorious saloon. And, on information and belief, he even spent some time in Cesario's of an evening.

He was a joiner, a volunteer, a promoter, a drumbeater, a promulgator, and he always seemed to be coming up the street at the head of a parade. You will find none of these things in the New York papers.

But over this most glorious summer weekend just past, a Father Martin J. Biglin stood up in the Holy Name of Jesus Church to pray over Peter Mustich. Now this Biglin is a most rare and highly unusual person who, when he puts on his Roman collar, is actually able to speak in entire graceful sentences and elegant paragraphs of the English language almost as well as most other priests of the Roman church recite the ancient Latin.

"He always did unto the least of these ...," said the white-haired priest. And after quoting the Carpenter's Son, who was altogether so perfect, he flung holy water on the casket of Peter Mustich who spent eighty-eight years saying nice things about his neighbors, most of them obscure sidemen in orchestras long dispersed. But to Peter Mustich they were all A-listers.

This is a WVOX commentary. This is William O'Shaughnessy.

Broadcast June 27, 2011

Nelson: A Child of the Neighborhood

The phone rang after midnight. Joseph Wood Canzeri, president of the Greenrock Company, which runs the Rockefeller estates, was calling from Pocantico, in the hills above Tarrytown. "Billy, Nelson died last night."

It is bad timing. Saturday is a day for jeans, chores around the house, errands, trips to the dry cleaner and the greengrocer, and shopping at the A&P. It is not the sort of day I feel like getting on the radio to announce that Nelson Aldrich Rockefeller had died. He deserves better than our Saturday edition.

But last night Nelson Rockefeller collapsed at his office in New York. He was one of the neighbors' children. All night long, and into these early morning hours, the newspapers and the radio prepared bulletins and obituaries to tell you this fabulous and zestful man's heart had stopped on him. In cold, clinical, medical language, he had a massive heart attack. It would have to be a slammer to take out this particular seventy-year-old man.

This weekend, there will be a great deal written and broadcast in the national media about Nelson Rockefeller. But if you want an objective, arm's-length report, you'd better tune in elsewhere, for you'll not get an unbiased version here at his hometown radio station—or from me. We were with him at countless political dinners, dedications, functions—"events," as they called them. Over the years, we rode with him in airplanes, helicopters, and golf carts.

It started with Louis Lefkowitz and Jack Gilhooley, down at Ratner's on Delancey Street in New York City. It was outside the famous old Jewish delicatessen in a Puerto Rican neighborhood where I first discovered the great squire of Pocantico Hills. As the men from the neighborhood looked on, this patrician—an aristocrat from Westchester—plowed into the crowd of Hispanic faces that were yelling, "Señor Rocky!"

For over ten years, we followed Rockefeller as he dominated New York state politics—settling garbage strikes, battling with John Lindsay, building colleges and a great state university, pushing bond issues, and building roads and expressways. He was always the best story of the day—even just sitting up there on the dais at the Westchester Republican dinners at the old Commodore Hotel with the late Fred Powers and telling his neighbors, "Good to see you! ... Nice to see you! ... Wow ... you look faaabulous!"

He loved to tell about the time old Boss Ward, the legendary Republican leader, put him on the Westchester Board of Health. And just last Thursday, as Henry Kissinger spoke at this year's county dinner, I was reminded of the time Fred Powers gave him a huge replica of the great Sword of Excalibur, which the Wilkinson Sword people had made up. Nelson Rockefeller, like a kid, just loved it! "Are you suggesting I'm a great swordsman?" he responded.

There were so many nights and speeches and trips, so many arrivals at the county airport. The governor would come down out of his Gulfstream in the middle of the night—exhausted. He might finesse an interview with the networks, but he never waved off a WVOX microphone. And when he left Albany, he gave us the last question at his final press conference as governor. We used the occasion to inquire which of his predecessors, of all those staring down at us in the Red Room, had "inspired" him. Nelson said a lot of great men had been governor of New York, but Teddy Roosevelt had really inspired him "as a young boy."

And there was the time *Air Force Two* brought a tired vice president home from a long trip around the world. As the national press and television camera crews clamored for interviews, the "governor," as we still called him, made straight for the news crew from our local station.

On this terrible, sad morning, my mind also drifts back to the time we accompanied him on a swing through the Deep South. David Broder and I were finishing a drink with Nelson as *Air Force Two*, a DC-9, hit the runway with a hell of an abrupt jolt—landing "hot," as the pilots calls it—at Columbia, South Carolina. For a brief, nervous, fleeting moment, Broder and I were reminded of our own mortality. But Rockefeller never even winced. He winked, bounded down out of the plane to meet Strom Thurmond and about fifty Southern belles in hoop skirts, and said, "Wow!"

On this same trip, down on Mobile Bay, Nelson Rockefeller even charmed old George Wallace and his lady, Cornelia. Eastern, patrician, aristocratic, wealthy, Yankee: Rockefeller wowed even the rednecks down South. We saw it; we felt it—and we remember.

Rockefeller could never, of course, make the great, formal speech in front of a television camera. But in a room with a crowd, or one-on-one, he was superb when he was informal. In 1968, in Miami, he had just delivered an uninspired formal speech to the delegates to the Republican National Convention. He didn't come across. But then, after his formal presentation, he joined Walter Cronkite in the CBS broadcast booth for a more informal discussion. The great Cronkite was trying hard to be his usual, objective self when Nelson reached over, put his hand on Walter's arm, and said, "Just a minute, Walter. I'd like to thank you, sir, for all that you do. The way you conduct yourself is an inspiration to me and to our country!" An astonished, but flattered, Cronkite went over like a giant oak!

I will remember lots of moments with this neighbor of ours, but none more than the day just before Christmas 1974, when Nelson Rockefeller walked into the Oval Office to be sworn in as vice president of the United States. America, which had just been through Watergate, felt good again about itself, having this extraordinary man at center stage for a while. I also remember President Gerald Ford telling us, over drinks in the White House: "Don't worry, Bill. I agree with you. Nelson and I are a good team. He'll be on my ticket—and we're going to win." That, of course, was before Bob Calloway and the mean, narrow southerners and the Rockefeller-haters started after him. Most men would sell their soul for the vice presidency or to sit in the Oval Office. But Rockefeller—he took himself out of it with style and class, and with that sense of grace that came so naturally.

On this morning after he died last night in New York City, it is Nelson Rockefeller's sense of humor that keeps coming back to me. I heard him once say, "My lawyer just sued me!" I didn't understand, until Bobby Douglas, his counselor, explained that Louis Lefkowitz, the New York attorney general, had just brought suit against Mobil Oil.

He was in great, good form at his last public appearance here in the county at Purchase College, where he showed slides of his art collection to a very tony group—members of the Westchester Arts Council. As he quipped, joked, raised his eyebrow, and moved his blocky shoulders, his eyes twinkled. It was vintage Rockefeller. As he greeted this staid, artsy crowd, an exceptionally well-endowed lady—falling out from a plenty revealing dress—came through the receiving line. Nelson's eyes lit up. Then, when he noticed that Joe Canzeri and I had also tuned in on the display, the governor threw a sly, mischievous wink to us—and to Happy, standing next to him—and said to the lady: "Wow! How are you? . . . Yes, sir! Good to see you!"

Nelson Rockefeller was a man of great enthusiasm. Although he could find humor in almost any situation, he had to have been hurt by that number done on him and his art reproductions by the reporter in the *Times* last month. And this weekend, I expect James Reston will write a sweet, affectionate column about him in the mighty *New York Times*—while Anthony Lewis, who shares the same page, will predictably find some way to tell us he never forgave Nelson for Attica.

Many Catholics, of course, will never understand Rockefeller's stand on abortion. Indeed, they have already declined to pray for him among the formal petitions on Sunday at Holy Family Church in New Rochelle. But in the same city, the Christian Brothers of Ireland will remember the soul of Nelson Rockefeller at a Mass for fathers and sons at Iona Grammar School.

There was a big, broad range to the life of Nelson Rockefeller. He was a high roller who was as much at ease with the emperor of Japan and the shah as he was with Meade Esposito of Brooklyn or any Yonkers politician. As a wealthy man—as a Rockefeller—he had a lot of material things: Kykuit, the house at Pocantico; an apartment on Fifth Avenue; the place at Seal Harbor, in Maine; and his newest project in the desert near Brownsville, Texas. He would sit at "21" and jet off to Dorado for vacations or with Happy to visit an Italian princess named Letitia in Rome—but he also had great enthusiasm for some of the ordinary pleasures.

I discovered this the night we flew to Cleveland so Rockefeller could campaign for Governor Jim Rhodes. A busy tour had been arranged: television interviews, a visit to the publishers of the *Plain-Dealer*, and a rubber-chicken political dinner. Just before the supper, however, we stopped at a slightly run-down Sheraton Hotel, where anti-abortion pickets were screaming outside. The governor's hosts had provided him with the "presidential suite," high above street level where we might retreat for a brief rest stop before dinner. As we cased the room, the governor spotted a portable bar stocked with Dubonnet and milk, which suited him just fine. (I personally could have used a Canadian Club!) There also sat a gleaming silver tray of Oreo cookies, all grandly wrapped in cellophane and ribbon. "Wow," said the governor of New York. "Look at that!" And so there we were—sitting in our shirtsleeves eating Oreo cookies, sipping Dubonnet and milk in the presidential suite—while pickets chanted on the street below. Today, the man has his name on tall buildings in Albany and New York, and has left around his state a lot of soaring architecture that will remind us and future generations of Nelson Rockefeller. But I will think of him every time I encounter enthusiasm and energy and optimism—and every time I see a kid eating an Oreo cookie.

As I sit here at this microphone, I can still hear and almost feel some of the rejection that met the man as he pursued his dreams across so many years, the rich man's son who could have been quite a glorious bum instead.

There will be a huge turnout at Riverside Church next week when the Rockefellers bury their most dazzling son. But as dying is something you have to do all by yourself, there were no crowds to cheer him last night on 55th Street. In countless radio editorials over the years, I've tried to tell you what he has done for our state and for our nation—his accomplishments. They are many and known to you. You can read about them all weekend in the public press, and when you are old, you can see all of it in the history books. But this morning, I merely want to say that I am glad he was our neighbor—and friend. He lit up our lives.

Nelson, you were faaabulous!

January 27, 1979

The Last Townie

A WVOX Commentary
by William O'Shaughnessy

"Don" Dominic Procopio was an agreeable and beloved presence in our city for as long as we can remember, and he was powerful.

He owned a wine company and was chairman of our Civil Service Commission. Mr. Procopio was also the Padrone of the Casa Calabria over whose annual dinner he presided.

The Calabria dinners would begin promptly at 6:30 p.m. and continue until well past midnight with the main course not being proffered until 11:30 p.m. The organizers and exhausted waiters would then mercifully push a rolling Venetian table onto the floor in the wee small hours loaded with sweets and cappuccinos laced with anisette.

Many hundreds of our neighbors and a posse of judges attended these soirées to toast and pay tribute to "Don" Dominic. One of them, Mr. Justice Frank Niccolai, served as master of ceremonies at the specific request of "Don" Dominic.

Among the honored guests were Billy DeLuca, a child of the West Side who is now one of the most important beer and beverage distributors in the country, and Nick Trotta, who ran the Presidential Protective Division of the U.S. Secret Service. At table were also any lawyer who ever aspired to a judgeship in the region.

By day, Dominic Procopio presided daily at a Posto 22 luncheon that was attended by police commissioners, city managers past and present, and all the elders of city hall whose ranking could be determined by how close they were seated to Mr. Procopio.

I've accused him of being "beloved." And he was that. "Don" Procopio was a politician the way those of our fathers' time imagined them to be as he constantly did favors for the less fortunate and those without standing or stature in our home heath.

He was also a great patron and supporter of this particular radio station, wvox. And we loved him for it.

With "Don" Procopio's passing an era ends in the Queen City, which now officially and forevermore becomes a "make it happen … do what it takes … gettin' it done …" aging city … firmly fixed in the so-called modern era with its uncaring, unfeeling … at arm's length … way of doing business.

The man was up there in years and he battled multiple-myeloma, pneumonia, skin cancer on his handsome head, and, near the end, Covid, all of which ultimately combined to overwhelm and take down this good and widely respected soul.

I'm writing a book called *Townies*, and you can be damn sure there will be a chapter on one "Don" Dominic Procopio.

But right now, I'm just very sad, as is our entire city.

December 15, 2020

Remarks of William O'Shaughnessy

Prepared for the Dedication Ceremony Designating the
Wykagyl Branch of the U.S. Postal Service as The Robert Merrill
Postal Station, New Rochelle, New York

Marion Merrill ... Bob's accompanist ... his partner ... his muse ... his beloved.

And Nita Lowey, our superb and absolutely inexhaustible congressional representative who serves us so well. She is now one of the ranking "cardinals" in the House and one of the four or five most powerful members of that body whose inhabitants know of her dynamism, her keen intelligence, and her effectiveness. All of us ... also know of her ... goodness.

We thank Mrs. Lowey for using her influence and stature to persuade the Congress to unanimously enact Public Law 110-102, which brings us to this wonderful occasion: the renaming of the Wykagyl Branch for Robert Merrill.

And so we are here today on this dazzling spring morning because of Marion ... Congresswoman Lowey ... and our brilliant young mayor, Noam Bramson, who is another gift of Mrs. Lowey's and with whom we are all so pleased. They all worked so hard for this day.

We thank the officials of the U.S. Postal Service: our own "postmaster general," Jerry Shapiro ... and the district chief, Mr. Joseph Lubrano, in whose care and keeping reside several hundred post offices.

It's a thrill to be here with Yankees greats Roy White and Mike Torrez ... and Mr. Steinbrenner's personal representative Deborah Tyman and her associate Greg King. Bob Merrill was so proud of his long association with our beloved Yankees. He often wore his World Series rings and, sometimes, even his pinstripe uniform emblazoned with his "official" number, 1½, which was conferred on him by Billy Martin.

I'm reminded that we've had three illustrious Yankees in these precincts. The great Mariano Rivera favored New Rochelle with his own restaurant. And for many, many years this was the home . . . lest we forget . . . of a Yankees immortal: Lou Gehrig. So Bob Merrill wasn't the only guy around here entitled to wear pinstripes. And like Mariano and the great Lou Gehrig, he was also beloved by his neighbors.

Being somewhat culturally challenged, I never heard Robert Merrill sing at the Met or in those grand concert halls all over the world. I knew him only as a neighbor. And as a cherished friend who never denied my importunings or pleadings to appear or attach his famous name to various charitable events . . . both in our home heath and for national organizations like the Broadcasters Foundation of America.

He—and Marion—was always there . . . for the Sound Shore Medical Center and for local Westchester opera groups.

This was his neighborhood . . . with his trees . . . and his sidewalks . . . and his shopping center with his bagel store and his A&P and his deli and his newspaper store. And . . . with his neighbors.

I often wondered why he chose to spend so many years with us, including his final ones. Surely this was a highly successful individual of means and international fame and personal wealth who made over fifty albums alone. And like Ossie Davis, another famous and beloved neighbor of sainted memory, Bob could have easily settled in a more tony, upscale neighborhood like Rye or Greenwich or Bedford or Bronxville or Scarsdale.

And you know why he chose New Rochelle? When I asked him, he gave me the same answer as that dear man Ossie Davis. "This is mine . . . this is real . . . these are my people."

And when the glory years were behind him and he was well into his eighties, Mr. Merrill loved to walk around this neighborhood . . . on lovely spring days like this one and even in the winter. In every season of the year . . . this was his.

He also loved to go into town for meetings of the fabled Dutch Treat luncheon club. All the writers, artists, and publishers belong to Dutch Treat. (It was founded about eighty years ago by James Montgomery Flagg, a New Rochelle resident, who was one of the most famous illustrators of the day . . . back in the 1920s, when Norman Rockwell also lived here.) Bob was an elder of the club as he was of the Friars Club.

He would call me at the radio station at about this time of the morning to inform me that our presence was urgently requested at that luncheon club ... after which we would sometimes continue our "discussions" concerning the great cosmic issues of the day at Pete's Tavern and, occasionally, at "21."

We were always graciously received by Marion when we made it back to New Rochelle by nightfall. Or at least in time for dinner!

It was during these delightful sessions that I heard some wonderful stories ... and I will share just two with you ... only very briefly:

I once inquired of the famous baritone, "Bob, who was the greatest tenor ... Pavarotti ... or Placido Domingo?" Without missing a beat, Merrill said, "That's easy ... *Frank Sinatra!*"

We know he often gave Sinatra singing lessons—on the phone! One day when I came to pick him up, Marion said, "He'll just be another minute ... he's giving Frank a little 'vocal tune up' on the phone. But you can go in." Even I wouldn't dare intrude on that! After his telephonic lesson with the great Sinatra, I asked if Sinatra said anything. "Yes ... he called me a showoff!"

I also have a baseball story ... about the day Bob was "managing" the Yankees Old-Timers' Day squad.

And when the great Joe DiMaggio himself came to the plate ... the infield dropped back ... and the outfield went deep ... for the great DiMaggio. Everybody in the stadium waited to see once more that magnificent, legendary, incomparably graceful DiMaggio swing that was like no other.

However, "Manager" Merrill then flashed the bunt sign (which was something akin to asking Sinatra to go and sing in the chorus!).

Well, the Yankee Clipper, Bob loved to recall, laid down a "perfect" sacrifice!

Speaking of which: I'd like to respectfully ask Deborah Tymon to petition Mr. Steinbrenner to start playing Bob's stirring rendition of "God Bless America" during the 7th inning stretch! Like ... enough with Kate Smith!

You can hear Bob's tribute to our country every afternoon at 6:00 when our colleague the great Bill Mazer, another fellow of a certain age but still vital and strong, always ends his WVOX program with Bob's recording of "God Bless America."

His voice thrilled millions all over the world. And, as Mrs. Lowey pointed out, he sang for every president since Ronald Reagan. During his brilliant career he performed in opera halls, in movies, on television, on radio, and on almost sixty albums. And during his lifetime he received every award for the arts our presidents could bestow.

Robert Merrill had a glorious voice ... and a glorious life ... so much of which he shared with all of us.

But after all the applause and the curtain calls and all the encomiums ... it was to this neighborhood that he repaired to love us and to be loved back by us.

June 2, 2008

"Colonel" Marty Rochelle

A WVOX and WVIP Commentary
by William O'Shaughnessy

One of Westchester's most beguiling and colorful characters passed away over the weekend. Marty Rochelle left after seventy-eight years, and with his departure everything becomes duller, flatter, and less vibrant. The fun is taken right out of our humdrum, everyday existence here in the county.

He was out of Damon Runyon and Ring Lardner. Jimmy Cannon could also have written of him. To no one's surprise at all, "Colonel" Marty Rochelle, as he was known far and wide, came out of Yonkers ... where true love conquers. I mean he had to come from Yonkers. For you could never place him in Bedford or Rye or Pound Ridge for very long. And certainly never in Bronxville or Waccabuc.

At about 325 pounds, he was (no pun intended) the biggest bail bondsman on the entire eastern seaboard, which line of work brought Mr. Martin Rochelle into almost constant daily contact with criminals, crooks, and deadbeats just as soon as they were about to become "defendants." As the preeminent bail bondsman of his time, that's what he did for a living. He would bail them out. He would spring them. And in this endeavor it helps if you know the judge.

Marty Rochelle knew the judge. Every judge. He also knew every law clerk, every secretary, every marshal who keeps order in every courtroom. The range and weight and depth of his Rolodex matched his ample girth.

And, if you can believe it, he was a real, actual colonel in the Air National Guard (New York state really does have one), which is where the "Colonel" comes from. That's what our fellows at WVOX called him when he arrived, always several hours early, for his weekly radio program bearing two dozen Dunkin' Donuts — one dozen for himself, of course, and one for the studio engineers and staff. I know of this because — full disclosure — he always brought a butternut-covered doughnut for me. "Don't touch that one ... it's for the boss!"

He would also come accompanied by the very latest behind-the-scenes political gossip, often mixed with rip-roaring tales of wrong-doing and skullduggery in just about every city hall in Westchester. He just knew of all these things.

But his specialty was the courthouse. And he knew every judge who ever donned a black robe to go up and sit in a courtroom under the "In God We Trust" sign. And there wasn't one jurist or magistrate who wouldn't come off the bench to take his call.

Recent years were not kind to this marvelous old character, who was in and out of many hospitals as he fought what Mario Cuomo and the great Jesuit philosopher Teilhard de Chardin called "the diminishments" we all suffer. It's a great word: *diminishments*. And yet despite those diminishments and infirmities, Marty Rochelle kept going. First with a cane. Then with a walker. He did his last few radio shows from a hospital room propped up on a pillow, raging into the phone as usual. And I do seem to recall him calling out His Honor, the Chief Judge of the entire Court of Appeals, the highest judicial tribunal in our state, for some "error"—real or imagined—that didn't sit quite right with Colonel Marty. He could do this and get away with it because all the judges loved him.

And if they didn't actually "love" him, well, they knew that when they next had to submit to the nasty and altogether unpleasant rigors of re-election to keep their standing and high estate in the judicial system, they knew that the man who knows everybody would be right there to tell any and all who would listen just exactly what great judges he knew them to be.

Marty was also capable of delivering an extra line or two on the ballot come election day, which prowess also no doubt commended him to the favorable judgment of a most grateful magistrate or two over the years.

If you doubt the man had real clout and influence ... I will leave you only with an actual scene just last year at the White Plains Hospital ... when one evening during visiting hours Marty's hospital room was filling up like a political convention. And according to several who were there assembled by his bedside on that very night ... the head nurse burst in at one point and said, "You're only supposed to have two visitors at any one time.... There are ten people in the room ... we can't have this!"

Colonel Marty looked up from his bed and said, very politely, "Ma'am ... six of them are Supreme Court justices ... two are county criminal court judges ... and the other two are family court judges. Who do you want me to throw out?" The nurse retreated and the "party" went on.

There will be many Marty Rochelle stories told at the Riverside Chapel in Mount Vernon on Wednesday and in every courthouse south of Albany. But the little "gathering" up in White Plains that night is my favorite.

The man had his "enthusiasms" during the seventy-eight years he pumped life and energy into his profession and Westchester itself. Among them were the casinos of Las Vegas, Atlantic City, Foxwoods, and the Bahamas, for he was a gamblin' man. But his favorite venue for games of chance of an evening was always Tim Rooney's Empire City right in Marty's home heath at Yonkers Raceway. "They're honest people, the Rooneys ... you really have a shot there!"

Marty also loved Jeanine Pirro and never gave up on "Judge Jeanine" even after she dumped everyone in the old neighborhood and went on to FOX News to display her famous lips and toned arms, among her other attributes.

He also would not permit anyone to do injury to this community radio station or its inhabitants—even divorce lawyers. Especially divorce lawyers. And as my mind drifts back through the hundreds of conversations we had, usually over those damn fattening doughnuts, I can't recall him ever saying anything really mean or hurtful about any of those who inhabit the judicial world that he knew so well or the body politic.

We can't really afford to lose too many Marty Rochelle types around here.

Because, like I said, only dullness will prevail ... everywhere.

I just hope Saint Peter likes Dunkin' Donuts.

But don't give him the butternut, Marty. Save that one for me.

This is a Whitney Media commentary. This is Bill O'Shaughnessy.

November 24, 2014

Alvin R. Ruskin

We'll Never See Another Like Him

Alvin Ruskin was mayor of New Rochelle back in the 1960s and then had a long, distinguished career as a justice of the New York Supreme Court. He was one of the most sincere, decent, and endearing politicians I ever encountered in public life.

RUSKIN: AN UNLIKELY HERO

Alvin Richard Ruskin, the mayor of the tenth-largest city in this state, is an imperfect man in an imperfect world. But Westchester will never see another like him.

In just a few days, Nelson Aldrich Rockefeller will accelerate the wheels, which are already in motion, and Alvin Ruskin will realize his dream. His father, whom he adored, was an acting city judge in New Rochelle, and one of Alvin Ruskin's brothers went to Yale and became the first Jew on the board of an important company. His brother Bobby Ruskin is in the limelight as John Lindsay's investigations commissioner. But Alvin Ruskin will soon be Judge Ruskin, and that would have made his father happy indeed.

He is a unique man, this Alvin Ruskin, and I believe that our city will miss him. He is a man of style, humor, warmth, and honesty. I have seen him in action with great financiers at restaurants on 52nd Street in New York—trying to drive a hard bargain for our city as we slept and worried about ourselves and our own. I have seen him at the Lincoln Day Care Center, and I have seen little Black children with icing and cake on their faces walk up to him and kiss him, because the other politicians forgot them at Christmas—but not Alvin Ruskin.

Ruskin was magnificent when he had to be. He could do it with pomp, according to rite, and he had great dignity; he gave the job his own stature. Yet, he was a man who lived simply. The car dealer Peter Griffin put it well when he said, "Ruskin's lifestyle and living habits fit the job so very well." That means: Where in hell are you going to find an honest man who will work as hard at it as Alvin Ruskin?

I don't know about "lifestyles." I just know that Ruskin could handle a man like Norman Winston, who used to come up here and tell us he had danced with Rose Kennedy at the Plaza only the night before. And our mayor likes to spend Saturday night in his bathrobe with sandwiches from the delicatessen. Other men dream of a good table at "21" or Toots Shor's, but Alvin was happy at Manero's in Greenwich. Contractors and hustlers and sharpie lawyers would come to his office on the eleventh floor of the Pershing Square Building to get him to handle a "contract" — and he would throw them out. He would vote against the son-in-law of his powerful friend Wolfie Duberstein when he had to. And when someone told me, "Check out your friend Ruskin on a certain real estate transaction down on Davenport Neck," and I mentioned it in jest to the mayor—well, frankly, I've never felt like such a jerk who touted me on the bogus story.

I can also remember a wheeler-dealer crossing the street at Pershing Square and saying to me as he looked up at the Pershing Square Building: "You know, if that guy Ruskin was smart he could take about fifty thousand a year out of city hall. And if he was just a little dishonest, he could pocket about thirty thousand." "In fact," as the advice went, "if Ruskin was just a little shady he could cozy about ten thousand that nobody would ever know about." I listened to this revelation, and I was not surprised when the hustler said, "But this guy must be stupid. He's so damned honest, he'll die broke!" When I mentioned this to our mayor after a few drinks, he got very serious and the tears flowed as he said, "You only take your cuff links with you—your cuff links and your integrity."

And so, as we bid farewell to the mayor and the man Alvin Richard Ruskin, I believe no one ever got close to him. No one ever got to him. And what a hell of a triumph in this day and age. As our mayor all these many years, he has been a one-man publicist for the virtues of our city while excusing our faults as a people.

There are people in our city with scrambled-egg minds who believe Jews run this city, and yet, I have seen Alvin Ruskin, a Jew, give three Catholic monsignors the biggest nights of their lives at testimonial dinners. And for the $13,000 we pay him, Alvin Ruskin had to read the mail we sent to the kid who dispatched the letter to the newspaper about the Christmas wreath at the high school. It talked about putting a "special mark" on businesses in our city that are run by Jews. Alvin Ruskin got sick. So did you.

As you look back, there was the time Ruskin got hold of the reporter from the *New York Times* who had just been rebuffed by the police commissioner and who was about to make a racial incident out of the high school fire. And you remember Alvin Ruskin talking to the reporter, saying it was not a racial proposition.

I loved Joe Vaccarella, the former mayor of Mount Vernon. I was thrilled by his style and by the sirens and the flags and the bodyguards and the drivers. But Ruskin heard a different music. His city car got so bad the neighbors made him turn it in for a new one. And the title "mayor" meant he had to let crummy amateur artists hang their awful paintings in his office at city hall and then bring all their relatives to see their works. He did not move like John Lindsay or Nelson Rockefeller, but late at night, at the Thruway Diner, there was no one greater or more ardent in his love for New Rochelle than Alvin Ruskin, who is leaving us in a matter of days to become a judge. He is a minstrel whose music was heard and understood in every neighborhood and on every street in our city.

So there you have a few reminiscences about a man named Alvin Ruskin. He is, I believe, an unlikely hero in this day and age. The mayor of New Rochelle is not nearly, I suppose, as handsome as John Lindsay. He doesn't have the extensive training, background, and breeding of Ogden Rogers Reid—whom, by the way, his father loved and whom he greatly admires. Not one single suit fits him quite right in the collar. But I believe him to be a most exceptional man. His own splendid integrity has elevated our city and given us strength.

Soon we will have to turn to someone else, as you have heard. And Alvin Ruskin will join the other mayors on the wall of the long hall outside the city council chamber on the first floor of city hall. He has some golden shovels in his office, which I hope they'll let him take. But these are too puny and meager to be his trophies. I believe the kiss from the little Black child at the day care center is a better trophy for the minstrel whose music is heard on every block and in every section of our city. New Rochelle: You will surely miss Mayor Ruskin.

1970

"Joe Slick"

*A WVOX and WVIP Commentary,
by William O'Shaughnessy, President*

He was known far and wide as "Joe Slick." Somewhere, however, there exists a birth certificate from ninety-five years ago that tells you his real, given name was Joseph L. Vitulli Sr. By any name, he was the last colorful character of the West End of our town known as "the Fourth Ward."

Rocco Bellantoni Jr. ("Rocky Bal") is gone. So too are John Fosina, Tony and Sal Tocci, and Nick Donofrio. Only "Goombah Sal" Generoso and Dominic Procopio linger to remind us of New Rochelle as it was in the 1960s and '70s. This was all before the Portuguese and Mexicans came and, one is hard-pressed not to observe, made it richer and better and even more vibrant.

The *Journal News* newspaper, which is still called the *Standard Star* in these parts, slapped the sidewalk this soft winter morning with a paid obit of Joe Slick's passing and tells of his exploits in the Great War. The rakish picture of Mr. Vitulli in the local daily newspaper is as classic as he was. Neither Mario Puzo nor Scorsese for all his Academy Awards could conjure up a better visage of this marvelous man.

His activities in places of death and heroism like the Battle of the Bulge earned him considerable honors given by a grateful nation: the Silver Star, a Bronze Star, the Purple Heart ... just to name a few ... and the French Croix de Guerre medal, which was bestowed for a little bit of business he did on the Germans at Verdun.

Joe Slick came back to New Rochelle and sixty-five years ago married a girl named Rose. And together they raised four kids, as a result of which Joe Slick presided over an extended family that includes doctors, lawyers, and realtors. Many of them now live in tony places like Bedford and Kent, New York, upstate.

Among his passions were the Republican Party, which he served as a major fundraiser. In this endeavor he had quite a bit of success as he caused many to reach into their pockets thinking all the while "Who the hell can turn down Joe Slick?" Not many did.

His enthusiasms included Anthony B. Gioffre, the great old state senator from Port Chester, and Frank Joseph Garito, who looked like Dean Martin and came off a bulldozer and made it all the way to the mayor's office in the city hall. He also had a wife named Rose.

Vitulli also loved Alvin Richard Ruskin, who was a dynamic liberal Republican mayor until Nelson Rockefeller made him a Supreme Court justice of the state of New York and put him into black robes sitting up in White Plains under an "In God We Trust" sign, where he presided over nasty, contentious divorces driven by vitriol and vengeance.

He also put his blessing and imprimatur on Nelson Aldrich Rockefeller and Judge Richard Daronco of sainted memory. And I once heard him say many nice things about the father of Andrew Mark Cuomo. He also favored Malcolm Wilson, Joseph Raymond Pisani, Mario Biaggi, and Anthony J. Colavita Sr.

One day many years ago, I received a call at this local broadcasting station from "Commissioner" Vitulli. I was "encouraged" to address him by that appellation because of his work on the Waterfront Commission, which he took most seriously.

"I have a breaking news story for you, Mr. O'! My liquor store was just robbed. Could you please send somebody over to interview me. It just happened." As our reporters of the day were otherwise engaged, I decided to handle this "assignment" myself.

So, tape recorder and microphone at the ready, I mounted the steps of the Edgewood liquor store over in that fabled area known as the Fourth Ward. As I put the microphone right up in front of his face, here is what Mr. Vitulli proceeded to say for the record. (We still have the tape somewhere in our archives.)

"Well, you see, Mr. O'Shaughnessy ... I was standing right here behind the cash register when this perpetrator entered upon these particular premises ... pointed a damn gun right at me and said, 'Give me yo' money, Bro.' (Right away you knew it was not an Irish kid!) I said, 'No problem.' Then the perpetrator told me to take off my belt and drop my trou! That, Mr. O'Shaughnessy, was too much! I then proceeded to reach under the cash register and took out my own gun ... the one I have for just such an unfortunate eventuality. Actually, I'm not supposed to have one, but the police commissioner kind of looks the other way, if ya know what I mean. When he saw my gun was bigger than his ... that young 'bro' took off down the street. And because he had sneakers, those high top ones, I couldn't catch the SOB."

No attempt was ever again made to disrupt business at Edgewood Liquors since that day so long ago. It's a small story, one of many I know about Mr. Vitulli. But I do also recall a very clear message from the police chief asking that we not run that "damn tape" anymore.

As I think of Joe Vitulli, my mind drifts back to a New Rochelle that has all but disappeared. Most of the political business and ordinary commerce of the town in those days was done downtown at P. J. O'Neill's saloon on Lawton Street or at dear, departed Schrafft's on Main Street, where you could get a whole carafe with your whiskey sour or martini, or up in the North End at Cesario's bar, which later was run by Lou Saparito and his wife, Loretta, before they split.

But Joe Vitulli stayed pretty much to the streets of the West End, where, with his brothers, he also owned a small oil company. None of their Edgewood Fuel trucks were ever bothered either.

I miss the old men of that neighborhood. The greatest compliment they could conjure up was to tell you someone "stays." This word was usually accompanied by the movement of a flat right hand, palm down, thrusting toward you, chest high. "He stays." Eloquence. Message delivered. You need an explanation?

Joe Slick had the back of this particular radio station. And this town, in every season. And for that he "stays."

They will pray for "Slick" at St. Joseph's Church in the neighborhood at 11 a.m. on Tuesday, February 28, another winter day on which our city instantly and irrevocably becomes lesser.

And fewer. And duller too.

This is a WVOX commentary. This is Bill O'Shaughnessy.

February 27, 2012

Masters of Media
and the Arts

Vincent Bellew

THE BARD OF THE REAL PEOPLE

*Vin Bellew was a high school coach, bank chairman,
and columnist for the Martinelli weekly newspapers.
He wrote with his heart on his sleeve.*

Eastchester has the strongest sense of community among all the towns, villages, and hamlets we are privileged to serve. And until this past weekend, Eastchester also had Vincent Bellew.

Vin was the quintessential "Townie" in one of the few Westchester places that haven't forgotten where they came from. In Eastchester, there is no Starbucks where people in designer jeans drink hazelnut café lattes. But there is a volunteer ambulance corps, a fire department, and almost a hundred civic associations and fraternal organizations. Patriotism and love of country are the national religion of the place. Eastchester is relentlessly, unabashedly, and resolutely Middle America.

It was here in Eastchester that Vincent Bellew lived out his eighty-four years. He died over the Memorial Day weekend, and I feel tremendous sadness about the passing of this dear, sweet man. For among his enthusiasms were these radio stations.

The local newspapers recited for you his many achievements: coach, teacher, banker, bank chairman, recreation superintendent, civic leader. Vin was also one of our favorite writers. He wrote of his neighbors as if they were the most important inhabitants of the planet. Week after week in the *Eastchester Record* he exalted the everyday accomplishments and celebrated the milestones of the ordinary struggling men and women of his home heath in columns filled with passion, admiration, and love. Vin wrote with his heart on his sleeve in an extravagant style as dated as the sentiment that came from his mind and heart. He created words that strung together into paragraphs that made people reflect and smile—and sometimes cry.

While other writers squandered their talents on the so-called great issues of the day, Vin wrote of Little League fields, the Eastchester Ambulance Corps, Memorial Day parades, flags, banners, band concerts in the summer, cemeteries, hero cops, volunteer firemen, Italian civic associations, high school graduations, Mike the Barber, Harry Truman, Ed Michaelian, Andy Rourke, Nat Racine, the cadets at West Point, Nelson Rockefeller, Cornell's Hardware, Vinnie Natrella, his wife, his students, his teachers, his daughter, his son, his town.

The only pedigree you needed to qualify for this man's imprimatur was a street address in the ZIP code 10709. He wrote of priests and nuns, and of nurses and doctors who still make house calls in the middle of the night. He celebrated Eagle Scouts and Big Brothers, and he loved books and snowfalls and blizzards and the flowers that come with springtime of the year. This bard of the simple folk noticed everything, and he gave us the gift of times we never knew: when Tuckahoe was a quarry and trucks brought coal to warm us in the winter and wagons dispensed blocks of ice to cool us in the summer.

Those of pretense and standing and high estate were not deemed worthy of his pen. Vin could find no magic in the lives of those who merely use Westchester as a bedroom, the ones who take and put nothing back. His love and attention were reserved only for the Townies and their children.

His editors referred to the product of his generosity and genius as "columns." Rather, I think, they were love sonnets that resemble, more accurately, the written history of life in Eastchester for the last fifty years. And as we recently suggested to Mary Angela and Robert Bellew, they must be preserved. Some merchant prince or banker or rich individual should promptly dispatch scholars to go through Vin's lovely legacy and publish his reminiscences and reflections for future generations.

All his life, Vin tried to tell us what we had. But all I can think of, as I sit at the microphone this morning, is what we lost.

And I'm also recalling a marvelous, but all too true, observation by the auto magnate B. F. Curry, who is also my father-in-law. He said: "It seems like people are dying these days who aren't supposed to."

Vince would have loved the line.

May 29, 1996

Louis Boccardi

THE DOWN-HOME PRESS LORD

*Down at the corner gas station in Westchester, they know
Lou Boccardi has a big job in the city. But they're not quite sure
what this quiet, self-effacing man really does for a living ...
or the immense power he has to shape public opinion.*

In the 1920s, the grand incorporated city of New Rochelle, New York, was the home of Frankie Frisch, Eddie Foy, the Seven Little Foys, and a struggling artist named Norman Rockwell. Glen Gray's Casa Loma Orchestra played every night at Glen Island Casino.

Today, it is a different city, and the civic boosters do not often use the phrase "Queen City of the Sound." But even now, Ossie Davis calls it home, as does Ruby Dee. Robert Merrill gets his mail here, and E. L. Doctorow is our writer-in-residence. There is even an extremely rich man, Nat Ancel, who owns a huge furniture company named for a patriot, Ethan Allen. And there are a lot of millionaires absolutely nobody knows about, including Barry Schwartz, who owns race-horses and 50 percent of a textile company that makes blue jeans and underwear. Every morning, this Schwartz from New Rochelle says hello to his partner, Calvin Klein, as soon as he arrives at their office on bustling Seventh Avenue, where, together, they make about a million dollars a week. But most of the tony people and the up-wardly mobile Yuppies in their BMWs and Buick station wagons have gone north—up Route 684 or over into Connecticut. And each night they roar along the Hutchinson River Parkway as we sleep. But New Rochelle, the dowager city, still hangs on as a place for certain discriminating individuals of influence, standing, and high estate.

Many ask why Barry Schwartz and the rest of them live in this tired, fading Lorelei of a city that belongs in the 1920s. I asked myself the same questions about Louis Boccardi when he came out of his house in the rain last night to go downtown to the public library to talk about his job with the neighbors of the town in which he lives.

Louis Boccardi is president and chief executive officer of the Associated Press. He is the most powerful working news executive and professional journalist in the free world, and he does not live in Bedford or Pound Ridge. Watching him stand there in the glare of hot white-and-pink lights in our library's amphitheater, you get the idea that Boccardi would not be too comfortable in Cos Cob or Old Greenwich either.

A League of Women Voters banner hung over a table that also held a single glass of water, as Boccardi presents himself to his neighbors—these ladies with blue hair and not a single smile across their earnest, serious faces. Where, I wondered, were the other lions of our national press on this fall night? Walter Cronkite was in the warmth of the Arizona desert, preparing to go before 1,100 journalists at a convention. Dan Rather, his successor, was finishing up the CBS evening news in a studio on 57th Street. A. M. Rosenthal of the *New York Times* was at Mortimer's restaurant queue. Helen Gurley Brown was at "21." And Mr. Arthur Ochs Sulzberger was at the White House, being called "Punch" by the Prince of Wales.

But here in a public library on a rainy, drodsome night in our town was Boccardi, who signs paychecks every week for 1,400 writers, editors, and photographers. Abe Rosenthal and Sulzberger can influence only one newspaper, but Boccardi sends words and thoughts and ideas out to more than 1,300 papers and 5,700 radio and television broadcasting stations. He has a bureau in every major city in the world. One of his employees is being held right now by madmen with guns in a remote, hidden valley in Lebanon, and Boccardi has been meeting with prime ministers, kings, ambassadors, CIA operatives, and even—if you have to know—some gangsters, in order to spring his Beirut correspondent, Terry Anderson.

Slowly, patiently, thoughtfully, Boccardi covered for his neighbors all the chapters of his calling: the First Amendment, the public's "perception" of a free press, the proper way to cover a disaster or a madman, the handling of terrorists, invasion of privacy, confidentiality, national security. Then it was the turn of the women, with their glasses held by lorgnettes, as he stood before them defending Mike Wallace, the *New York Times*, the Gannett chain, William Randolph Hearst, the *New York Post*—and WVOX.

Louis Boccardi spoke easily and politely to his neighbors about "the times we messed up." He stood there like a lightning rod and gathered "grievances" from the ladies who had come out in the rain to put some questions to the chief executive officer of the Associated Press. While Punch Sulzberger stood in a receiving line in Washington next to Nancy Reagan, Louis Boccardi, journalist, talked of "checks and balances" and square, unexciting things with dullness in them like responsibility and democracy. "My profession," he said, "makes it work." At one point in his talk, he addressed these people as "citizens."

I have seen Boccardi rake leaves in his old clothes, but on this night as a warm rain fell over our city and he stood there justifying his existence on this planet, Louis Boccardi was dressed up in his best suit and, predictably, in a neat white shirt.

Following Boccardi's presentation, the entire audience gathered in an adjoining room for refreshments, which consisted of exactly one jug of cider, one large plastic bottle of Diet 7-Up, and 108 small doughnuts, freshly baked that day. Boccardi sipped cider from a paper cup, while a woman named Nikki Shelton asked him for a job as a travel writer, as she liked to see the world. I left him standing there defending William Randolph Hearst in front of Mrs. Feldman from Pelham Road, who'd heard something very bad about Mr. Hearst in her journalism class at Adelphi in 1940.

In New York, Dan Rather had just arrived at "21" for a late supper. Rupert Murdoch was ordering up his helicopter for an early-morning getaway to Columbia County. Jim Hoge, the central casting, handsome publisher of the *New York Daily News*, was leaving a black-tie dinner on Park Avenue. And at the Associated Press, a reporter who works for Louis Boccardi was pounding on a keyboard, issuing words that would travel over writing machines and up into the sky to ricochet off satellites and come down to Earth again to be read and heard by most of the inhabitants of the free world.

Having performed his little talk about what he does for a living, Louis Boccardi went out of the library and drove his own car straight up North Avenue in the rain, across wet, slippery leaves, to his home. The next time somebody raps our town, I will tell them that Louis Boccardi does not live in Greenwich.

November 15, 1985

The Last Public Remarks
of Ossie Davis
Lincoln Hall, Annual Dinner Introduction

Welcome to the Lincoln Hall Annual Dinner. Thank you for the generosity of your purse and your willingness to leave hearth and home for a noble purpose. I'm reminded—as the late New York Governor Malcolm Wilson once observed—that I am, as the program indicates, the only one standing between you and your dinner (laughter), and I plan to extricate myself from that position promptly and expeditiously, if not deftly. (*applause*)

We're here tonight, ladies and gentlemen, because no one in my home can resist a summons from Nancy Curry O'Shaughnessy, our dinner chair. (*applause*)

The towering reputation of your president, Jim Nugent, also compels our presence. For thirty years, he has served Lincoln Hall with relentless devotion, a personality flaw also shared by your vice president, Douglas Wyatt. (*applause*)

In the last few years, Lincoln Hall has raised over $100,000 for the McCooey Scholarship Fund, an organization providing grants to deserving young men after they leave your care and keeping.

Lincoln Hall, named for our greatest president, was founded some 139 years ago and has quietly compiled a remarkable record. Except for a small group of family judges, youth counselors, social workers, and Catholic officials, no one really knew anything about Lincoln Hall until just a few years ago. Of course, the chairman of the board today is Edward Cardinal Egan, the Archbishop of New York. And Monsignor Sullivan, the head of Catholic Charities; Cardinal Cooke and his protégé, Monsignor Terry Attridge; and our beloved John Cardinal O'Connor have always known of Lincoln Hall and its wonderful work. Over time, however, Lincoln Hall has built a national reputation as a haven for the restoration and renewal of troubled young boys twelve to seventeen.

So the Abraham Lincoln Spirit Award commemorates our greatest president. In his first inaugural address, Mr. Lincoln called for "a new birth of freedom," precisely the meaning of Lincoln Hall for thousands of young people. Today, Lincoln Hall eschews the punitive measures currently so popular and focuses on rehabilitative strategies to achieve lasting change.

Most of Lincoln Hall's boys come from turbulent neighborhoods, teeming with squalor, drugs, poverty, illiteracy, and from streets filled with prostitution, degradation, and little hope. Most of them, as the great Mario Cuomo once so stunningly observed, "knew the sound of gunfire before they ever heard the sound of an orchestra."

Your presence here tonight and your generosity directly benefit the 232 boys who are now putting their lives together at Lincoln Hall's spectacular campus in Lincolndale. So on behalf of these young men, I thank you.

Allow me a moment to tell you about this year's honoree. He's an actor, a star of stage, screen, and television; he's a playwright, an author of children's books, a director, a churchgoer, a lecturer; he's best described as a citizen-activist, probably the greatest and most succinct appellation I can give him.

Malcolm X sat in his living room and sought his counsel. Governors and presidents did the same.

He has been bestowed with many titles and roles in his long, illustrious life. A former New Rochelle police commissioner once labeled him a "subversive" during the '60s because he hung out with Pete Seeger. (*laughter*) And Paul Zuber. And I. Philip Sipser. And Paul O'Dwyer. In fact, the New Rochelle Police Department had a special file on him, and it omitted any mention of his priceless gifts to the theater or how he inspired the nation with his plays, writing, acting, directing, and books, in addition to his civic activism. He is, by all accounts, one of the most versatile and valuable citizens in our country.

I tell my grandchildren there are still some heroes around. And ladies and gentlemen, here is one of them, the recipient of your Abraham Lincoln Spirit Award, Mr. Ossie Davis. (*applause*)

OSSIE DAVIS: Ladies and gentlemen, friends, fellow citizens of the world, I'm thankful for this opportunity to meet with you once again because we bear a close kinship and serious responsibility.

We are "citizens," a very serious category, and one of the most important aspirations in our beloved country.

My heart is light because I have the great pleasure of bringing with me tonight my partner, and the one who made it possible for me to attain the Abraham Lincoln Award. And she is ... Miss Ruby Dee. (*applause*)

The last year was tumultuous for us because my mother passed away in June. Mama was 105, but as I stood over her body giving her eulogy, it was not an easy thing. And it was a serious responsibility to assume. As is my message to you tonight.

Ladies and gentlemen, we, in our world, in our time, in our universe, are confronted by the face of horror, of death, of pain, by the blood of young folks and children. What is our response?

Certainly, one part is merely "good manners" ... and charity.

But just as certainly, you cannot respond to what's happening in the world today without considering the whole nature of existence and what our responsibility must be when faced with such overwhelming tragedies. I often don't know where to begin.

Of course, we understand the meaning of charity and the obligation of filling the helpless hand with whatever bread we can spare, of rushing in with all our resources to bind up wounds caused by natural disasters. I thank God for His mercy and for the reputation of this country over the years. And yet, we look; we pause; we wonder. And we ask ourselves the deepest questions of all.

What is this life? Where does brotherhood and sisterhood begin and end? "And this, ye know that ye are My disciples." What is the true nature of love?

I'm honored you think of me as someone who's been responsive to the needs of ordinary citizens, problems solved by Lincoln Hall and other charitable, front-line institutions that understand the true meaning of America.

As I look beyond the horizon, I try to perceive what the future will hold. I say to myself, surely there must be much more we can offer as human beings during times of trouble, besides giving bread to beggars and soothing those who need comfort. Is there not something else in our ability? Is there not something else in our gifts? Is there not something else beyond the technical capacity to respond?

Who more than we are capable of feeding the hungry? Who more than we are capable of flying from one tragedy to another? Who more than America should the world look to in a crisis? And yet, is that our only assignment? Is it our responsibility to interrupt our joyous occasions only when tragedy calls? Is there any other way we can, as Americans, prepare ourselves?

We have not yet escaped our bondage to nature. Has America a special responsibility? Look you, America, and be prepared! Is it enough we are able to send money, food, clothing, and shelter only after the disaster has struck? Can we not somehow detect when it is on the way? Is there no way we can bring this wonderful gift we call America and say, "It is for this that God put you in this world"?

I don't know. I have no answers. I ask you because you are my friends. I ask you because you are my neighbors. I have lived for a long time here with my wife and my family and have been granted God's gift to end my citizenship on this prosperous ground.

I am pleased to accept this honor and further the mission of Lincoln Hall. I speak with particular gratitude because I know some of the young boys Lincoln Hall has helped. It's also my privilege, at least once a year, to visit the young prisoners at Sing Sing. So I know the feelings of young boys, young Black boys in particular, for whom the world has no hope, no helping hand, no meaning to discern.

Sometimes, perhaps, they might perceive us as the last hope, the last chance. So I'm glad to support your generosity and your heart. And when I meet struggling young men in the future, I will tell them about you.

And they will respond; they care; they love you; they still want you to succeed. And you want all of this. For them.

I'm glad to participate in that opportunity. And I will continue to do so for as long as I am able. But it seems to me that the time has come to think wiser and deeper thoughts about all of this and about our world.

What should we do in the future, Oh Lord, to face the hammer nature can wield? How can we avoid, by our greed and selfishness, adding to her destruction?

We must look; we must think; we must relate to all that is human within us. Perhaps what we need now is a new definition of human being.

Maybe, we already are too small for the world we have created. Perhaps, our own technology has reduced us to the verge of insignificance. Maybe, we need a new vision, a new model, a new Lincoln, to remind us of our deeper obligations. If that is the case, then I would like to, at the end of my day, be among those who responded. (*applause*)

You honor me tonight; you honor yourselves. God bless you. God bless us all. And let us never forget our capabilities are greater than we imagine.

Sometimes, if we search again, the little gift we overlooked might be the very one, that if called upon, might help save humankind!

Thank you very much. (*applause*)

Ladies and gentlemen, these microphones rarely convey a more meaningful talk than we've heard this winter night. I was looking over Mr. Davis's shoulder, and it was almost as if the roiling, swirling tide in the East River turned and started running upstream. So, we're very grateful to you, Ossie Davis, our neighbor and friend, for your insights and graceful heart.

You've given us a special gift. With your life. With your example. With your wisdom. With your friendship. (*applause*)

The Water Club, New York City
(original speech, January 7, 2005)

Ruby Dee

Interview with William O'Shaughnessy

WO: "Tonight another famous citizen of our home heath. She is possessed of a worldwide reputation in her field, in her craft. She's an actor of breathtaking range and soaring talent and a great writer. Ruby Dee."

RD: "I'm delighted to be here."

WO: "Do you know you're going to give people whiplash ... when you run and jog along Pinebrook Boulevard!"

RD: "I don't run anymore ... but I do walk. I try to walk fast."

WO: "I see more people going down Pinebrook Boulevard in our city saying, 'Is that Ruby Dee?'"

RD: "I started maybe about twenty years ago ... running. And then one icy morning I had an argument with Ossie ... not a serious one ... but I went out all 'perturbed.' It was a Saturday and I broke my ankle and since that time I've just been walking."

WO: "Did you blame Ossie Davis?"

RD: "Yes! But also I blamed myself ... because I met Dick Gregory, who is a very well-known runner/walker and he had told me not to run on Saturday. I don't know why he said that but it stuck with me. It was a Saturday that I broke my leg! It was a Saturday that a dog bit me! It was a Saturday that I tripped and fell another time!"

WO: "When you're walking along Pinebrook Boulevard you're not on stage or you're not before the camera. It's just you all alone. What do you think about?"

RD: "You know what I'm trying to do now? I'm trying to learn lines or I'm listening to a novel because I'm mad about books on tape. I've recorded quite a number of books myself and that's what I do. But if I'm trying to get ready to do a play or a film it helps me to try to walk and do the lines at the same time. Walk and just talk to myself ...."

WO: "You and Ossie Davis have lived here and graced our neighborhood for so many years ...."

RD: "We've lived in Westchester for thirty years. Actually, in New Rochelle for thirty years, in Westchester for forty-three!"

WO: "You and Ossie Davis are very accomplished in your field. You do television, you write books, you appear all over the country ... why did you pick New Rochelle? I can maybe see you in Greenwich."

RD: "You know what, Bill? When I was living in a group in Harlem and Ossie was in the Bronx in a house that was just about to fall down after we got married ... we were going to move to Long Island because everyone was moving to Long Island and I never will forget an actor, a tall guy whose name is Stretch Ellis, said, 'Why are you going to move to Long Island? Why don't you move to Mount Vernon?' I hear the voice just as clearly ... so Ossie said, 'Why don't we?' We hadn't any idea where to move. So we began to look in Mount Vernon. We found a little house on Cooley Place. It was owned by a German woman. In those days you could buy a house for $13,000."

WO: "But you're making big bucks now. You can live damn near anyplace."

RD: "It depends upon what you call big bucks. We're very fortunate. We thank God there's nothing we think of that we need. Our main concern is the resources to do the things we want to do beyond the jobs we do. So we earn the money to be able to afford to do some of the things we want to."

WO: "This is a rare treat for me to have you all to myself. Ossie Davis is out of town. Where is he?"

RD: "He's in Memphis now ... doing *Evening Shade*. He's also doing a part in a film called *The Quiet*. And he's done *Grumpy Old Men* with Jack Lemmon and Walter Matthau."

WO: "What is the story on Burt Reynolds? Does Ossie like him?"

RD: "Oh yes. They are very fond of each other. Maybe it's because they're from the same neck of the woods. They've worked together on a number of films. And it pains us ...."

WO: "About the marriage falling apart?"

RD: "Because it was so unexpected."

WO: "It didn't surprise you?"

RD: "I think it surprised a lot of us. We like Loni [Anderson] so much and we like Burt and we like them together. And Quinton, the son.

It was a surprise and a hurt. I remember when I got the news I had an emotional reaction."

WO: "Is it tough to keep a marriage together? You have two famous actors, two playwrights. You have your career. Ossie has his. But you've been together for a long time now."

RD: "Oh yes .... I don't think there is anything easy about human relations worldwide ... or in very small units like a family. I think love is a process. We learn to live together. The wedding is the *fait accompli*. But marriage is something that we continue to do every day over something or other ... subconsciously or consciously. Of course I think the more things we do to make the marriage successful, if they outnumber the times we divorce in the course of a day or a week or a month ... then we're ahead of the game. But love is hard, I think."

WO: "There are few men I admire more than your husband. He knows that and you know that. But I don't live with the guy. Do you two argue? Do you fight?"

RD: "Yes, we have arguments. I'm trying to teach him to argue better ... don't change the subject when I'm winning!"

WO: "You mean you have to play fair even when you argue?"

RD: "Yes. And so I want him to be able to fight better!"

WO: "You are a great dramatic actor. I'll bet you can be a force to be reckoned with if you were angry or upset."

RD: "Yes. Yes! Who of us is not a force to be reckoned with when we are angry? I've learned to be calm and tame that part of me. I grew up in the streets of Harlem. Early on you see yourself in different perspectives. I learned to fight and beat up people and be tough and all that ... but I try not to do that now. I try to control those impulses."

WO: "There's a new book by Ruby Dee."

RD: "Yes. Those are short stories and anecdotes. Ossie calls me a humorist and indeed I discovered that I guess I am. I like that book. I'm about to re-issue it with some additions and perhaps do a one-woman show based on my one good nerve."

WO: "You and Bobby DeNiro did a commercial for David Dinkins. What about the other guy ... Giuliani?"

RD: "I guess I have not really investigated him. There's a gut reaction to the man. There's something about him. I shouldn't say this because it's based on feeling and that's not good enough. I should look at the man's record but I'm committed to David Dinkins. There's something about Giuliani that I don't trust. When I've not obeyed my instincts I've run into trouble. I apologize for saying that because when you say that you don't trust somebody you should base it on some concrete proof, but as an actor I beg tolerance on that point because a great deal of things come to me just through the sensing of them and when I ignore it, it's to my peril."

WO: "You and Ossie are always opening your home to all kinds of politicians, but most of them are Democrats, I noticed. Did you ever meet a Republican you liked?"

RD: "Oh yes. As a matter of fact I know Lionel Hampton. I really don't think there's much difference between Democrats and Republicans."

WO: "Lionel Hampton is the only Republican you could think of?"

RD: "No. I know other people who are Republicans, but I don't think the differences are that marked."

WO: "You also give a lot of money to politicians. Do you think Clinton is all right?"

RD: "Yes I do. I like his intelligence, his compassion, and I think he's trying to govern with wisdom. I think he's intelligent ... and I believe he's wise. And he's married to a good woman."

WO: "You like Hillary?"

RD: "Yes, I like her."

WO: "Why?"

RD: "First of all, people that I know admire her. And I like her concern for people. The people in our world don't have many champions now ... and I think that she's a champion of people and people progress. I think our world is becoming so involved with mechanics and technologies that we're not paying attention to the human spirit. That's why we need a revolution."

WO: "What do you mean a revolution? You got a lot of people nervous."

RD: "A revolution in terms of our values. We need to care about ourselves and not what we can consume. And not what we can get. We have to move away from 'give me, give me' and 'I got, I got.' We have to look at the divinity of the human spirit. There is something absolutely astonishing that we're overlooking in our search for the irrelevancies."

WO: "Your husband goes out on Sunday mornings and preaches in churches. Are you pretty religious? Do you believe in all that?"

RD: "I think everybody is religious. Where your thoughts and your mind are determines religion. What we dedicate ourselves to is a religion. I'm fascinated by the fact that we're human beings ... and we can't make ourselves. We can't make anything like us. We can't even make a chicken or a butterfly or anything ... let alone people. What a marvelous instrument we are. And how dare we overlook and expend this miracle. How dare we. We always come up with a new technological advancement. I think we should stop progressing and progressing and just coming up with new products. And the obsolescence of this and that and get on with trying to even the equation. These things that we're inventing are not worthy of us. I don't think there's anything to compare with the human mind, and we're treating it as if it's absolutely nothing ... ordinary. The human equation needs to be worked on in relation to the things around us. Where is the human being? Where is the human spirit? We don't seem to care about that. My value system is all tied in with what I own and what I have and how I look and the human spirit .... I'm hoping that it's not beginning to wither from lack of use. No matter what we're doing with the moon and outer space and satellites and rockets, I believe that the human mind is capable of all such calculations and trips just like that you see."

WO: "Do you talk to God?"

RD: "I try to. Sometimes I'm too lazy. Yes, I talk to God. I'm talking to God right now ... I'm talking to you. Each of us is a product with instructions ... our piece of God programmed into us, and before you use the instrument you should read the directions and the instructions and I think that's what life is all about ... getting a hold of those instructions. So yes, I talk to God."

WO: "Malcolm X sat in your living room. You knew Martin Luther King and Jackie Robinson. Are there any great heroes anymore? Anybody like those mythic figures?"

RD: "You mean that has not been killed off? They've managed to kill

off our hopes. And it sends a message to the generations: Don't try
... don't rock the boat or you will get shot. There are always great
people around and they will come forth, I believe. But more than
anything now ... as my husband says ... it's not the man, it's the
plan. It's not the map, it's the rap. So I believe that these people are
going to become manifest in more of us so it's going to be impossible to shoot one person and alter a certain human thrust toward
some kind of righteousness. If one person is killed ... twenty will
take up that spirit."

WO: "Do you ever get hopeless about the whole thing?"

RD: "As Lorraine Hansberry said once in an essay I read, 'How dare
you despairing ones think that only you have the truth. How dare
I despair about human beings? Who am I to despair about this
wonder ...?'"

Jean Ensign

Jean Ensign was a classy woman, a first-rate broadcast executive ...
and a hell of an actress.

She stood out from the pack in our own profession as a woman of
breeding, manners, and erudition.

An inspiration and role model to hundreds of young people, she
had her own special vocabulary. If Jean was not enamored of something, she would pronounce it "quite drodsome" (which marvelous
word is not to be found in any dictionary, but is absolutely perfect).
And she once described a broadcasting station in her care and keeping as "a pristine jewel of a radio station ... with just a touch of ragtime in its soul."

What a lovely line ....

She would know.

May 5, 2004

Music Man

He was in his eighties and he looked like Ed Koch.

Murray Grand wrote witty, literate, highly sophisticated songs for obscure Broadway revues. He was a poor man's Noël Coward.

I discovered him back in the '60s sitting behind a piano at a smoky downtown joint called the Village Green. He sang his own songs; actually "croaked" is a better word to describe his thin, whispery voice.

"Guess Who I Saw Today" was his most requested song. It's a song of heartbreak and betrayal. Eydie Gormé had the best version.

> *I went in town to shop around for something new.*
> *The waiter showed me to a dark, secluded table.*
> *And as my eyes became accustomed to the gloom ...*
> *I saw a couple who were so much in love ... that even I could*
>   *spot it clear across the room ...*
> *Guess who I saw today, my dear?*
> *I saw you.*

Although Murray Grand was a stranger to fame, he was revered by his own tribe. Songsters like Michael Feinstein and Darrell Sherman knew how special he was.

As he sat alone in those smoky joints explaining songs like "I'm Too Old to Die Young," he would look out into half-empty rooms to find the most lovely, hurting soul.

A few nights he found me.

Murray Grand, famous composer, lyricist, and performer, died today, March 7, 2007, near his home in Santa Monica. He was eighty-seven.

Murray Grand, eighty-seven, born in Philadelphia, Pennsylvania, started his career playing piano at private clubs at the young age of fifteen during the Depression. He continued to play through high school and textile school and hit the local piano-bar scene after the repeal of Prohibition. He brought his love of piano to the Army Infantry during World War II, where he played with Betty Grable,

Gypsy Rose Lee, Beatrice Lillie, Alberta Hunter, and other stars touring with the USO.

After returning from the war, Murray studied composition and piano at the Juilliard School of Music, where he fell in love with New York City and began playing at the Fireside Inn in Manhattan (1949) for regular customers including Tennessee Williams, José Quintero, George Schaeffer, and other Broadway patrons.

He played at the top New York nightspots. Trendy locations such as Upstairs at the Downstairs, Bon Soir, Jack Delaney's, and The Village Green. His wit and lyrics made him a staple of the New York piano-bar scene for more than four decades. Grand never exactly retired, but instead took his passion to Fort Lauderdale, where he was surrounded by friends at Burt and Jack's restaurant. His final endeavor, a yet-to-be-published book of recollections, is appropriately titled after his iconic song, "Guess Who I Saw Today."

Some of Murray Grand's most popular songs include:

"Guess Who I Saw Today," recorded by Eydie Gormé, Nancy Wilson, Carmen McRae, and Sarah Vaughan, whose rendition is included in an anthology of the twenty-five best nightclub songs of all time.
"Thursday's Child," recorded by Eartha Kitt, Chris Conner, and Abbey Lincoln.
"Come by Sunday," recorded by Jeri Southern, Norene Tate, and Earl Grant.
"Not a Moment Too Soon," recorded by Mabel Mercer, Peggy Lee, and Marlene VerPlank.

His writing credits include:

New Faces of 1952 (Broadway)
Triple Galo (Théâtre La Bruyere, 1953, Paris)
Four Below (Cabaret, 1955)
New Faces of 1956 (Broadway)
Chic (Off-Broadway, 1959)
The Dancing Heiress (London, 1960) (also as co-author of the book)

New Faces of 1962 (Broadway)
New Faces of 1968 (Broadway)
Caesar's Palace Revue (1969, Las Vegas)
Good, Good Friends, written with Patrick Dennis of *Auntie
Mame* fame (San Diego Dinner Theater, 1971)
Fountain of Youth, book by Pulitzer Prize winner Ketti Frings
First Lady, book by Patrick Dennis
Murder at the Gaiety, book by Robert Elston
Grand Slam, a nightclub revue, 1987 winner of the MAC
(Manhattan Association of Cabarets) award
"Ladies Please" (Jan McArt's Dinner Theater, Boca Raton, 1991)

Feature film performances included:

Jamboree (1953)
Diamond Stud (1969)
Tempest (1987)
Moscow on the Hudson (1989)

The Herald Tribune
DEATH ON THE NINTH FLOOR

The New York City newspaper world had been shrinking steadily in the twentieth century, from fifteen daily papers in 1900 to seven in 1950. It came about in large part because of the great exodus to the suburbs at the end of World War II. When the middle class moved out of the city, it subscribed to the local suburban paper and began watching TV instead of buying and reading two or three city dailies.

The newspaper unions then began to demand a bigger share of the shrinking pie and went on strike to make their point. They shut down the papers for short periods in 1953 and 1958. In 1962–63, however, the strike lasted 114 days and killed Hearst's *Daily Mirror*, even though the paper sold a million copies every day.

Just two years later, in 1965, a twenty-five-day strike led three dailies—the morning *Herald Tribune*, the afternoon *World-Telegram & Sun*, and the *Journal-American*—to combine into one twenty-four-hour operation. But before even one edition came out in April 1966, the unions struck again.

When the strike dragged on into the summer, the owner of the *Herald Tribune* folded his newspaper, one of the best in the country. It happened on August 15, 1966. Here are some thoughts from the morning after.

There was a funeral yesterday on West 41st Street in New York City.

It is 1966, and we are now an entire nation sitting in front of a television set, which is an electronic instrument that does not impose on us any serious burden such as having to use our minds to think about anything more difficult than a headline or a baseball score.

The New York *Herald Tribune* was founded by Horace Greeley. It was a civilized newspaper written by men and women who sat at typewriters to string words together. That meant you had to think a little bit when those words appeared before you in print.

It happened on the ninth floor. The television crews and the few radio reporters who are still out on the streets came to tape this funeral for their six o'clock news. The cameramen from NBC were there first to wire up the room, which responded to the bright lights set high on their tripods—no dark funeral parlor on Queens Boulevard for this victim. The *Herald Tribune* would go out in bright lights as a media event, because it is 1966, and the electronic age, the wired nation, is here.

A tall, shy man named John Hay Whitney came riding down 41st Street in a vintage dark green Cadillac, known around here as "the green hornet." Minutes later, up on the ninth floor, this well-bred patrician, a former ambassador to the Court of St. James's, read some graceful words over the fallen newspaper. Jock Whitney, as he is known in London, Saratoga, Manhasset, and Thomasville, Georgia, received the largest inheritance ever probated in this country, which means no father ever left his son more cash. He stood there in the bright lights in a rich woolen suit made by Davies and Son of London—Savile Row's best bespoke tailor. John S. "Shipwreck" Kelly, his friend and court jester, calls Whitney the "Aga John." Yet, it was this fine, bright man who left the rarefied atmosphere of London eight years ago to try to save the *Herald Tribune*.

A lot of him went into the paper. He squandered his reputation and his money—$40 million of it—trying to keep the paper afloat.

"The function of the press in society," said A. J Liebling, "is to inform, but its role is to make money." Even a Whitney could understand that. So he stood there yesterday with Walter Nelson Thayer, the president of the *Trib*. The *Gallagher Report* newsletter calls Thayer "Wily Walter." Richard Nixon says he is the toughest, shrewdest individual in the country, which is rather like praise from the Master. But the *Tribune* was hemorrhaging badly, at a rate beyond Whitney's cash or Thayer's genius and toughness. "It is a bitter blow to finally have to abandon the *Herald Tribune*," Whitney told the newspaper reporters in the big room on the ninth floor

You stood and watched all this, and your mind drifted back to Sunday, October 4, 1964, when this quintessential Republican newspaper stunned the nation by endorsing Lyndon Johnson over Barry Goldwater. It did many things that surprised people.

The *Trib* provided a forum for strong writers such as Tom Wolfe,

Dick Schaap, Pete Hamill, John Crosby, Eugenia Sheppard, and Walter Kerr. Not many of them were around to hear Whitney's eulogy, but Tom O'Hara, the old reporter, was there. And Jimmy Breslin— who, in this decade, is the finest, strongest writer for any newspaper —was there cursing and muttering that "the newspaper game will never be the same, because Whitney and Thayer were owners who happened to be Big Republicans." "But," Breslin said, "I could write a column and murder one of their friends, and they would just smile. Whitney ran the paper with great class and grace. Jock Whitney was the only millionaire I ever rooted for."

And the great sportswriter Red Smith was there—an icon of this calling. His hands shook as he dragged on a cigarette and watched this all happen. Red writes about the games men play, but he told us that this day he was going to damn well write an obituary about the newspaper. He sighed and said that he was sick of writing obits about his friends. But as you'd expect, this was heart-tugging. "What it means here," Walter "Red" Smith wrote, "is that my best girl is dead."

The whole funeral took twenty minutes. When Whitney finished his statement, the room emptied out fast, and he and Thayer did not look back as they walked past Archie's newsstand in the lobby. The proprietor, Archie, had run the place for the *Trib* people for twenty-five years. He refused to close down, even during the newspaper strike. But late yesterday afternoon, when the *Herald Tribune* folded, Archie was gone, too. It was the first time he closed early in twenty-five years.

Next door at Jack Bleeck's saloon, known on the sign over the door as the Artists and Writers Restaurant, the newspaper people came in for a drink. The pub owner has been sitting on more than $6,000 in bar tabs for the liquor consumed by the *Trib* people on their bar bills as a "show of good faith." And now they would drink again and talk about newspapers.

John O'Hara, the author, wrote some lines that fit this strange, bittersweet afternoon in New York: "When a journalistic institution is allowed to die ... every man and woman who has ever read a single word in that publication—in agreement or disagreement—is the loser. The loss to nonreaders is incalculable, and the loss to freedom is absolute."

Jack Gould put it better in the *Times*: "Every independent voice is a national asset."

Our piece on all this ends with the writers and editors, the rewrite men and proofreaders, some messengers, secretaries, and the switch-board operators sitting in Bleeck's. They had all just come from a funeral. The deceased was 125 years old.

August 16, 1966

Nancy Q. Keefe

SHE'S STILL THERE

Nancy Q. Keefe is the distinguished writer-in-residence of
Manhattanville College. Her wisdom, insight, and friendship
have been so important to me over the years.

Nancy Q. Keefe, the preeminent journalist during our time in Westchester, is throwing herself a party on Saturday night to celebrate just
being alive. A better reason I could hardly imagine—for this Mrs.
Nancy Q. Keefe is absolutely so damn special.

You may recognize the woman by another name. Some of the haters who call on our "Westchester Open Line" radio program to register their great, unqualified lack of admiration for her wonderful,
bright newspaper columns refer to the Larchmont lady simple as
"that goddamn Nancy Keefe." This appellation is usually delivered
without pause or breath.

Well, Mrs. Keefe is still around after having confronted, five years
ago—and every day since—the cancer a woman fears most. She did
this with the help of her husband, Kevin, her kids, and more than
a few friends. I can tell you one in particular—the former head of
the Cancer Society in Queens: Matilda R. Cuomo, who had the state
health commissioner of the day personally threaten to revoke the
charter of John Spicer's magnificent Sound Shore Medical Center in
the event anything should happen to Mrs. Keefe. And Matilda Cuomo's husband, who has nothing else to occupy his time, was not a
pretty sight himself, worrying about the illness of the woman who
"reads" *him* better than anyone in the national press.

I, of course, being a fair-weather friend, could not deal with any
of it. So I closed my ears to any talk of Nancy Keefe's operation or
things like radiation or chemotherapy. I did this by refusing to take
Cuomo's calls inquiring about her condition, and I even crossed the
street when I saw Miriam Curnin, the mayor, or Nita Lowey, from
Congress, because I just knew they would want to talk about the terrible thing that had befallen Nancy Keefe. But unlike those caring

and concerned souls, I was out in La-La Land for most of it. For you see, it was for me simply *unacceptable* that Nancy Keefe should cease to be around—in my morning paper three times a week, and in my life all the time.

So this "survivor" business was a solo flight, which the woman did without any brave words or prompting from Bill O'Shaughnessy, who was nowhere to be found, because he is basically a selfish person who could not accommodate even the slightest suggestion that Nancy Keefe might not exist to make me think, and smile, and even on occasion cause me tear-duct problems with the graceful words that come out of her head and through her fingers onto a typewriter to be laid down in a newspaper that lands on my sidewalk at 5:30 in the morning.

Which reminds me that fellows who really *should* rejoice in the lady's accomplishment are a Mr. Ken Paulson and one Gary Sherlock. They run the mighty Gannett suburban newspaper company, which, if anything should happen that might leave Mrs. Keefe unable to continue her columns three times each week, would almost surely find itself presiding over a new entity known as The Gannett Westchester *Bowling Alley*! She is that strong and that good, as I expect Paulson and Sherlock know without any prompting from me.

Of course—and I must at least attempt some objectivity about Keefe—she does have some major character flaws. The lady does not listen to me when I attempt to lay magnificent stories at her doorstep that might help one of my friends and thus increase my own importance around here. That is *one* great failing of the woman. Another is that she does not automatically like every Republican—which will hold her back in this county.

And her worst trait is that she sometimes *worries* about those she covers and writes about. Like when she told Mario Cuomo that she did not want a good man like the governor for president, because you couldn't do it and—are you ready for this?—*keep your soul*! So, because she worries about some aging, failed baseball player's *soul*, there goes our invitation to the White House! Maybe even an ambassadorship for the Honorable Kevin Keefe!

But I guess the woman does the best she can with the limited talents God gave her—those unique gifts she brings to her writing, which include intelligence, toughness, integrity, and that commodity only Mario Cuomo, among men, speaks of these days, *sweetness*.

It's hard for me to be objective about Nancy Keefe. I like her writing, and I love the woman.

Those of you who don't, check Sunday's paper. *She's still there!*

June 10, 1994

Nancy Q. Keefe

A Remembrance by William O'Shaughnessy,
WVOX/Westchester 1460 AM, WRTN/ReturnRadio 93.5 FM

Nancy Q. Keefe was the preeminent print journalist of her time in the New York suburbs.

The woman would sit at a Gannett typewriter and fashion words into strong, muscular sentences that would cause people to think and move toward each other.

She championed a lot of worthy and often unpopular causes, like housing for the homeless, and supported political candidates who did not immediately set off her exquisitely tuned "Bozo" meter. And for a good long time, maybe fifty years, she wrote for her beloved *Berkshire Eagle*, based in Pittsfield, Massachusetts.

Keefe loved Mario Cuomo and pleaded with the governor not to run for president for the most meritorious reason that a good man cannot keep his soul and be president of the United States of America under any circumstances. In advocating this line of thinking, she ruined a lot of invitations to the White House for me and mine.

Nancy Q. Keefe was a brilliant social commentator. And; this takes nothing away from her Gannett colleague Milton Hoffman, she also had a keen eye for matters political in our entire state.

She loved the little people. And what a contagious fury she directed to their betters.

I was out in the streets of Manhattan when the call came from the editor Meryl Harris that Mrs. Keefe had died last night in an ambulance in Westchester.

I went with my cell phone to sit in the late winter sun on a slab marble bench next to CBS, just down the street from "21," where a certain lady print journalist would occasionally hoist a libation with a Republican radio station person who needed to be enlightened of an evening.

As I sat in the warm sunshine trying to speak into the phone, Mario Cuomo was at his desk a block away looking at a picture of St.

Thomas More that was given to him by Nancy Keefe on the very day he was defeated in his final run for governor.

Cuomo and I make our living with words … he much more artfully and gracefully than I. But we couldn't think of anything to say that would be worthy of the woman who used words better than any of us.

March 12, 2004

The One-Night Stand
of Charles Osgood

Tourists gawked in the glare, the glitter, and neon of Times Square, while a few blocks away at number 315 West 44th Street a man of culture and erudition sat at a piano in the great temple of jazz called Birdland.

His given name is Charles Osgood Wood. He is the last great writer of the English language to sit in front of a microphone. He does this every weekend on "CBS Sunday Morning" and during the week on the radio, which makes him a beloved icon of his profession. He is the Noël Coward of our tribe.

He is better at putting words and thoughts into graceful sentences and elegant paragraphs than Lowell Thomas, Eric Sevareid, James Van Sickle, Reid Collins, or the great Charles Kuralt of sainted memory. All of whom could paint pictures with the spoken word. Writing for the ear, they call it. And this particular practitioner of the dying art even does it in rhyme and meter.

But on this autumn night in the theater district of Manhattan, Charles Osgood wanted to make some real music. And so he came to Birdland for a charity gig with Vince Giordano and his entire Nighthawks Society Orchestra to back him up.

"Nijinsky is dancing in the hallways of Times Square to the sound of a kazoo," a lovely, haunting line from the great Jimmy Cannon, kept coming back as you listened to this Charles Osgood sit at a piano in this faded old jazz club and play his music into the New York night.

It was a benefit for one of Osgood's favorite charities to which he has been devoted for years—the Broadcasters Foundation of America.

Not everybody in this calling makes the big salaries like Oprah, Imus, or Howard. And thus the Foundation assists those broadcasters who have fallen on hard times, most of them obscure sidemen in orchestras long dispersed.

The tunes he chose for his "One Night Stand" were marvelous old loreleis from the 1920s and 1930s, most of them, appropriately, show tunes from Broadway.

The seventy-nine-year-old poet-broadcaster crooned "Young at Heart" after reminding his Standing Room Only audience that it was introduced by Jimmy Durante (and you thought it was Sinatra).

He then swung into a saloon song, "One for My Baby," with the marvelous line, perfect for the moment, "Buddy . . . you may not know it . . . but I'm a kind of poet." He sure is.

In addition to his enormous talent, and the Nighthawks band, Osgood also brought with him the television anchorman Harry Smith. The follically challenged, bespectacled, and altogether delightful Smith actually played the damn tuba, quite well, in fact. "You wouldn't laugh if I had a violin," said Smith, as he ran the scale.

Then the elegantly attired Osgood brought forth a rising young CBS colleague, Mo Rocca, a sartorial disaster of a comedic genius who sang a witty and beguiling tune, "Rhode Island Is Famous for You," an intoxicating paean to the diminutive Ocean State made famous by the late Blossom Dearie. It was written by Arthur Schwartz (fabled father of deejay and musicologist Jonathan) and Howard Dietz and performed to this day by the luminous Christine Andreas.

Then Osgood sat again at the piano, adjusted his glasses on the bridge of his nose, and sang Johnny Mercer's "Moon River." "I'm off to see the world . . . there's such a lot of world to see . . . . " The song has been done too many times in too many venues. But never better than by the man with the bow tie hunched over a piano whispering into a microphone this splendid autumn night in Manhattan.

He even called up his amanuensis, Liz Powers, who belted out two numbers. And guess what? She can certainly do more than type and answer the phone. The kid can sing too.

Charles Osgood himself has written six books and tens of thousands of rhymes and couplets. He has performed with the New York Pops and the Boston Pops, all since he came off the Fordham campus early in his seventy-nine years.

Toward the end of his graceful, lovely turn in the old, faded jazz club, he even paid tribute to Steve Jobs for caring "not just about the nuts and bolts, but also about the beauty of the thing."

Speaking of which, the next time one despairs after watching all the vacuous talking heads and bimbos—male and female—reading from teleprompters and staring into television cameras with teeth gleaming under perfectly coifed "do's" . . . remember the graceful broadcaster who famously ends each television show: "I'll see you . . . on the radio."

There still is . . . someone.

POST SCRIPT

He won't at all approve of me telling you this. But after being informed of the night's "take," which was substantial and all of which went to the Broadcasters Foundation of America, the CBS icon handed over another check—his own—for triple the amount.

In case you haven't figured it out by now . . . he's a graceful guy. On the air. And for real.

W.O.
November 1, 2011

Hugh Shannon: 1921-1982

St. Monica's Church, New York City

In the few moments of your lives that are given to me this morning, I want to talk about and remember Hugh Shannon, a joyful, elegant man with a touch of ragtime in his soul.

It should be night when we talk about the man we have just prayed for. He deserves more from us, I think, than a Saturday morning by daylight.

His name was Hugh Shannon, but those who knew him best called him Hugo. And Helen Tubs, who is not even a countess or a princess, sometimes called him Erwit, which goes way back to DeSoto in eastern Missouri.

Hugh needs no defining. His life of sixty-one years requires no explanation in its telling. It is not necessary to position or fix him against the canvas of his own calling—or in our own lives or in our hearts. He was joyful and, as Mabel Mercer told me yesterday, "He was warm." Hugh was an entertainer, a singer of songs, a minstrel of the night. The words and the tunes were those of Cole Porter, Noël Coward, Cy Coleman, Johnny Mercer, Hoagy Carmichael, Rogers and Hart, and, occasionally, of Billy Joel, Stevie Wonder, and Stephen Sondheim.

Hugh was not the greatest singer or even the most terrific piano player. He did, however, have the greatest left foot in the history of show business. He wore out more Lefcourt velvet slippers and Belgian shoes than any other piano man.

John S. Wilson of the *New York Times* wrote that Hugh's voice was "aged in saloon smoke and warmed to a glowing hoarseness." He called him the "last of the breed, the last, great saloon singer, and the progenitor of a whole new generation of cocktail piano players." And Whitney Balliett, who wrote so lovingly of Hugh in his *New Yorker* profile, observed that "there are really only four great saloon singers: Mabel Mercer, of course, inimitable Bobby Short, Blossom Dearie, and Hugh Shannon."

Hugh touched chords in our hearts that no one ever touched before. Mabel said, "You sing to everybody, because everybody has feelings. They react inwardly; they react inside. You just get up and sing." And you give; night after night after night, you give. That's what Hugh did for a living, and that's how most of us came to know him. *W* magazine said:

> He extracted from life all the emotions and put them
> into songs.
>   He articulated our feelings.... He was witty and
> we laughed.
>   He was sad and we cried.

"You sing to everybody," said Mabel. But, and perhaps you had the same reaction when listening to Hugh, he always seemed to be singing just for me and mine. And that was his genius. Others who worked at his calling "performed," "appeared," "sang," "played," or "danced"—and the songs were technically perfect and skillfully done. But they were for the artist in his own private world—not for us or ours.

Hugh, on the other hand, beamed! He reached out—beyond the microphone, beyond the pencil spotlight, and beyond the piano. He made people happy with his music. He loved! Hugh Shannon's songs were an expression of that love and, as he squandered his talent across more than 10,000 nights over 40 years, he became the greatest saloon singer of them all—and it was all because of the love he had for everyone and everything.

Capri, London, Rome, Cape Cod, the Riviera, St. Thomas, Nassau, the Hamptons, Palm Beach, and, finally, New York. So many swell places. So many elegant nights. So many sweet songs. So much love. Other singers had fans who were "customers" or "patrons" of all those joints in which they displayed their well-hewn talents. But the ones who came night after night to hear Hugh came as friends. They came to be with him. They came to love him back. Like I said, he was different and unique. He loved!

There was a big, broad range to the life of this itinerant minstrel. From the 22 Club in Woodside, Queens, and the Blue Haven in Jackson Heights, where his first admirer was that bus driver who would double-park outside in order to hear Hugh sing a few tunes, which always had to include the driver's favorite anthem: "It's a Big, Wide, Wonderful World," to the titled, the privileged, the well-founded, who came in season to Numero Due in Capri, to Bricktop's in Paris, to Francis Carpenter's Bull's Head Inn, to Grace and Rainier's Café du Paris in Monte Carlo, to Carol's, to David Keh's, to the International Club in London, and, finally, to his last stand, the final booking of his life—to Peter Sharp's Café Carlyle.

They will miss Hugh, too, all those elegant, sophisticated ladies and gentlemen of high estate who adopted him and took him into their rarefied world and made him theirs. They had names like Cordelia and Bibi and Doris and Ruby and M'liss and Rebecca and Peggy and Diana. And there were Biddies, Dukes, Cushings, and Whitneys, and even a "Bang Bang" Rutherford, who, I understand, was "persistent," if nothing else, in her fabled attempt to have Hugh all to herself.

Some of them are here today in St. Monica's, and I hope they won't take offense, but Hugh had another life, too. It was here, in this neighborhood, in these streets, in the shops with the cobbler and the greengrocer. It was in the park with the children, and with the construction workers in their hardhats. It was with the nurses at Lenox Hill and in Dressner's bar telling tall tales. And here, with his God, in St. Monica's. Just as he lit up our nights, so, too, he illuminated their days. Thus, it is fitting that so many of Hugh's neighbors are here today as well.

There really was a lot to his life. There was Betty and there was Gus and the Osmunds, Joanne and Jerry. And Bob and Patrice and Helen and Sheila and Kathleen. And you, Father Leone. There was Dick Gelb's mother and the Conroys and the Savitts and the Millers, who took him in. And the Erteguns and Millie and Sheldon and Bricktop—he called her "Brickie." And there were so many others who gave him their friendship and shelter—and always love.

Hugh gave us a lot: the songs, his love, his friendship. And now, the two nice men who run Audiophile Records in Atlanta told us this week that a two-record album will be in the record stores "in the early weeks of November. It was lovingly and carefully recorded by Wendell Echols and George H. Buck Jr. last fall when Hugh was at the Carlyle. There was some uncertainty about a fitting and appropriate name for the new album. Many suggested: Hugh Shannon at the Carlyle. But I'm pleased to tell you that it will be titled, simply, as he would have it: Saloon Singer. So his music will live on after him.

But Hugh is gone. He died, as he lived—with style and grace.

October 30, 1982

Michael Scott Shannon

Notes Re: The Legendary "Z Morning Zoo"

I'm a radio guy.

I write books, editorials, and commentaries about the great issues of the day.

And I've occasionally been introduced as an "author." But I flee from that lofty description.

Breslin was a writer. So too are Malcolm Wilson, Sam Roberts, David Hinckley, Daniel Silva, Robert Harris, Pete Hamill, Lance Morrow, Bill Saroyan, Tracey O'Shaughnessy (no relation), Michael "Lionel" Lebron, Phil Reisman, John McKenna, and Mario Cuomo. Also a lawyer named Michael Assaf. *They* are writers.

I am a hack who earnestly tries to move around words and fashion them into coherent paragraphs. But I struggle mightily and unsuccessfully with the Mother Tongue English language.

So I'll gladly embrace the appellation "Radio Guy" any time, even in my dotage.

And I've always had great respect for disc jockeys who get up each day to strap on earphones and go into a radio studio to entertain and inform.

Some of them view the instrument of communication over which they preside for a few hours each day as more than a jukebox.

A few even resemble social commentators and, lacking that, they aspire to be agreeable companions.

In high school in Buffalo I loved Fred Klestine and the five guys who all used the moniker "Guy King."

And then, much later I discovered a guy from Babylon, New York, named William Bernard Breitbard, which given name he didn't use. Instead, he addressed a microphone as *William B. Williams*.

He went to work in a room called the "Make-Believe Ballroom" that was housed at an iconic radio station with the legendary call sign WNEW.

William B. became a wonderful friend to a young Irish guy from

Westchester. And it was a sad day when *Variety* asked me to eulogize Billy as he left us with the music still playing.

And then, speaking of legends of the air, I became a fan of one *Michael Scott Shannon*, who presided over an obscure New Jersey station, z-100.

Scott is a lot more than a hippy-dippy, finger-snapping "Rodney Radio" disc jockey.

In his best moments he's also a gifted and skillful social commentator, knowledgeable and worldly about the great issues of the day.

And so he assembled a marvelous and beguiling cast of characters to populate his now legendary "Z Morning Zoo."

They played Cyndi Lauper. I had no idea who the hell Cyndi Lauper was. I *still* don't ... but I understand she's pretty, talented, and a big deal on Broadway now.

This Scott Shannon, who has become the preeminent radio guy of our time, was the ringmaster, the interlocutor, the glue and seasoning that drove the inhabitants of the "Zoo," and his genius held it all together.

I can still remember some of the most delightful off-beat personalities from that show. *Everyone* on my block ... including Yours Truly ... was in love with a dame named Claire Stevens!

And the *most* beguiling of all, of course, was one absolutely outrageous but endearing character named "Mr. Leonard," who wore a lime-green leisure suit and cherry red pumps. He was always getting into trouble ... like when he covered the visit of Princess Diana "on assignment for Mr. Scott Shannon" and got rousted by the British Secret Service when they caught Mr. Leonard hiding in the bushes with his "Z Morning Zoo" microphone! ("Don't you know who I am ... ?")

And we remember when he charged out of the radio station in high dudgeon to "have a word" with someone who had had the "audacity" to take his personal parking spot. The confrontation didn't last long, however, when Mr. Leonard found out the car belonged to Hulk Hogan!

"Oh, sorry, so sorry Mr. Hulk Hogan ... I didn't mean nothing by it when I said those terrible things to you and threatened to *beat* you ... I was just kidding! Hah, hah, hah ...."

So many delightful moments ....

So much fun.

Such great radio.

I didn't just *enjoy* their antics. Many nights I would stand at the "21" bar and pummel one and all who would listen with my admiration for this Scott Shannon.

Apparently, I was not alone in my enthusiasm. In a short time, the station had a meteoric rise and went from "Worst to First" in the New York market.

Scott then moved on to also program WPLJ and re-invigorate the iconic WCBS-FM.

He is the best of what we are.

And he is equally at home with high rollers like Ken Langone, the late Jack Welch, his "patsies" at Westchester Country Club, and the swells at the exclusive Lost Tree in Palm Beach.

Shannon is also possessed of those generous genes which inhabited William B. Williams. He has raised hundreds of thousands of dollars for Blythdale Children's Hospital and tees off with his sketchy 18-handicap at our Broadcasters Foundation of America and many other charity golf tournaments.

An observation: You've heard the phrase "He's got a *face* for radio."

I don't want you to think I'm "sweet" on the guy. But Scott Shannon, with those beautiful cheekbones and exquisite jawline, indeed has a face for ... *television*.

But maybe, just maybe, that would ruin everything. He's so damn good at what he does on the radio.

I'm glad he's my friend.

He's a *great* entertainer.

And a class act in every season.

(Oh, and his daughter works in the White House for the president of the United States.)

P.S. These days there is also another mega-jock based in New York. Elvis Duran and his business partner, David Katz, have been absolutely wonderful to our Broadcasters Foundation of America. Duran's airborne genius can be heard on today's version of Z-100 and around the country via our friends at Premiere Networks.

Talese the Writer

A Whitney Radio Commentary by
William O'Shaughnessy, WVOX and WRTN

Maybe you think you've got a budding "author" in the family ... ?

Well, O.K.... it only costs around $50,000.00 a year—just for the tuition—at the Columbia School of Journalism. If you have a kid thus inclined ... you could always attempt to get him or her enrolled at the "J" School come September and try paying off the tab for about the next five years.

Or ... you could just shell out twenty-six U.S. dollars right now and give that youngster a copy of *A Writer's Life* by Gay Talese, the great New York journalist, reporter, and author.

Mr. Talese, whose earlier magazine pieces on Sinatra, DiMaggio, and Floyd Patterson are the stuff of legend, has finally written about Gay Talese.

The son and heir of a master tailor from Calabria who in his day used needle and thread to run up exquisite haberdashery ... Gay Talese now uses graceful words and elegant sentences—as well as over fifty years of listening, questioning, and observing—to fashion a modern damn masterpiece of a book.

He's previously written several bestsellers *The Kingdom and the Power* about the *New York Times, Honor Thy Father* about the Mafia, and *Unto the Sons* about the immigrant experience in America. Also a collection of his magazine and newspaper gems (*The Gay Talese Reader*), which, up until now, was my favorite.

The high-brow *Atlantic Monthly* says, "He has written some of the best American prose of the second half of the twentieth century." And David Halberstam, in the *Boston Globe*, accused Talese of being "the most important nonfiction writer of his generation." (It must, of course, be pointed out that this is the very same daily newspaper owned by Sulzberger that swelled Mario Cuomo's head by calling him "the great philosopher-statesman of the American nation.")

Forget all that stuff. After you save yourself $49,974.00 in college tuition for the gifted kid, buy another copy of *A Writer's Life* for yourself and stay up for two nights like I did reading this exquisite, perfect (there, I've said it) book.

Colorful characters abound. But Talese is clearly the star this time. A meticulous craftsman, he is somewhat famous (or infamous) for taking years to actually complete and deliver a manuscript. This one, which took him only sixty years to assemble, was well worth the wait.

Much research was done over his preferred dry gin martinis at the tables of Elaine Kaufman (Elaine's), Frank Pellegrino (Rao's), Bruce Snyder and Bryan McGuire ("21"), and Maestro Sirio Maccioni (ringmaster of the once and future Le Cirque).

Talese has also logged some time with a rather nefarious group known as The Skeeters, a questionable organization founded as a drinking society by the late Ted Husing that, according to its bylaws, "exists for no good or useful purpose." Current members in good standing are Hugh Leo Carey, Brendan Byrne, Jerry Cummins, Mike Letis, John Hennessy, Jack Landry, insurance moguls Flynn and Moran, William Plunkett Esq., Nelson Doubleday, and Bill Barry the FBI guy, and the son of Sonny Werblin. There is also a Mara, a Quick, and Tony Rolfe. With the possible exceptions of Carey and Byrne, the ex-governors, not one of The Skeeters has ever written a coherent sentence. Most have never even read a book from cover to cover except for the *Daily Racing Form*, with which they have a keen and abiding interest. And thus Talese's talent is barely tolerated in this august fraternity. Top-secret meetings of The Skeeters are held at various racetracks and at Yankee Stadium and at Shea, courtesy of George M. Steinbrenner III and Fred Wilpon, whose lawyer Richard Cummins is an unindicted co-conspirator of this society of "sportsmen." But Talese is right in there too.

A relentless researcher and voracious gatherer of facts and textures, shades and tones, Talese has a brilliance as an observer and interviewer that is the foundation, the underpinning, for his talent as a writer.

Indeed, he blames his remarkable ability on "my natural, though at times misguided, affinity for people and places that exist in the shadows and side streets of the city and other overlooked places in which there are untold stories awaiting my discovery and development!" He doesn't miss much in this wonderful book.

You've no doubt seen Gay Talese around town of an evening. He has a dazzling, powerful wife—the former Nan Ahearn, a Westchester girl (Rye Country Day, Convent of the Sacred Heart, and Manhattanville). She is an important publisher, and he dresses like a fop and a dandy. Don't let the beautiful clothes fool you. Underneath the finery struts an American master of the written word.

Funny thing about this book ... as you amble through *A Writer's Life* you never want the damn thing to end. You never want Gay Talese to end.

Now, at last, we know who he is.

Alfred A. Knopf is the publisher. It goes right on the shelf next to Breslin, Hamill, Mr. Cuomo, Saroyan, Jimmy Cannon ... and Gay Talese's other books. But this is the best one he's ever done.

April 14, 2006

Legends of Arthur Avenue
(and a Publican)

Joseph Migliucci, Pizza Maker

A Remembrance by William O'Shaughnessy

On the sixth day of April, 2020, 731 people in New York died and went to another and, we are sure, better world. One of them was a Joseph Migliucci, who made pizzas. He had existed around here for eighty-one years.

Actually, this man Migliucci did a hell of a lot more than spin pizza dough in the air. Never, in his eighty-one years did he ever spend a single second in Italy, whence his forebearers had come. Instead, Joseph presided over the most beloved Italian restaurant in the great City. Known for five generations, it is actually called Mario's and is heralded and quite beloved far beyond Arthur Avenue in the Little Italy neighborhood of the Bronx.

He was the son of Mario Migliucci, a slim, elegant man who moved through a dining room before him like Fred Astaire. His mother, who was widely known as "Mama Rose," was a Bochino girl, the most beautiful in the Roman Catholic parish of Our Lady of Mount Carmel.

The restaurant over which Mario and Rose, and then their son Joseph, presided was unlike any other eatery abroad in the land.

Arthur Avenue is a place of myth and legend. Many venues these days are run by Albanians. But the Italians like Joseph still hold their own as fishmongers, butchers, greengrocers, bakers, and cannoli makers. Also as restaurateurs.

"Interesting" characters still abound on the streets of Belmont, as this part of the Bronx is formally known. I once inquired of Joseph Migliucci if he was "affiliated" or "associated" with any of the two famous neighborhood "associations" or so-called social Clubs. And after pondering the question, he said, "No ... I'm not 'with' anybody ... but, let's put it this way ... nobody bothers me."

Although you would occasionally encounter some of those "interesting" characters at table during Joe Migliucci's time, there were also federal judges like Jed Rakoff, Westchester judges like Mary Smith and Tom Dickerson, and former Yankees like Bucky Dent.

Mario Cuomo loved the place, and so did Bronx legend Mario Biaggi. A picture of "The Three Marios"—Mario Cuomo, Mario Biaggi, and Mario Migliucci, Joseph's father—still hangs reverently near the front door.

Before Joseph took his leave to that better world on Monday of this week, he and his devoted daughter Regina installed faux leather, saddle-colored banquets along the dining room's side walls where once were displayed hundreds of pictures of Joseph and his family and friends that were recently removed as a gesture to "modernize" and spiff up the place. It is expected that the family mementos will now, with his passing, return to their places of honor.

He sure had a following, this man Joseph Migliucci, which included the rich and well-founded from Westchester and Connecticut ... Fordham Jesuits ... an exterminator ... a 107-year-old named Joe Binder, who was written up by Corey Kilgannon in the *New York Times* itself. And Karen and Judge Jeffrey Bernbach always came down from Westchester for their weekly "lemon squeeze" with Joseph.

It was the place to go—before and after—the Bronx Zoo, the Botanical Gardens, or the Stadium, which is home to our beloved Yankees. And each year Fordham's graduation was the busiest day of the year.

You would often see Frances Fusco, the beautiful Bronx legend, and busloads of white-haired ladies who came from all over the metro area to bask in Joseph's warm and welcoming hospitality. Julian Niccolini, the colorful proprietor of the Four Seasons, would also pick up a pizza on the way home to tony Bedford.

And on other spring days better than this one, Margaret Noonan and Fred Nachbaur and the elders of the highly regarded Fordham University Press would leave their old building and stroll down the avenue in the sunshine to visit Joseph, where the pizza, which never existed on the menu, was the best to be had in America.

I also came often to Joseph's table ... just to be with the guy. In recent years, the "diminishments" (it's a word Cuomo and I stole from the Jesuit Father Pierre Teilhard de Chardin) nibbled away at his legs and lungs and heart. And yet Joseph refused to cede his title as Patriarch of his extended restaurant family.

They even won a James Beard Award. And last year Mario's, the restaurant, had its centennial. I knew the proprietor for forty of those one hundred years. My grandchildren still remember riding on the serving carts when the usually crowded dining room would allow. Joseph and Mama Rose always would "allow."

He spent a lot of time bailing people out and getting them out of trouble. Joseph knew every judge . . . and every important doctor. Doctor Philip Ozuah, the graceful and influential new head of the huge Montefiore Health System, with whom everyone is so well pleased, moved right in to help Joseph scramble at White Plains Hospital before he gave up and left us on Monday.

And so as I sit here the very next day over a legal pad on my own eighty-second birthday, I can only tell you I really miss the damn, wonderful guy.

I make my living with words (in my case they usually appear awkwardly, inartfully, and imprecisely). But I don't really have the words to tell of how much I miss this particular man, the Pizza Maker.

It's much easier to write about people who are just acquaintances and exist from afar rather than someone who always called me "Brother Bill."

Only one other gave me that elevated appellation—a failed baseball player with too many vowels in his name who was a governor.

I give the last word to food critic and author John Mariani, who called Joseph "one of the great men of Italian-American food . . . a big, sweet giant beloved by everyone."

I think he got it just right for my brother Joseph, the Pizza Maker.

April 7, 2020

Mama Rose Migliucci

"THE FIRST LADY OF LITTLE ITALY"

May it please you, Reverend Father Eric Rapaglia ....

Your posting as pastor here at Our Lady of Mount Carmel is a great gift from His Eminence ... for the Parish ... and for the neighborhood.

And Mama Rose would have been so pleased by the presence on the altar of Monsignor Bill O'Brien, the legendary founder and chairman of Daytop Village, who enjoys a well-deserved international reputation ... and also Father Sebastian, the Parochial Vicar of St. Pius X, where he serves the "underprivileged," the "poor," and the "distressed" of Scarsdale, New York ... with another great priest, Father John O'Brien.

Actually, we've been here before in *this* great Bronx church on *another* bittersweet occasion and accompanied then as now with a rich admixture of sadness and joy.

It was one month shy of ten years ago that we prayed for and remembered "Pop" ... *Mario* Migliucci. On that day, January 27, 1998, the people of the neighborhood came together as you have now to bid farewell to another legend of the Bronx. They came out of their shops on that winter day ... the greengrocers ... the bakers ... the breadmakers ... the fishmongers ... the butchers and cheesemongers. That day was for Mario.

And so we are here again ... to pray for Mario's beloved Rose Bochino Migliucci ... to remember our incomparable "Mama Rose."

But it is right, I think, that we also mention Pop as we pray for Mama, because you can't really assess the life of one ... without the other.

They were always, it seems, *together* ... ever since that day when a young girl named Rosie Bochino peered out the window of her tenement house, which, incidentally, was directly across the street from Mario's Restaurant. She took one look at Mario, who moved like a graceful ballet dancer, even when waiting on tables or twirling pizzas ... sending them airborne ... with great *élan* and a certain finesse ...

at his father's Neapolitan restaurant. His father had come from Cairo to establish a life for himself in these undeveloped, wild and wooly precincts in the early 1900s — 1919, in fact.

This was all happening during the days when actual *farms* existed in the Belmont section of what was becoming known as the "Little Italy" we know today.

We all know the story of their courtship ... how when Pop started dating Mom ... the popular lore of the neighborhood has it ... that Mom had *another* suitor who was, in fact, an usher, a very upstanding fellow, who took the collection every Sunday in *this very church.*

And then one day Mario — "Pop" — now greatly taken by and deeply in love with Rose Bochino, went to pay this fellow a little "visit" here at the church ... (I don't think Mario came here to pray that particular day) ... and legend has it that the man somehow saw fit to transfer his genius at passing the basket to *another* parish! And the rest you know. They lived and loved and flourished for more than seventy years together. Rose and Mario. Mario and Rose.

Right here in the Bronx. Right here on these streets, in this fabled neighborhood they call "Little Italy." Or "Arthur Avenue," as some would have it. And, always, on Mondays ... by the ocean in Montauk. The two of them.

The papers that wrote stories of her passing last weekend at ninety-four called Mama Rose a "restaurateur." Well, those of us who knew — and *loved* — her know she was *much* more.

Rose Bochino Migliucci was essentially, a *teacher.* She taught us all the oldest virtues and verities. She never preached. Rather, she instructed by living — by example, by fortitude, by consistency, by dedication.

She had a quiet charisma ... presiding over her domain and her family from that old, wobbly stool near the cappuccino machine from which were drawn the famous "Bochino Cappuccinos" ... (I could use one tonight, Dominick ... and you could spike it too!).

Incidentally, Joseph was *thinking* about closing down in Mom's honor ... for at least one day. Then he realized that Mama would have been the first to say, "Don't even *think* about it, Joseph!" So he got the message delivered from on high!

To her favorites at the restaurant she would proffer her pickled carrots ... her "Mom salad," which she made herself, and her chopped liver. (You have to remember ... this was an *Italian* restaurant!)

She was always there ... in every season ... until late into the night. Feeding people and loving them. And when life turned sad and difficult, when things were spinning out of control, we would repair to her counsel, to her warmth, to her wisdom.

The rich and privileged came from Westchester and Connecticut and even from New Jersey. They came down from their country clubs in Bronxville and their yacht clubs in Rye, because Rose and Mario gave them something they couldn't get in those rarefied precincts.

Mama's goodness and charm brought them to this neighborhood ... judges, magistrates, food critics, journalists, merchant princes, civic leaders, the people of the neighborhood who loved her, even a few competitors—other restaurateurs.

One of Mama's admirers, Julian Niccolini—the owner of the fancy, formidable Four Seasons, one of America's most elaborate venues— came every Sunday night to spend his one day off with Mama and Joseph. On other days Julian feeds tycoons and power brokers at his famous landmark Manhattan restaurant ... the Rudins, the Bronfmans. But when *he* wants to dine ... he comes straight away to Mario's because, I think, there's a "realness" ... an authenticity about the place. He also came for Mama. And I expect he will still come because her spirit is still everywhere apparent.

Mama was so strong, so dignified, so intuitive. Every mother is wonderful and glorious, I know. Yet, even after you carve away the excess, you know this one was special. When she walked down Arthur Avenue every afternoon to the bake shop ... you knew something very wonderful was coming at you.

She used to regret her lack of education. Maybe it's better she didn't know cybernetics from a salami slicing machine—or megabytes instead of the struggle for survival. She was better with her intuition than you were with your education and intelligence.

She knew *only* this—that no one could have assembled all this magnificence and all this complication if it weren't going to come out all right in the end. She knew this, and you could not have a mother like this without being awestruck by her strength. She was not of a world where Porsches are parked next to BMWs.

Rose's success as a restaurateur was enough to earn her *respect* ...
but not enough to earn her *love*. She was loved. So today we remember Mario *and* Rose ... the charity of their souls and the largeness of their hearts.

I only want to quote from the Book of Proverbs: "Her value is far beyond pearls. Her husband, entrusting his heart to her, has an unfailing prize. She brings him good all the days of her life. She rises while it is still night and distributes food to her household. She has strength, and sturdy are her arms. She reaches out her hands to the poor and extends her arms to the needy. She is clothed with strength and dignity, and she laughs at the days to come. She opens her mouth in wisdom, and on her tongue is kindly counsel. Her children rise up and praise her. Give her a reward of her labors, and let her works ... praise her at the city gates."

So it is a remarkable story! A story of generations. A story of a unique Bronx woman as endearing as she was enduring. And, finally, a story of a marriage as strong and remarkable and resilient as any of us have ever seen.

But it was always about family.

And if you didn't have one, or if your own was falling apart, you could come and appropriate her family—and make it your own. You could throw your arms around Rose and have Joseph, who is his father's son, call you "brother" and give you a big, wet kiss on both cheeks. His son, young Mario, has learned that pretty well too!

So she now leaves us Joseph ... and Barbara. And Diane ... and Michael. And nine grandchildren ... and fourteen great-grandchildren. She could not have existed without that family ... without all of you to love.

And she leaves us knowing that, essentially, her work was done.

Even to her last day, Mama, with everything in her being, loved that family she clung to with a fierceness across ninety-four years.

All of you in that family have your own stories, and you will go off now to share them with one another ... and for days and years to come.

Finally, those of you here assembled may not be aware that just before she left, Mama waited up for Joseph to come home at 12:30 from the restaurant last Friday night.

To the very last she made sure everyone in this amazingly strong family was all right.

And then ... what happened ... my own wife, Nancy Curry, explained, with great sureness, when *she* heard the news that caused us all such exquisite sadness this week: "Mama Rose just wanted to spend *Christmas* ... with *Mario*."

And that's what really happened, I think, just as Nancy said ...

What a remarkable life. What an extraordinary woman.

So, smile for us, Mama. The years are behind you.

And try to make a little room ... and set a table ... for us.

Our Lady of Mt. Carmel Church,
Bronx, New York (December 17, 2008)

Mario "Pop" Migliucci: 1914–1998

Our Lady of Mount Carmel Church,
Little Italy, Bronx, New York

This is what I know about Mario Migliucci, about "Pop," a Bronx legend.

I will begin in Montauk, where he would revive and restore himself by the sea on weekends alone, with the wind and the light and his beloved Rose. Then, each Tuesday morning, he would return to what he was and where he had to be, always to these streets, to this neighborhood, and to the landmark restaurant that bears his name.

Pop's goodness and charm brought them to this neighborhood. Judges, magistrates, food critics, journalists, merchant princes, civic leaders, and the people of the neighborhood who loved him, even a few competitors—other restaurateurs. The rich and privileged came from Westchester and Connecticut and even from New Jersey. They came down from their country clubs in Bronxville and their yacht clubs in Rye, because Pop gave them something they couldn't get in those rarefied precincts. He gave them realness.

Pop provided an agreeable venue, a warm, beckoning place, where they could sit at a table with their families and eat and drink and talk—and laugh—through the night. "*Vera real*," he called it. Authentic! Everything about Pop was authentic.

What an attractive man he was! What a handsome man! He would move through the dining room with that lean, lithe, taut body like Fred Astaire. He was always imperially slim, while the rest of us put on too many pounds as a result of the abundance of his hearty, earthy Neapolitan food! He moved with a grace not found in men of his years.

And his hands were beautiful, graceful, and elegant—the hands of a craftsman, an artisan. Especially when he would send the pizzas swirling skyward, borne aloft by those beautiful hands. He let me try once. The pizza is still on the ceiling!

You saw him across eighty-four years. You have your own stories, and you will go off to share them with one another. You know he was a man of great subtlety, great warmth. Mario's Restaurant, during his time, was the quintessential family restaurant—and it still is. There were always children, in-laws, and out-laws! And, always, someone who was related to Rose. It was always about family.

If you didn't have one, or if your own was falling apart, you could come and appropriate his family—and make it your own. You could throw your arms around Rose and have Joseph, who is his father's son, call you "brother" and give you a big, wet kiss on both cheeks.

And Momma—you cannot tell the story of Mario Migliucci without Mama. They were always together, for more than fifty years. Since that day he saw a young Rose Bochino looking out the window across the street, a few blocks away. It happened on Arthur Avenue, most of this story. She was with him in all good times—for all the weddings, for all the children, for all the grandchildren. She saw it all. She felt it all.

But all those times in Montauk, on Arthur Avenue, were just a prelude to their last year together. Momma was there every day; so were her children, Joseph and Diane. But the love of Rose for Mario, and Mario for Rose, in those hospitals, every day, was something never witnessed by the attending physicians or nurses at Stony Brook or at our Lady of Mercy across the parkway. The good and gifted Cardinal Archbishop John J. O'Connor talks often and eloquently of couples who remain together for fifty years or more. He even gives them prizes and bestows medals. But if Cardinal O'Connor sent to central casting for vivid, contemporary, perfect examples of fidelity and commitment and devotion, central casting would send you a profile of Rose Bochino and Mario Migliucci: Mom and Pop. We, who look through a glass darkly, can't see it yet. We can't yet realize or understand it. But the last, not yet final, chapter of their love was absolutely their best, most memorable work together.

Mario lived his life in these streets, with the butchers, the fishmongers, the greengrocers, the bankers, the old women of the neighborhood in their dark shawls, the priests, and the students from Fordham University.

Our religion, when we listen and when we are still, tells us to try and see the goodness in every face we encounter. It's not always easy.

But every once in a while, we do come upon a face that radiates the goodness and sweetness within that person. Mario—Pop—had such a countenance. Rose has it. When they entered a room together, you knew there was something special coming at you. And that something good and very sweet was going to happen.

I asked one of the merchant princes of Little Italy to tell me something about Mario. "He was there for about seventy-five years!" the merchant said. But we loved him, and we mourn him—not because of his longevity. Mario's life, however enduring, instructs us in the old-fashioned, eternal values. They are the lessons of a man who stayed at his task.

Another man named Mario—who wrote to Pop in the hospital—once reminded us: "Don't let us forget who we are and where we've come from. We are the sons and daughters of giants," said Mario Cuomo. The governor spoke not of physical stature or the magnitude of our purse or the resonance of our voice and reputation or of our high estate and standing in the community. Rather, he spoke of other strengths, other attributes, other qualities, and sweeter truths—harder, more difficult to define, but nonetheless real. He was identifying for us, and leading us toward, those men and women who live their lives out of the glare of celebrity, but not removed from the rest of us. He was leading us to Mario Migliucci, to the kind of man he was, to the way he lived his life, even to the way he died.

So it is a remarkable story! A story of generations. A story of a unique Bronx institution as endearing as he was enduring. And, finally, a story of a marriage as strong and remarkable and resilient as any of us has ever seen.

And it is a story about the unique goodness of Pop. Some of us move toward things, things we can control and maneuver like instruments. Others move toward people, people who breathe and think and feel—and love. The restaurant business, where Mario chose to spend all his years, is about people—about feeding them, giving them sustenance and drink. Like the reading this morning: "You spread the table before me...." Some see it as a business. Others, like Mario, view it as a calling, a way to bring people together, and love them—and to be loved in return. So how could he have chosen any other venue for his genius, for his love, than the restaurant? It was his podium, his forum, his theater. He was its interpreter, its impresario, its steward. It was his calling. But it was merely an entity to bring him closer to people.

Pop fed everyone: rabbis, baseball players, failed priests, Steinbrenner, Fugazy, Biaggi, DiMaggio, Rockefeller, and the great Cuomo himself. Neal Travis, in the *New York Post*, recalled when Lee Iacocca would dispatch his jet to New York to pick up an armload of Pop's pizza! Mario's hospitality was natural and unforced, a product of a good heart and a generous soul. He was a good man. He was always there. He stayed.

And he is glad you came today.

January 27, 1998

Jimmy Neary

BELOVED PUBLICAN OF THE GREAT CITY

A Remembrance by William O'Shaughnessy

A rich man who is head of an international
Gourmet Society once told me: "The Best Restaurant
is the one where they know you the best."

I always looked forward to a warm greeting from Bruce Snyder at "21" ... Joe Migliucci at Mario's in the Bronx ... James O'Shea and the late Charlie Kafferman at the West Street Grill in Litchfield ... Sirio Maccioni at the mighty Le Cirque ... Bruno Dussin at Circo ... Sergio Vacca at Harry Cipriani ... Julian Niccolini and Alex Von Bidder at the Four Seasons ... Michael DeLullo at the Venetian in Torrington, an old Connecticut mill town ... Gerry Biggins at P. J. Clarke's (the Mother Ship on Third Avenue) .... I also loved seeing Joe Valeant of Bernie Murray's and Tommy Moretti in upstate Elmira ... Franco Lazarri of Vice Versa on the West Side ... Tony Federici, the Parkside maestro and his deputy Alfredo Chiesa in Corona, Queens ... Gerardo Bruno of our beloved San Pietro and Dino Arpaia of Cellini. Also Samantha Tilley of Mockingbird (a *cooker* and a *looker*!) ... ditto Alyssa Potts, proprietor of the Fife and Drum in Kent. And we've recently discovered Lisa Burnett and Suzanne Pond at La Tavola in Waterbury and Gigi D'Amico and Michael Cavallo and a knockout named Lucy Tiche at Mangia in Watertown, also in Connecticut.

New York is littered with ersatz Irish pubs. A few stood out from the pack of touristy joints: Gerry Toner's Kennedy's; Des O'Brien's Langan's, where Neal Travis and Steve Dunleavy hung out when Rupert Murdoch picked up their checks; and Costello's, where James Earle "Jimmy" Breslin would preside with his unique facility with the mother tongue.

And even those private clubs that abound for the rich and famous have some stellar practitioners of the Cordial Welcome: Teddy

Suric of the Harvard Club ... Colin Burns Sr. of the greatly heralded Winged Foot ... Tim McCormick of the New York Yacht Club ... and Anne-Marie Fillipini of the Torrington Country Club. All hear the same music of how to make people feel welcome when they are lonely, hurting, or just hungry.

But there was only *one* Jimmy Neary. He was the most beloved *publican* of the great city. *Sui generis* is the word. And he was also *sui generous*. This gregarious, gracious Irishman had a unique gift for hospitality that drew governors, writers, publishers, bishops, moguls, presidents, senators, mayors, and the rich widows and denizens of tony Sutton Place to his care and keeping at the legendary saloon on East 57th Street.

He gave them food for sustenance ... and booze, tho' he never partook of the demon. And everyone at his bar always looked like Pat Moynihan, Hughie Carey, or James A. Farley.

At table there was usually Pat Barrett, the upstate New York politico who made a score with Avis; D. J. Carey (nephew of the governor); Kevin Barry McGrath and "Don't Worry" Murray Richman, the power lawyers; and Tom Werblin, son of Sonny ... *and* our magnificently gifted and articulate Cardinal Timothy Michael Dolan, who was a frequent—I'd better make that *occasional*—visitor. Also Jonathan Bush, who was as nice a *patron* as Jimmy was a *host* ... a regular from the neighborhood.

Jimmy was keen on a Queens guy named Donald John Trump, who became president of the United States. And Neary didn't waver or apologize for it. Speaking of which, he forgave me for my own enthusiasm for Mario Matthew Cuomo, another Queens guy. Neary much preferred George Elmer Pataki.

Jimmy was there every night and especially looked forward to working weekends with his spectacular daughter Una Neary who, in real life, is one of the preeminent international bankers in the city. She is also, as one Irishman observed, "easy on the eyes."

Regulars at Neary's breathed a huge sigh of relief when it was announced yesterday that Jimmy's podium and forum—his beloved saloon and restaurant—will continue under the watchful care and keeping of Una.

Bloomberg staffers Kevin Sheekey and Dan Doctoroff hung out

with Jimmy. And their boss, Michael Bloomberg, who has a habit of doing nice things for people, took Jimmy to Ireland on his personal plane to meet up with relatives.

Cardinal Dolan took him to Rome, to the Vatican. And on Saturday at Saint Patrick's Cathedral, he'll introduce him to Heaven on high, where he'll present Jimmy to the *Celestial Maître d* ... whose name, I believe, is *Peter*, who will almost instantly recognize Jimmy Neary and escort him to a very great table, indeed.

"Ah ... yes ... the Cardinal Archbishop of New York personally made your reservation, sir. Come right in. Incidentally, the owner, who is in charge of everything here, has been asking for you!" It has to happen that way.

There was only one Jimmy Neary.

He was the most beloved publican of the great city.

And a dear man.

October 4, 2021

This Sporting Life

Ann T. Mara

Eulogy by John Mara, Co-president,
New York Giants, New York City

Your Eminence Cardinal Dolan, Cardinal Egan, family and friends, thank you for being here to celebrate the life of our mother. Your support and friendship has meant the world to my family over the past few weeks and we are deeply appreciative.

I have to also thank and acknowledge all ten of my brothers and sisters for taking such good care of our mother since our father died more than nine years ago, especially my seven sisters. The care you gave her over the last two weeks was extraordinary, as only daughters can do. She was never alone for one minute. Most nights, two of you stayed all night with her in her hospital room. You held her hands, caressed her forehead, and constantly told her how much you loved her and were grateful for everything she had given us. Our father would have been so proud of you, as I am.

It was fitting that my mother chose Super Bowl Sunday to leave us. As embarrassed and uncomfortable as my father always felt about being the center of attention, that was *not* the case with my mother. When the doctors disconnected her from the ventilator this past Saturday around 10:30 a.m., they predicted she would last for maybe an hour or two. But nobody was going to tell *her* when it was time to go. It was the first time in her life when she was not in a hurry to get somewhere. We should have known she was not going to be yesterday's news. She was going out on Super Bowl Sunday for the whole world to see. It was also fitting that she lasted so long because she kept us all together in the same room for an entire day and night. Her children and grandchildren all in and out of her room saying our goodbyes. We went from tears to laughter, to telling stories about her and about each other. And then finally to tears again. But we were together, loving and supporting each other the way she would have wanted. It was her final gift to us, yet another lesson in how to be a family.

My mother was very specific about her funeral arrangements. The wake had to be at Campbell's and the funeral, of course, at St. Ignatius ... this church where they met, were married, and where so much of our family history is, was so special to her. My parents were married here on February 10, 1954. I was born nine months and two-and-a-half weeks later. And yes, I did the math a long time ago!

My mom's Catholic faith was so important to her and shaped so much of her life. You have already heard how she went to Mass every day. She observed the Sacraments so closely and expected her children to do the same. Just like my father before he died, I could always count on a phone call from Mom to remind me that it was a Holy Day of Obligation and I'd better get to Mass. My mother's hospital room over the last two weeks was a place of prayer, constantly visited by priests. I lost count of how many times she was anointed.

Although she followed the teachings of the Church closely, she sometimes played by her own rules. For as long as I can remember she parked in the same spot on the Resurrection Church driveway in Rye. She wasn't supposed to park there, of course, and eventually they put up a sign: "Thou shalt not park here." Well, that sign might just as well have said, "Reserved for Ann Mara," because she kept parking there right until she was hospitalized. I asked her about it, and she dismissed me by saying, "I've been parking there for years."

My mother had many endearing qualities. She was kind, loving, and compassionate. Patience ... however, not so much. She supported many charities. With eleven children, forty-three grandkids, and sixteen great-grandchildren, she attended more baptisms, first communions, graduations, school plays, and the like than anyone I will ever know. She never wanted to disappoint any of us.

She was never afraid to speak her mind, as I am sure many can personally attest. Several years ago we were playing in San Francisco and before the game I escorted my mother to the owner's box. As I was getting ready to leave (we rarely sat together—for good reason), a security guard approached and said "Speaker Nancy Pelosi would like to come in and say hello to Mrs. Mara." As fear ran through my entire body, in walks Speaker Pelosi, who goes right up to Mom and says, "Mrs. Mara, welcome to San Francisco." My mother thanked her and said what was really on her mind. "I just want you to know I'm a Republican and I don't agree with most of your political views . . . ." I would tell you the rest of what she said, but I wasn't around to hear it. Frankly, I was too afraid, so I got out of there as fast as I could.

And of course she will forever be remembered for the encounter with Terry Bradshaw. It is difficult to put into words the paralyzing fear that ran through me, being on national TV and watching my mother charge the stage, with that determined look in her eyes. knowing there was nothing I could do to stop her. Many people would be embarrassed by the amount of attention she received. But not her. She became an overnight sensation and loved every minute of it. Fans sent her letters, cards, and gifts, including a pair of boxing gloves she proudly displayed in her home.

As many of you know, my mother delighted in telling everyone she was my boss. "You are just an employee, you know, and you can be replaced." She would sometimes heckle me if I was speaking at some event, and she didn't particularly like what I was saying. "Don't forget, I'm your boss," she would yell from the audience. It got to the point where she would be asked to sign a football and she would sign "Ann Mara, John's boss." In fact, maybe the last words she ever spoke to me were when I walked into her hospital room shortly after she was admitted. Susan was with her and asked, "Mom, do you know who this is?" She looked up at me, her eyes barely open, and answered, "John . . . my employee."

Many people—and institutions—will feel the loss of my mother. Nobody I know attended more charity dinners and events than she did. She felt it was her obligation to support all of these charities, and she did not want to disappoint anyone. And I'm reminded of Saks Fifth Avenue, which will undoubtedly announce a reduction in earnings in 2015! And there is Rocco, my mother's personal hairstylist, who gave her that Ann Mara trademark look. I think she would walk into Rocco's salon at 5′1″ and walk out at 5′9″! Nearly every week during the football season, Mom would call my assistant, Ann, and say, "I need two more tickets—for *Rocco*—please don't tell John." Mom . . . I knew . . . I knew.

Mom rarely missed a game. The team meant so much and she lived and died with our successes and failures. I would sometimes try to convince her to stay home from a long road trip or a night game. "I can't," she would say, "the team would notice and I don't want them to think I have given up on them." The sight of her holding up the Lombardi Trophy from Super Bowl 46, broken shoulder and all, with a big smile on her face will live with us forever.

It was difficult to watch our mom deteriorate so quickly over her last two weeks. She was always so strong and feisty, and I thought she would outlive us all. She had every intention of going to the Super Bowl until that fateful day she slipped on the ice. As troubling as it was to watch her go through that, we tried to take comfort in realizing how fortunate we all were. My daughter, Lauren, kept saying to me, "Dad, do you realize how blessed we all are because of all that your father and mother had given us?"

The eleven of us (and our extended families) are so fortunate. Think about it. We had Ann and Wellington Mara as our parents. How much more blessed could anybody be than to have had the two most loving, caring, and supportive parents anyone could ask for? The ideal role models. Parents who gave us such a large and loving family, who loved us unconditionally, and had such strong faith. No amount of fame or fortune could compare with that.

There is a poem called "Her Journey's Just Begun" (by Rhonda Baker):

Don't think of her as gone away —
Her journey's just begun,
Life holds so many facets —
This earth is only one.

Just think of her as resting
From the sorrow and the tears.
In a place of warmth and comfort
Where there are no days and years.

Think how she must be wishing
That we could know today
How nothing but our sadness
Can really pass away.

And think of her as living
In the hearts of those she touched ...
For nothing loved is ever lost —
And she was loved so much.

Thank you, Mom, for everything you gave us ... and taught us. You were the best mother and role model for all of us.

I may not have always shown it . . . but I was proud to be your employee.

And I am even more proud to be your son.

February 6, 2015

Mr. Mara

He went out a winner.

On Sunday, the New York Giants came from behind in the final minutes to beat the Denver Broncos 24–23. And at his home at 67 Park Drive South in Rye, the eighty-nine-year-old Wellington Mara watched the game through a haze of painkillers and medication. The elderly man with the cherubic smile and dancing eyes was in the final hours of an extraordinary life. He was comforted by those who loved him the most, but dying is something you have to do all by yourself.

After he left us early Tuesday morning, October 25th, Mr. Mara's passing was covered on the front page of the *New York Times*, whose editors knew that the man transcended the raucous, and often brutal, game of football. The life of Wellington Mara was more than just a sports story.

The pages where they celebrated his gentle genius bombard us daily with schedules, scores, and statistics. But the patriarch of the New York Giants was about more than touchdowns, win–loss records, championship rings, or even the Football Hall of Fame in Canton, Ohio, where Mr. Mara is permanently enshrined.

He was the son of a bookmaker when that calling was right, honorable, and legal. And he became an icon of his sport, a pillar of the Roman Church, and a stalwart of the pro-life movement.

If Mr. Mara despised anything during his eighty-nine years, it was the taking of vulnerable, innocent, defenseless life, because he believed, with absolute certainty, it possessed Divine potential. And Mr. Mara cared about this cause more than the exploits of his football team.

He was always courteous to doormen, limo drivers and cabbies, waiters, delivery boys, parking-lot attendants, store clerks, and crossing guards, and he always smiled at the caddie at Winged Foot. No one ever had a bad or nasty thing to say about this ontologist, a lover of life.

Possessed of great intelligence, as well as humility and gentleness, he would engage in robust philosophical discussions with Mario

Cuomo and other prominent leaders on the great theological and ecclesiastical issues of the day. But he always stayed civil and kept an open mind.

The patriarch of the Giants was the last surviving scion of great football families and legends such as George Halas, Art Rooney, Leon Hess, Sonny Werblin, George Allen, Paul Brown, and Vince Lombardi. Today, few gentlemen remain to preside over this game of choreographed, physical battle, with its players operating on the frontier of rage.

Mr. Mara went to all the high school and Catholic church rubber-chicken dinners, along with the Plunketts, the Smiths, the Gills, the Currans, the Joyces, the Conways, the Egans, the McCooeys, and the Mastronardis. He attended almost every NFL owners' meeting and was generally the last to speak. But Art Modell and Commissioner Tagliabue will tell you his shy, gentle wisdom invariably carried the day.

Mr. Mara hung around Westchester during the football season and visited Winged Foot Saturday nights with his dazzling, luminous wife, Ann. And you would see him at a corner table at Emilio's in Harrison with his daughter, Susan, and her handsome husband, John McDonnell, and, every morning, on his knees at Resurrection Church in Rye.

Mr. Mara made his living in the stadiums and amphitheaters of a ruthless professional sport built on big money. But his neighbors here in Westchester would encounter him on soft, sunlit afternoons in the springtime, as he discreetly perched on one of those tri-corner leather stools at the Pinebrook Little League field, watching his grandson Timmy McDonnell play shortstop. And when North-End parents from New Rochelle would spy the man in an Irish tweed bucket hat, they would inquire, "Aren't you Wellington Mara, the owner of the Giants?!" And the gentle patrician from Rye would tip his hat and say, "Today, I'm only a grandfather!"

And the summer was one of his favorite seasons, when he could bunk with his grandson Timmy at the Giants' training camp, near the headwaters of the Hudson.

Mr. Mara wasn't a suave man who moved in a dazzle of haberdashery. But he could make a grand entrance at "21" and at Sirio

Maccioni's LeCirque with the glamorous grandmother of his forty grandkids. And their charisma and presence were very real, drawing from a great reservoir of goodness without haughty glitz, phoniness, or hype.

Edward Cardinal Egan will pray for the soul of Wellington Mara at Saint Patrick's Cathedral on Friday morning in a ceremony worthy of the great City. And as he takes the pulpit, the articulate Archbishop with the big, booming, resonant voice will proclaim that Mr. Mara went out a winner in the game of life, regardless of the numbers on the scoreboard.

Original broadcast, October 26, 2005

Remarks of William O'Shaughnessy for John Scully, "A Sailor and a Gentleman"

It comes as no great surprise that John Watson Scully was a high church Anglican. I mean, everyone at the American Yacht Club on Milton Point in Rye, New York, a most famous sailing club in the County of Westchester, when informed of the passing of this John Watson Scully did not have to hesitate before pronouncing him a gentleman. It was not even necessary to read his obit in the *Times* and the Gannett daily newspapers last week.

A gentleman he was. And that is now required to be carved by the stonemason and placed with him in the Anglican cemetery in Vero Beach, Florida, where he will go for all time to come.

John Scully was eighty-two. He came at you before hedge funds with their derivatives and well before Yuppies invaded Westchester and his beloved Rye with their tasteless, out-of-scale McMansions that lumber oppressively behind wrought-iron electronic gates. As you look at Scully's life and way of operating, you also have to put him before iPads, cell phones, reality shows, Lady Gaga, and the Kardashians.

He was of the American Yacht Club of George Gibbons, Jim and Leggy Mertz, Ogden Reid, Rudy Schaefer, Walter Nelson Thayer, T. Garrison Morfit a.k.a. Garry Moore, the Isdales, the Jamisons, Tinker Myles, George Bryant, the Mundingers, the Hibberds, Ann and Richard A.R. Fraser, Dick Pinkham, Wally Elton, Bill Ketcham, Rick Clark, Drake Sparkman, the Weins, Diana and Peter Gonzalez, and Charles Brieant, whose name is on a federal courthouse in White Plains where once he sat in a black robe under an "In God We Trust" sign.

John Scully was, in every season, a cultured man who existed in

our frantic "Between You and Me" society where most flunk the in-
terrogatory: "I'm fine ... " and never mind the ... "And how are you?"

Scully sold pension plans and retirement funds, which enabled
him to shuttle between Vero Beach and his beloved Rye. And for the
last sixteen years he battled the prostate cancer inside him with the
relentless assistance and loving care of one Howard Scher of Sloan
Kettering, which is the New York Yankees of cancer hospitals. And
so Captain John Scully made it to his eighty-second year to bring his
boat up from Florida for the very last time this summer.

A young John Watson Scully made his biggest score when he
married a spectacular woman of great lineage in these parts named
Suzanne Marechal, and together they raised a whole posse of little
Scullys who were given impressive middle names of substance, car-
riage, and nobility that conveyed an aura of considerable heritage,
provenance, and breeding.

These offspring of John and Sue Scully are now parents of yet another issue of little Scullys, each, of course, endowed with a formidable middle name just as John Scully would have it.

He will be remembered next Monday, the seventeenth day of September, 2012, at precisely 1500 hours at the American Yacht Club,
where once he served as Fleet Captain. I don't think he ever made
commodore or won any major sailing races. Thus no silver trophies
adorned his mantle. Nor is his name carved in any wooden plaques
above the yacht club bar. But few of the accomplished, actual winning yachtsmen there commemorated will be as fondly remembered
by the sailing fraternity. Or by the people who pour the drinks, cook
the food, wait on tables, and haul the boats at this iconic sailing place
hard by Long Island Sound in our home heath.

It is also to be here noted that one John Scully associated his name
with the application of the very first Jewish member of said legendary sailing organization. As memory serves, that particular individual was also proposed by a Richard M. Clark and has since preceded
them to a place where such designations, categories, and labels are
no longer remarked upon. But Scully and Clark put up the first one.

The great philosophers, social commentators, and many of our
statesmen speak often of a "coarsening of the culture." And Scully's
departure surely gives them another chapter for their sad assump-

tions and bleak prognostications as they preserve the story of our times and lack of civility and manners.

But for eighty-two years there was a John Watson Scully.

September 15, 2012

Higher Powers

Father Terry Attridge
Interview with William O'Shaughnessy

wo: "Tonight someone with a strange looking collar. I am a poor, stumbling, staggering, faltering Catholic. But I do call it my own 'personal' Roman Holy Catholic Church. We've had Brother John Driscoll, head of Iona College, and Monsignor Ed Connors, the great preacher from Immaculate Heart of Mary Church. Tonight, I'd like you to meet someone who is the pastor of Sacred Heart Church in Dobbs Ferry. He is a former associate superintendent of schools for the Archdiocese. He's a police chaplain. He gives retreats. He's a central casting, handsome priest. I think he's a model priest ... Father Terry Attridge. Father Attridge, no one believes this, not even Nancy Curry O'Shaughnessy, but you and I are the same *age*."

TA: "That's what they tell me, Bill. I was listening to all the guests you are going to have in the future and it's really great to bring me in here to try to boost your ratings ... so your vast audience will be ready to watch all these great celebrities!"

wo: "We're off and running ... Father T.! I remember when you were a young parish priest. You look the same. You'll be ninety years old and you'll look like that. Can I mention that you're fifty-four?"

TA: "You just gave away the great secret of the county, and the rest of the world. But again, Bill, if you started to live my life ... *you* might be able to work the thing out and look more respectable."

wo: "You were a youngster when you first climbed up into the pulpit at Blessed Sacrament Church in New Rochelle, as a young priest. Do you remember those days?"

TA: "I had this white-haired gentleman sitting out in front with these three good-looking kids ... and that's how we began our friendship ...."

wo: "And do you remember Charlie Wendelken?"

TA: "I do. A great man. It's too bad that he's not well now. He's a

[211]

deacon in the Church and he does a great deal of wonderful work there."

WO: "What about the Church today? It's been under siege in a lot of ways."

TA: "Well, I think it's very exciting to be very active in the Church. We have a program now called The Right of Christian Initiation for Adults for people who had been baptized but were not actively involved in the church and they are just now beginning to get involved. And I think it's because the value system that the Gospels and the Scriptures offer is really something that is desperately needed in our society. With a lot of the issues in our society and the violence that is taking place ... it's too bad so many people sit back and tolerate and become indifferent to what is happening in our society. The Church is willing to take a stand on a lot of these issues and, hopefully, wake a lot of people up."

WO: "Is this whole society going to hell in a hand basket? I don't know what that phrase means ... !"

TA: "The basic issue in our society rests upon life issues. When we have a society that is willing to tolerate the killing of babies before birth through abortion. When we have people who will do anything to their bodies to get high rather than deal with issues. When you have a society that looks back and gets upset over violence ... but is not willing to do something about it. When we have so many people in our society who are hungry ... and it's not that these people are not working, it's just that they can't take the meager income they are getting from their salaries and be able to feed themselves after they are paying rents that are out of sight ...."

WO: "Didn't the Bible say, 'The poor you will have with you always'?"

TA: "The Bible also talks about justice, Bill. I think we have to be able to look at these justice issues in our society today as well."

WO: "I forgot to mention that you were the head of the DARE national drug program. You started it. Is the drug thing really behind a lot of this?"

TA: "The drugs are part of a *symptom* that is a big problem in our society. If you look back to the decline of the basic sub-community of our society today, family life, and if you look back over the last thirty years, you see that as family life begins to decline ... we see crime and the drug problem beginning to escalate. I don't think a lot of our society is willing to deal with it. A lot of people will say that it is not happening in their community. We are *all* affected by the drug problem. I lived in a community before I moved up to Dobbs Ferry. I lived there fourteen years and was robbed fifteen times!"

WO: "You were robbed?"

TA: "The place I was living in ... I managed to talk myself out of it four times."

WO: "But you're the police chaplain. They've got to be *dumb* robbers!"

TA: "That was the way I was able to talk my way out of it! It's really a problem when we deny that we have a problem. The number one health problem in our society is addiction. To be aware of that and to be aware of the killers ... like alcohol, say, that alcohol is not the primary killer. We say it's heart disease and cancer. But if we look back at the source for those diseases, you're going to find alcoholism involved in that and cigarettes also. People say they can deal with legal drugs ... and they're looking at illegal drugs and then the misinformation and the studies that come out and say that the drug problem is declining. That's really not true. Being involved with law enforcement for twenty-five years and dealing with the people in enforcement, they can very easily tell you that it's not. The heroin problem today is higher than it was in the past. And the quality of the heroin coming into the country today is better than in the past."

WO: "But we are sitting here in pristine Westchester. You're talking about downtown New York."

TA: "The problem is here, but you don't see the crime. Maybe in some cities in Westchester County you'll see the crime escalating but, in other cities ... the Larchmont–Scarsdale area ... it might not be reflected, and even talking to the young people there you'll find out that pot is in the house, pills are certainly there ... and the abusive prescription drugs ...."

WO: "In Larchmont?"

TA: "In a lot of affluent areas."

WO: "Are you fingering booze as a killer? As much as heroin and cocaine?"

TA: "I think it's as destructive. If you look at it ... I think more people die in that particular area than they do from heroin. Cocaine is involved in that, and for many people alcohol is a trail into cocaine. One of the key areas ... and it's a fairly recent area ... within the last twenty years ... the whole problem of adult children of alcoholics. You have a high possibility of becoming an alcoholic or a drug abuser. I don't think you find anyone under forty years old today as just simply an *alcoholic*. Most of the times it is alcohol *and* other drugs ... probably drug abuse. Male children have four times the potential of becoming alcoholics and females have three to four times. It's not scaring people. But to be forewarned is to be forearmed that you're in a high-risk group. I think people should be aware of that ...."

WO: "The Cardinal Archbishop of New York ... you were a great protégé of Cardinal Cooke ... the word is you were like a son to him."

TA: "He never said that ... and my father would get upset over it!"

WO: "What was he like ... Cardinal Cooke?"

TA: "I found Cardinal Cooke a very easy person to deal with. He was very sensitive to social issues. He was a social worker by trade. And he was very sensitive to the needs of people. In fact I had been associate superintendent of schools prior to going to the Substance Abuse Office ... and he pulled me out of that because he had set up a study to look at the problem of alcohol and other drugs among young people because he thought that was a priority. It was good working with him because he would give you a project and he wouldn't necessarily tell you how to do it. I began working with young people back in the mid-'60s. Denial is a great part of that problem. In that time it was heroin and alcohol. A lot of the young people, in fact *all* of the young people I dealt with at that time, are dead. Some of them were by 'contracts' ... others because of overdoses and so on. When Cardinal Cooke asked me to do this, I got myself updated by going into a treatment facility and working in there for a while and experiencing the problem from the point of view of the people in treatment. After being there for a while I came back out and I decided there are a lot of good treatment facilities, but the area we really have to address is the area of *education* and prevention, which people talk about as the demand side."

WO: "But tell me about Cardinal Cooke. Was he a saint? They're trying to make him one ...."

TA: "Right. He's a very unique person ... a very prayerful person. He suffered an awful lot over the years. For about twenty years he had the disease of cancer. A lot of people didn't know that. He was willing to confront a lot of issues."

WO: "Was he a saint?"

TA: "I think all of us are called to be saints, Bill. And if they designate Cardinal Cooke as a saint and if they are able to work that out.... I know people *are* praying to him ... people who have cancer .... Is he a saint? I think a lot of people die and are saints ... a lot of people are saints. To be declared a saint is a long process in the Church."

WO: "Saint Terry? Saint Bill?"

TA: "Yes. *Even* Saint Bill!"

WO: "What about his successor ... John Cardinal O'Connor?"

TA: "I think Cardinal O'Connor is a person who is really an 'adopted' New Yorker ... coming out of Philadelphia and spending so many years in the Navy. He was in the Navy for twenty-eight years, I think."

WO: "You guys call him 'The Admiral,' don't you?"

TA: "And they call 1011 First Avenue, the headquarters of the Archdiocese, 'The Flagship.' Cardinal O'Connor has a lot of very positive qualities ... because, being an admiral, he knows about delegating things too. He gives you a task and he'll just run with you. Sometimes in the area of substance abuse ... I was out there as a long-distance runner. I really didn't get too much support from people. Some people call you an alarmist. But Cardinal O'Connor would be always there to support me because he was the person in charge of substance abuse for the Navy! We would have DARE dinners and he would get up and say how important this particular area is. You might as well talk to the wind for some people ... and even in some cases with the American bishops ... because they're not personally dealing with it. This man here has had the experience in all this because he stands up in front of the camera and because he realizes New York is the big communications center for the world, he'll take a stand and he'll get abused because of it. I'm not just trying to defend him. But, for example, in the area of AIDS ... I don't think any diocese has done as much as the New York Archdiocese in the area of AIDS. Not only in treatment, but in the area of support groups. And this man very quietly ... and he never says it himself ... goes over to St. Clare's hospital and functions as a basin-Jason in working with those people."

WO: "Does he really change bedpans?"

TA: "That's what he does ... and he does it very quietly. He's not looking for the press."

WO: "Is that a story or is that true?"

TA: "That's a fact. You can call St. Clare's and talk to the administration down there and they can tell you what he does."

WO: "What about the contretemps with the Hibernians, the gays, and the St. Patrick's Day Parade?"

TA: "The parade itself is a religious thing. There have been gays and lesbians in that parade for many years. I think the Church takes a lot of heat. I personally have ministered to a lot of gay and lesbian people myself. No one condemns them. Their ground rules are exactly the same as we have as heterosexuals. The Church doesn't accept homosexual behavior. Sexually active people, just like a heterosexual person ... if you have a commitment as a celibate you're supposed to live up to that commitment. If you have a commitment as a married person ... you don't have any right getting sexually involved with somebody else. And if you do the Church welcomes you back. It doesn't ostracize you."

WO: "So you're saying the Church has been more sensitive than people know to gays and lesbians."

TA: "I think so."

WO: "You don't get the best assignments. You are now the pastor in Dobbs Ferry at Sacred Heart Church. There's also a little problem about abortion clinics in Dobbs Ferry ... people throwing themselves in front of bulldozers and picketing. How do you feel about this abortion problem? You're right in the middle of it."

TA: "The problem itself is one of the major life issues in our society. You're denying the basic right to life to the unborn. But I don't personally agree that the demonstrating in front of a clinic is going to solve the problem. The Church, and Cardinal O'Connor especially, has set up a whole program for any woman, or man who is a father of any of these children, if they need some help we have a *program* there. But people don't want to hear it."

WO: "Is that the Pregnancy Care Center?"

TA: "Pregnancy care is just one aspect of that. If a woman or a young girl finds herself pregnant ... I've dealt with a lot of them within the parish. People will refer people to us. I think, by ministering to that person at that time, no one condemns an individual. A person can get pregnant in a moment of passion ... but I think by having a person there to support that person ... instead of saying, 'Get rid of it,' saying, 'We can help you.' We can take care of an individual from pre-natal care through post-natal care. And we can relocate that individual if they feel self-conscious about going to their job. We can get a person a comparable job out on the West Coast or any other place. If a person is a student in a school we can get that person relocated in that area as well."

WO: "Should a woman have control over her own body?"

TA: "Not when it violates the right of the life that is there. That child, that baby has a right to ... and she violates that right."

WO: "So abortion is never acceptable?"

TA: "That's right. You also have a 'therapeutic' abortion situation. If for example a woman has cancer ... and they are performing an operation and the intention is to clear up that pathological condition and the side effect is an abortion ... well OK ... but your *intent* is not to have it. It's interesting you bring that up. Some people will say that if an individual that has been raped or [been the victim of] incest, we will go along with it."

WO: "We'll look the other way on *that* one?"

TA: "No, Bill. Less than 1 percent. So if a person says they are pro-choice and that's their purpose ... state your purpose. Don't come out generically and say you are pro-choice because all of this other is really unacceptable. There is a misunderstanding and a lack of communication in that area. I can honestly say ... and unfortunately because of my work I've dealt with a lot of women who have been raped and all of that ... in all those years ... I'm not saying that it's impossible ... in my own experience I've only had one ... and that was only a year ago ... where this woman was raped and it was an incest situation ... and because of fear she never ended up getting to a hospital."

WO: "In grammar school they told me you would take a bullet before you tell me what goes on in Confession. But did you not also tell someone once ... that women have told you ... in Confession, it's the worst day of their life when they have an abortion?"

TA: "That wasn't a confessional situation. That was a *counseling* situation. What do you say for example to an eighty-four-year-old woman who had an abortion when she was sixteen years old and she was forgiven by the Church but she has been unable to forgive herself? You take a person like Molly Yard, who will get up there and say that there is no emotional effect ... that's a crock, Bill. Molly Yard is the NOW lady ... former. And the whole thing is that you can justify a thing, maybe when you're seventeen or twenty-two, but what do you do later on when you realize what is taking place? It not only affects the female ... it affects the person who is aware of the fact that he is the father of this child. And the anxiety ... the Church is there to minister to that person as well after the fact of the abortion to help that person go through that healing process."

WO: "But the pro-abortion people ... and I can't believe that someone would want that appellation 'I'm pro-abortion.' I think everyone is against it but they'll say, 'How can you guys tell women what to do?' The Church, the hierarchy ... they're all men."

TA: "I agree with you, Bill. I think women should be in the forefront in saying this and I think it's too bad that more women aren't out there saying this. If you want to talk about the women's movement, and I think women should have a better position in a lot of situations, all over ... I mean why would a person be paid less because they are female! I think women should take the stand on abortion because this is one of the areas destroying women at this point."

WO: "I've asked you about the Cardinal. I want to ask you about another friend of yours ... from Rome."

TA: "That's a picture with the Holy Father, Pope John Paul, the Second. I was over in Rome for an international meeting on substance abuse and drugs and the Pope gets a lot of heat, as Cardinal

O'Connor gets a lot of heat, but very few people know of his true interest. Monsignor Bill O'Brien, who is the founder and president of Daytop, which I think is one of the best drug treatment facilities around, got a call at his office in New York on 40th Street and the person says, 'I'm calling for the Holy Father.' O'Brien says, 'Get off it!' and slams the phone down. He gets *another* call saying that the call is long distance from Rome and that the Holy Father wants to *meet* with him because he is concerned about the people who are coming through Rome and the young people in Europe who are devastated because of drugs. So Monsignor Bill and this Italian street priest meet with the Pope ... Bill speaks only English and the other speaks only Italian ... and guess who the interpreter was between the three in the group with the Pope himself?"

wo: "Really. So he was down to earth and with it."

TA: "He's very concerned about youngsters on drugs. He said to the Italian street priest, 'What do you want? I'll do anything to help you get something going in treatment or education or whatever it might be.' And the priest says to the Holy Father, 'I want your summer residence in Castel Gandolfo.' The Pope says, 'I just got it fixed up.' And my counterpart in Rome—the street priest—says, 'And I want the *pool*, too.' The Pope says, 'But I want to swim.' And the young priest says, 'We'll let you use it.'"

wo: "Wow."

TA: "He would get out of the Vatican and, from what I'm told, Bill, is that he has gone in there and he has made dinner for those people because he wanted to learn from those kids. That never makes the paper, Bill."

wo: "That's a great story."

TA: "This is just one of a lot of issues that the Church is involved in and that people don't talk about."

wo: "When you get feeling 'few' ... or confused—do you ever get scared?"

TA: "*Frustrated* probably is a better word."

wo: "What's a great *prayer*?"

TA: "I think the Serenity Prayer is great. Maybe it's because of my background with the treatment and AA and all of that. The Serenity Prayer is, 'God grant me the serenity to accept the things I cannot change ... the courage to change the things I can ... and the wisdom to know the difference.' It gets me through a lot of stuff whether it's Church stuff, parish stuff, or whatever it might be."

WO: "You're still a great salesman. We want to show one more graphic. When you were recruiting priests for the Archdiocese you came up with a memorable slogan ... 'The New York Priest ....'"

TA: "'... God knows what he does for a living.' It's interesting, Bill, that the person who did that was John Chervokis who did 'Don't *squeeze* the Charmin.'"

WO: "Do you think God knows what *you do* for a living?"

TA: "I hope so ...."

The Priest

An Appreciation of Monsignor Terence Attridge

Father Terence Attridge, a priest of the ancient Roman Church, lay dying in a hospital room at Calvary Hospital in the Bronx on Palm Sunday. And in Westchester at St. Pius X Church, Father John O'Brien, who had just recited the Passion and Crucifixion of Jesus Christ, went up on the altar and asked for prayers for Monsignor Attridge ... "who is undergoing his own final agony."

Father O'Brien's spontaneous petition only confirmed what everyone in the New York area has known for months. Monsignor Terry Attridge, with his easy manner and central casting looks, had a major problem, a form of cancer that even the best doctors at Memorial Sloan Kettering couldn't help him defeat.

And so he remains at Calvary Hospital beyond the reach of all those thousands who love him. The priest who made so many sick calls himself is now comforted only by his "immediate" family and parish associates like Claire Farrington and Sister Connie Koch, a Dominican nun.

Bishop Edwin O'Brien, the chief of all the United States military chaplains in the world, flew up from Washington to be with his old classmate from their days in the seminary. New York's newest bishop, James McCarthy, paid a visit and so too did Monsignor Bill O'Brien, who runs the Daytop program.

Officially, the newspapers will tell you Terry Attridge is pastor of Sacred Heart Church in Dobbs Ferry, a parish that is already in mourning. As pastor he performed weddings and baptisms, heard confessions, ran church socials, and raised money. He said Mass every day and several times on Sunday, the day of obligation.

He also ministered to state troopers, DEA undercover operatives, FBI agents, street cops, firemen, nuns, and other priests. And ... I'm probably not supposed to broadcast this ... a few months ago he even placed a call directly to John Cardinal O'Connor requesting that His

Eminence "give me a call ... if you just need to talk to someone." With Terry Attridge, it seems, even princes of the Church are worth saving.

As a young man he was a favorite of kindly, saintly Cardinal Cooke. And over the years Cardinal Cooke's popular protégé served as associate superintendent of schools and head of the DARE drug program. Father Attridge gained a national reputation as a wise, practical voice in the field of substance abuse and addiction. And, for a while, he was the pied piper of the Archdiocese in charge of vocations and recruiting young men for the priesthood. It was in this post that Father Terry developed the memorable campaign "The New York Priest: God Knows What He Does for a Living!" He also had a popular radio program on WVOX and was the "commentator" on some of the first televised masses.

As a PBA chaplain for many law enforcement groups, he drove around in a souped-up Honda equipped with pursuit lights and a siren that he never activated. On his belt was a beeper that was always chirping. And in his pocket the priest carried one of many badges that he never displayed. His handsome Irish looks and Roman collar got him everywhere he wanted to go.

He loved to play golf with Monsignor Charles Kavanagh, the vicar of development (or any other pigeon he could find!). And Jim Bender, the pro at Ardsley Country Club, even named a tournament after him. This year the 10th Annual Monsignor Terry Attridge Charity Golf Tournament is June 12th at Ardsley.

He was a natural, unassuming guy with a tremendous network of friends. And so the news of his terminal illness resonates with thousands of people in all walks of life ....

Rich, generous Catholic women—philanthropists like Florence D'Urso, Hope Carter, Mary D'Ablemont, Mary Jane Arrigoni, Josie Abplanalp, June Rooney, and Anne Mara—were great admirers of the candid style and no-nonsense commitment of this particular Diocesan priest. He moved easily in all the rarefied philanthropic circles and attended many dinners as an honored guest. But Father Attridge was not unlike Robin Hood in that he did his best work among those who were without influence, money, or high estate.

He got hundreds of youngsters into high schools and colleges after persuading the administrators to forgo or "finesse" the tuition. And he got countless people without insurance into hospitals and nursing homes. Just last month he called for the number of a grammar school official who had thrown out a kid because his mother's restaurant business had failed and she couldn't afford the tuition.

He was always getting youngsters off the streets and into drug programs. And I have lost count of just how many times he called my wife or her father, Mr. B. F. Curry Jr., the auto magnate, to waive a down payment or arrange a "little creative financing" for a nun "with bad credit" . . . a priest "who just needs to get back on his feet" . . . or a school teacher "whose husband just left her." There was always a "story." And some people who needed help.

It must also be fairly said that his enlightened, often courageous approach to many of the great moral issues of the day did not exactly endear him to some members of the hierarchy or the zealots of his own Church. He was a pro-life priest who once told me, "You've got to be for life in *every* instance." Meaning you've got to be against abortion *and* capital punishment. Although several women told him over the years that the day they had an abortion was "the worst" day of their lives, Father Terry fought against the current Slaughter of the Innocents right in his own back yard, not with civil disobedience but with something more powerful. While others picketed the infamous abortion clinic in Dobbs Ferry, Terry urged his parishioners to "pray" for the doctor who ran the clinic.

He was enormously respected by other enlightened priests like Ed Connors, the wise and beloved former vicar of Westchester, who said of Terry Attridge: "How sad to lose him at such a young age. But what a wonderful, full life he's had. And what a wonderful priest he was."

I can still see him here at wvox. Whenever I would inquire after him when Father Terry had finished his radio broadcast . . . the reply would come back: "Oh, he's out in the parking lot . . . talking with one of your announcers about a problem of some sort or another."

As Father John O'Brien said when we left Mass on Sunday: "He was a great priest."

And I expect God also knows . . . what he did for a living for thirty-five years.

Monsignor Edward Connors

THE PRIEST WHO SINGS

Monsignor Ed Connors lives in retirement at the
Stepinac residence in White Plains. Although his eyesight is
failing, he still says Mass at Our Lady of Sorrows Church.
And he can still carry a tune.

On Sunday morning in our pristine New York suburbs, the doors of Catholic churches are flung open to receive the faithful, most of whom, during the week, do their actual heavy lifting with the Franciscans, in hushed tones and quite anonymously, at St. Francis of Assisi Church on 31st Street in Manhattan. Even the governor of New York says, "We love the Franciscans, because they forgive us, gently and generously." Thus they are occupied for the purposes of salvation for the guilt-ridden castle Irish of Scarsdale, Bronxville, Eastchester, and New Rochelle—at least during the week.

But on the Day of Obligation, every Sunday, the action is at the Immaculate Heart of Mary Church in Scarsdale, where we are confronted in our rectitude, smugness, and fine clothes by a seventy-two-year-old Catholic monsignor named Edward Connors.

This is about Ed Connors, who has been a priest for forty-six years, according to the ancient rite. They come, these castle Irish, on cold winter mornings, to hear the old priest. And there are many ladies in mink coats who used to lunch at the Winged Foot Golf Club, until Donald Trump brought Marla Maples around. In some of the front pews you will see entire families with names like Rooney, Murphy, O'Hara, and Curry. In recent years, they have had to sit cheek-by-jowl with Indian, Hispanic, and Asian people, who also know something special is happening when this Monsignor Edward Connors steps out to open his arms and heart during the homily, which used to be called the sermon.

This must be called to your attention, you see, because a lot of clergymen and almost all the priests of my personal holy Roman Catholic Church resemble the rest of humanity when called upon to get up in front of a crowd. It is not a lovely thing to behold—or listen to. So it is a most unusual occurrence to encounter an actual person with a Roman collar who can take words and string them together in sentences that are always intelligent—and often lyrical.

Connors has been around a while. He had several high-profile jobs with the Archdiocese of New York: superintendent of schools, spiritual director of St. Joseph's Seminary, and vicar of Westchester. Some years ago, they even made him a monsignor, which is a step removed from bishop—but he doesn't use the designation, preferring just "Father Connors."

When he is not saying Mass or doing parish work, Father Connors dispatches subtle thought notes to all sides in the abortion battle, trying to get the zealots of both camps to a common ground in order to curtail the number of abortions. It is this endeavor which recommends him to Mario Cuomo.

Father Connors is probably not as close to His Eminence John J. O'Connor, the present cardinal archbishop, as he was to his predecessor, Terence Cooke. But on local cable television and in interviews in the public press, Father Connors is an ardent defender of Cardinal O'Connor's stewardship. He's like this in private too. I once heard him, over a drink, tell George Bush's brother: "You should know how hard the cardinal works. We had neighboring rooms at the seminary last year, and I used to see the fatigue and exhaustion when he came home late at night from his ceremonial rounds. Often I saw His Eminence sitting alone eating a peanut butter sandwich at midnight in his T-shirt. He's quite a human guy, with a wonderful sense of humor."

Over the holidays just passed, Father Connors stood right in front of the altar of his Scarsdale church, avoiding the towering pulpit to his right, and addressed people who were empty and groggy from the commercial Christmas and the New Year's holiday, which is another "Hallmark Hall of Fame" day on the phony, meaningless calendar of our years. This is some of what he said: "I listened to a Jerome Kern lyric, 'I told every little star,' and I wondered about that One Star, the Star of Bethlehem. God is often not the God we expect him to be. He came in poverty and weakness and in suffering, attended only by smelly shepherds. Human life has an intrinsic dignity of its own, a purpose. We find Christ in the events of lives and in our human relationships. It is about music—the music of our heart. In songs we are not looking for scientific accuracy; Christ is a paradigm, a framework, a model, a Master Plan for human living. The Star of Bethlehem is a star of faith to illuminate your journey. Listen for the music of the heart. This is the song we sing. This is what we tell every little star."

As an out-of-control three-year-old strolled across the altar in front of him, Father Connors, without missing a beat, also told his rich Catholic parishioners: "When the song of the angels is stilled, when the star in the sky is gone, when the kings and princes are home, where the shepherds are back with their flocks, the *real* work of Christmas begins: to find the lost, to heal the broken, to feed the hungry, to release the prisoner, to rebuild the nations, to bring peace among brothers, to make music with the heart."

All this without notes.

Then, moving from one side of the altar to the other, edging closer to his flock, the old priest spoke these words: "This Christ, I tell you, is not what we expected. We find him not in a palace, but in a cave. He comes not as a warrior king, but as a tiny, powerless infant. He is a strange kind of king who now has a manger and one day, a cross, for this throne. But he *keeps* his promises. We can *trust* him."

As Ed Connors talks, his hands come up from his sides and go out to his audience, palms open, as if trying to explain all the things he knows about a carpenter's son attended only by smelly shepherds at birth. The kindly eyes in his seventy-two-year-old face are a graceful and appropriate accompaniment to the music of his lips.

We hear about the smelly shepherds only at Christmas—but Ed Connors knows a lot of songs.

January 6, 1993

Monsignor Ed Connors

Interview with William O'Shaughnessy

wo: "Tonight I'd like to introduce to you a man well known to all
of us in Westchester County. He is a consultor ... that's a high-
class word for advisor ... to the Cardinal Archbishop of New York.
He was superintendent of schools for the Archdiocese ... and he's
held every top job including running the seminary at Dunwoodie
over on the hill in Yonkers. He is now best known as the beloved
and very influential pastor of Immaculate Heart of Mary Church
in Scarsdale. We'd like to welcome Monsignor Edward Connors
to *Interview*. Among those who present themselves in his church
every Sunday morning are some of the most influential residents
of Westchester ... David Hartmann ... Lou Boccardi, CEO of the
Associated Press ... Tony Colavita, the Rooneys of Yonkers Raceway ... you get a lot of influential types and you also get some low-
lifes like me occasionally over there. We're glad to have you with
us, Monsignor ...."

EC: "We're glad to have you with us on Sunday too, Bill. All of those
people come as simple people of faith. They don't come parading
titles or bringing anything with them ... but their desire for the
Lord and for friendship and unity with other people. And so we're
very happy to have them and all the people of various jobs that
make the county and the world run."

wo: "You don't suffer fools or compliments well ... but I'm going
to try my best. You don't like to refer to yourself as 'Monsignor.'
Rather, you prefer to say this is 'Father' Connors. You don't preach
from the pulpit ... you go out in the aisles and talk to people and
yet you've held all the high estates that the Archdiocese can bestow. Who are you? What do you see yourself as?"

EC: "I see myself as a parish priest who is there to help people, to be
there with them, to respond to their needs, whatever the needs
may be ... whether it's a young parent who is struggling to bring
up a child ... not that I can tell her or him how to bring up a child

... tell her how to handle some of the difficulties of his or her own personal life ... or whether it's an old person who is getting ready to meet their Maker ... it's just an infinite variety. But it's a person-to-person deal ... and I just like dealing with people."

WO: "You're a priest ... what do they call that ... according to the Ancient Order of Melkizadeh."

EC: "Melkizadeh from the Old Testament was one who didn't have a beginning or an end. He was without ancestors and he just comes across the stage of the Old Testament and it's the symbol of the Eternal ... that business of mediating between God and man."

WO: "But that right gives you a lot of power. You can forgive sins. Is there any greater power?"

EC: "In Christian teaching ... in Catholic teaching ... there is that Sacrament of Reconciliation or Penance ... whereby on behalf of the Church, when a person is properly disposed, through the mediation of the priest and through the assurance from the Church that God loves that person and God wants only the best for that person ... they are given God's forgiveness. Many a soul at a crisis point of life has been given God's grace and aided through that sacrament and through the ministry of the priest."

WO: "Do you see people coming back to the Church?"

EC: "We do see them coming back ... not in droves but steadily. And that is one of the things that any Church has to do ... to serve people and especially the marginal people. It's not just about serving the rich and powerful. People on the fringes of society, people who are poor, who have personal problems, people who are finding it difficult to cope in these difficult times of unemployment, these difficult times of raising children ... we have to have not just the highly successful and the influential ... they can usually take care of themselves and they know it ... and they're willing to help others. We have to try to bring people together to help one another on this pilgrimage of life."

WO: "Has the Catholic Church done a good job in reaching out to the unpopular ... to the despised?"

EC: "I think so. I think that in our own area, for example, there has been no greater outreach to AIDS paitents than that generated by the Catholic Church ... despite the vilification of a man like

Cardinal O'Connor. The number of beds, the outreach has been a very practical one and yet there doesn't seem to be that much appreciation for it."

WO: "Does he really, the Cardinal Archbishop, you are a 'consultor' to him ... does he really go down and do those bedpans or is that a press story?"

EC: "No, he does. Naturally he can't do it all the time ... but he does it and he does it to keep in touch with the poor and the marginal and he has so many who are hurting in so many different directions that naturally he can't be there every single day, but he does it with enough frequency and enough sacrifice for it to hurt. Of course he has the advantage of only needing four hours of sleep a night."

WO: "Tell us about the Cardinal Archbishop. You were a friend of his predecessor, Terrance Cardinal Cooke ... different types."

EC: "They were different men for different times in history. Cardinal Cooke came to office at a time when all institutions were being questioned and there were rumblings in universities and government and in the Church too. He was a man that could stand at the middle and unify people. He was not confrontational. He was more collegial. He was able to bring people together."

WO: "Whereas ..."

EC: "A lot of healing took place and now a new man comes who sees a need and another need ... it's to call it the way it is ... and to tell the world what authentic Catholic Christian teaching is in this age so there will be no mistaking it and he has a tremendous ability to do that. Cardinal O'Connor is a most articulate man ... and he calls it as he sees it. He's quicker and more impulsive than Cardinal Cooke, who was more laid back ...."

WO: "You're a consultor. Do you ever presume to slow him down on something? Do you ever disagree with him?"

EC: "Oh, yes. You disagree ... but you do it before the decision is made and once the decision is made it's right, you know? In other words, practically speaking, if you belong to a group and the decision is made ... he's very open to consultation ... but he's a strong man and he has an extremely brilliant mind and he takes everything into consideration. He has a lot of advisors, that's the other part, he has a lot of consultative groups that feed his decisions. As a matter of fact, people talk up to him more than they ever talked up to Cardinal Cooke. One man said to me, 'Cardinal Cooke was like God. You would never question something that he would say.' But this man ... there's something about him that makes you want to tell him exactly how you think."

WO: "You mean they talk up without fear of getting assigned to a parish in Poughkeepsie?"

EC: "Absolutely ... and that's the way it is now. This is no business for shrinking violets ... so they talk up. And I mean priests and I mean religious and I mean lay people at public meetings. Once in a while the Cardinal gets on his hind legs as a result of it ... but most times he's able to take it and assimilate it and build it into his decision-making process."

WO: "So you're saying he's human."

EC: "He's human."

WO: "The coat of arms of Cardinal Archbishop O'Connor has a line on it ... his 'slogan' if you will ... 'There can be no Love without Justice!' What does that mean and what does justice mean in terms of the Church?"

EC: "Justice means giving a person what belongs to him or her. If a person is working for the Church he has a passionate conviction that he or she should be given a living wage. It isn't enough to do considerably less than that and then have a Christmas party or give a little trinket around Easter time. That love is manifested not so much in giving people things that are not pertinent to what they are doing. They should be rewarded for their labor and given a living wage. The Cardinal is taking the position that, as a basis for charity and for love, the first obligation is to give them what their humanity calls out for ... respect, recognition, justice in that sense and then on top of that to show love for one another."

WO: "So as the Cardinal means justice ... it's not like the criminal justice system or the vengeful giving someone their due. That word seems a little jarring next to *love*. It's been suggested that of all things ... love is the most important. Is it?"

EC: "Yes, it is. But *justice* is the first step. It's the foundation on which love is built. Giving the person what belongs to him ... and what belongs to him is a recognition of his or her human rights and human dignity. When a person is exploited in any way ... young, old, male, female ... and that person is not given justice ... you can't say that love is present there. When they're given what belongs to them, that still doesn't mean that you absolutely are going out of your way to love them to give them a little bit more ... it just means that you are giving them what their humanity calls for ... the respect and the reward of their labor."

WO: "Cardinal Cooke, I hear, they're trying to make a saint now. Do you ever pray to Cardinal Cooke?"

EC: "I don't, but many do. My own feeling is that God has His way of taking care of it. If that's what He wants done He'll give some signs ... some strong signs."

WO: "You ran the seminary over on the hill, St. Joseph's at Dunwoodie, near Yonkers. There aren't many young men aspiring to the priesthood or women aspiring to be nuns. It's declining and it's a big problem, isn't it?"

EC: "It is ... but this has always been cyclical. There have been times when there have been an abundance of calls and vocations to the priesthood and religious life and other times when it's been slack. Perhaps the Holy Spirit is trying to say to us that we don't need quite this many priests and that the laity can now come into the picture? Maybe that's what God is seeking to tell us in the way these calls are coming. We're getting men who are a little older than they had been in the past. They might be in their mid-thirties or their early forties who are looking at a second career. There hasn't been enough in life for them in their primary career whether they were lawyers or engineers ... and they're coming in greater numbers later in life. The average age of ordination used to be about twenty-six ... now it's thirty-one or thirty-two."

WO: "You've been asked this question a thousand times. This will be a thousand and one. If you dispensed with that vow of celibacy, would you get a lot more?"

EC: "Probably. We're not a completely celibate clergy. For example, in recent years we have taken in a number of former Lutheran pastors and Episcopal priests and their families. They have been ordained and are functioning in the Catholic Church ... in Europe and in this country. We also have all the Eastern Rites who are in union with the Roman Catholic Church through the Holy Father. They have a married clergy."

WO: "Well, advisor to Cardinals ... if the Pope called you up and said, 'Monsignor Connors, should I let them get married?' what would you tell the Pope?"

EC: "It would be very easy to answer that one because he wouldn't call me."

WO: "But you send little notes to editors and people from time to time. You have enormous influence, in a very subtle way, here in Westchester. What's your opinion? Should they do it or not?"

EC: "I think they should study it a little bit more. We have a Universal Church. We have a very traditional Church. It's widespread throughout the world and I think it has to be studied a lot more and discussed a lot more first—in house—and then in the rest of the world."

WO: "You mentioned what God may be trying to tell us with the question of vocations. What is God trying to tell the whole world? How do you know that it's God speaking to you?"

EC: "It's always a problem. We believe that when we say God's *trying* of course we're being anthropomorphic. We're talking in human terms rather than in terms of God's Kingdom and God's reality ... because if He wants to make us listen He can make us listen, but that's not the way God has created us so He doesn't do it that way. Through the Scriptures, through the lives of other people, through the intelligence that He has given us in creating us ... He has given us a tremendous amount of material with which to work. In addition to that, we believe that He does send His grace in a mysterious way, that His Holy Spirit, which means God Himself, is present to us and speaks to us if we will just take a little time to pray and to listen and to reflect."

WO: "God speaks in whispers. Didn't you say that once?"

EC: "Yes ... and He speaks in mysterious ways ... He does. And the sincere desire to find His will may very well be rewarded by a clear notion of what it is. And in every case it will probably result in a person's being more humane, more helpful to others on this journey through life and with more regard and respect for other people as brothers and sisters of a common Father ... a common Creator."

WO: "You mentioned prayers. Are you talking about Hail Marys and Our Fathers?"

EC: "I'm talking more about just silence ... and thought ... and reflection on the Scriptures ... the Bible ... and seeing in what way God is speaking to us today in the events of our lives and in the Words of Revelation through the great Prophets of the Old Testament and through His Son, Jesus, in the New Testament."

WO: "Do you still read the Bible?"

EC: "Every day."

WO: "Don't you know it by heart now?"

EC: "No, you never know it by heart. It means something a little different every day that you read it."

WO: "You don't think it's outdated?"

EC: "Never outdated. It's the Living Word and it's as effective and powerful as a two-edged sword. It's for today ... and if we can recognize it as such ... it would be a much better world."

WO: "This is the Easter Time ... the Easter season. Why is that so important? I remember from grammar school they said, 'If Christ be not risen, then is not all our preaching in vain?' Did that prove that Jesus wasn't a con man?"

EC: "I think so. I think what you have here is proof in the sense of there being nothing to disrupt our faith in the awesome event. That our faith in the event is simply that God has spoken through this man Jesus who He sent, His Son, who shares the divinity and has shown all of us that death never has the last word. All forms of death in human existence don't have the last word. Life has the last word .... That's why Easter is important. There is no such thing as Easter without Good Friday. There is no such thing as resurrection without suffering and death ... and that's the road that we travel, and even nature itself repeats that cycle of death and resurrection with the seasons of the year. We're now seeing the season of Resurrection."

WO: "It seems the slogan of the Church is that you have to die before you can be born again ... but then others would say that God didn't intend for you to be unhappy."

EC: "That's correct. We believe that there was an original rebellion of man against God and that we are possessors of a human nature that is tainted. How can human beings who were created to be happy and meant to be happy perpetrate such things as the wars of our time, the Holocaust of our time, the genocide of our time. Why did God allow all that? God leaves us free to follow Him or not to follow Him. He has not created us as He created plants and animal life. He has created us as free human beings and called us to follow Him in that way. So we have within us, all of us, possibilities for great good ... and we have possibilities for great evil. And the call is through self-discipline ... through dying to self ... to rise above the evil impulses of our nature and to overcome them and to live in the manner in which God, through the Scriptures, through the Bible, has indicated we should live."

WO: "Allow me please to ask you about a contemporary issue which has so divided our republic. You preach every Sunday at Immaculate Heart of Mary Church and I've heard you talk on this issue. I'm talking about abortion. I've never seen you locked up in front of an abortion mill over in Dobbs Ferry. You are doing it in sort of a different way ...."

EC: "Yes. We try to do it by education and by whatever political action people want to do as a result of the education. We don't as a church indulge directly in political action. I believe firmly that you have developing human life from the moment of conception and anything else, I believe, is unscientific. You have those who would justify taking that human life in its early stages on philosophical arguments. They talk more about its not being a human person, its being a fetus instead of a child. I view abortion as the killing of a developing human being .... I would call it a violent solution to a human problem ... the human problem being an unwanted pregnancy. And yet the life of that child is not unwanted. There are thousands upon thousands of wonderful people who would be delighted to adopt and give a wonderful life to that child. We have five local pregnancy-care centers and many other groups ... in Westchester .... The Pregnancy Care Center is the one best known in this region. Cardinal O'Connor has put the guarantee of the Church behind providing the means for any young woman who is impoverished and would be seeking an abortion to avoid the expenses. All expenses will be taken care of to have that child."

WO: "Is it possible to be pro-choice *and* pro-life? To respect the right of a woman ... to believe that the state can't legislate where it has no power, e.g., in a woman's body. Is it possible to be both?"

EC: "I don't think it's possible to be both. I think it's possible to be pro-life in any number of directions ... because life is from the womb to the tomb. If it is a human life ... then society should do everything possible to protect that life. I would also be against capital punishment. And the bishops of our state and country are against capital punishment. It doesn't work ... and it doesn't give the protection to human life that it is alleged to give."

WO: "You disagree with Bishop Vaughn and the anti-abortion protesters ... ?"

EC: "I don't disagree with them. I think that they've enlivened the issue and they've kept it alive from the viewpoint of the pro-life people. I just choose other ways to go on this matter ...."

WO: "One day I was feeling 'few' and, as you know, I'm a stumbling, staggering, faltering son of your church, but I came in and I heard you recite something by Joyce Kilmer. Do you remember that? You said he wasn't the greatest poet but ...."

EC: "Joyce Kilmer was a young man who was a man of great faith, and he was killed in World War I in Flanders Fields. He once wrote a little poem, which is apropos of the Easter season ... about the house with nobody in it ... about suffering. It concludes:

> They say that life is a highway and its milestones are the years. Once in a while there is a tollgate where you buy your way with tears. It's a rough road and a steep road and it stretches broad and far but at last it leads to a golden town where golden houses are.

"It's the story of death and resurrection."

Father John O'Brien

The Simple Priest

John O'Brien was a priest of the Roman Church according to the ancient Order. He had a marvelous gift, and not since Monsignor Ed Connors have we had someone stand up in front of a Westchester congregation to preach about the Carpenter's Son with as much grace and eloquence.

O'Brien, a gentle man, spoke with a raspy, gritty croak caused by the thousands of cigarettes that killed him. But he reached into many hearts with that great gift of expression which accompanied him when he went to work in a church.

He was a Christian Brother for many years before entering the priesthood late in life. And so, instead of standing in a classroom before thirty-five rowdy kids, John O'Brien, in recent years, did his teaching and his preaching too in front of many of all ages every Sunday and on the days of Obligation.

He didn't speak with the brilliance of a Jesuit orator or the scruffy humanity and relentless compassion of the Franciscans. There was only a stark honesty to O'Brien, who spoke with some intimate knowledge of the long-remembered, timeless wisdom of the church fathers. You could hear the cigarettes, the wheeze, and the rattle in his soft voice as he whispered those ancient truths in stunningly simple homilies.

The old priest was uncomfortable presiding way up in the pulpit, lording it over everyone. He always did his best work at eye level on the floor up close to the people huddled in their pews.

I've seen the priest O'Brien in hospital rooms mumbling the Rosary for comatose patients who couldn't even hear him. And I observed him consoling a family following the untimely death of a beautiful young man. I also saw the Irishman with the Roman collar go after rich contractors and road builders from Scarsdale to persuade them to help his parish. He was something to behold when shaking the money tree.

[236]

But being Irish, John O'Brien was at his best at funerals ... praying and often shedding his own real tears over the deceased and dearly departed ranging in age from eighty-four to twenty-two. But he was gentle and kind and had a great way about him through it all in every season.

I remember one winter day, not unlike this one, when the priest stood in front of grieving relatives at a funeral Mass for that young man:

> Our lives teach us that courage is the opposite of fear. But it's not. Faith is the opposite of fear. Having that Faith is something that doesn't come easily or automatically into our lives. It comes by experience and by the awful grace of God.
>
> You're filled with sorrow now. But Faith tells us, assures us, all is well ... because ... His name is Emmanuel ... and I am with you always. Even to the End of the World. It was His name at the Beginning. And it is His name at the End.
>
> So, I come to do the Will of my Father. And this is the Will of my Father ... that I should lose ... nothing. That you should lose ... nothing.

He was not a high church kind of priest. And you could not imagine O'Brien strolling in some Vatican garden taking his constitutional clad in a finely tailored cassock adorned with a purple sash or scarlet trim speaking in hushed diplomatic tones with hands clasped casually behind his back.

And yet, despite his aversion to pomp and pretension, it was announced that several bishops and elders of the Church will pray over the Reverend John P. O'Brien at St. Pius X Church in Scarsdale this weekend, including the new Archbishop Timothy Dolan, who, one is sure, is O'Brien's kind of guy. Come to think of it, you couldn't imagine *Dolan* strolling in that Vatican garden with the Canon lawyers and diplomats either.

As he lay dying this week at New York University Hospital in the great City, someone sent the priest a note: "You are loved and respected." I hope he got it and understood it through all the tubes and painkillers.

And so Timothy Dolan himself will preside at Mass on Saturday.

The Archbishop brings a wonderful joy and dynamism to everything
he does. But who, I wonder, will reach out and grab people by the
throat and tug at their hearts to tell those assembled once more in
sadness and mourning just how very special the old priest with the
gravelly voice really was ... ?

Before he left us last week, the pastor of St. Pius X Church in
Scarsdale sat at his desk in the parish rectory to write a Christmas
message. It was to be his last homily. The priest was wracked with
pain. But there were many things to do to get the parish ready for
the holy season. He knew he was dying, and the very next day John
O'Brien would check himself into a New York hospital. So he worked
quickly, but carefully. This is what he wrote as he sat in loneliness
and silence on that cold day last week in Scarsdale:

Silent night, holy night
All is calm, all is bright.
A holy night to be sure, but hardly silent and anything but
calm.

The "silence" of that night was shattered by the blood-
curdling cries of wild animals roaming the hillsides. In a cold,
dark cave a young, frightened woman gave birth to her child
while her husband, a carpenter by trade, stood by helplessly.

Finally, amid the bleating of sheep and the braying of
animals, the newborn's first cry broke the stillness. This "silent
night" was filled with terror, pain, and the bone-numbing
exhaustion that sleep alone cannot relieve.

There was no "silence" that night so long ago in crowded,
chaotic Bethlehem, bursting with visitors who had come
for the great census. In fact, there was no "calm" in all of
Israel—only tension and conflict between the Jewish people
and their Roman occupiers. Ancient Palestine was hardly a
place of "heavenly peace." It was a land torn by oppression,
persecution, and terror. Madness reigned.

And yet ... on this noisy, chaotic, anxious night, our Savior,
the Light of the World was born. Amid the pain and anguish
of a devastated people, new hope was born. The Messiah came
at last with transforming joy.

Even though our world today may once more seem far from "silent," our Church far from "holy," our personal lives far from "calm," the Prince of Peace has blessed our flawed and fractured world by walking upon it, by loving those in it relentlessly and unconditionally, and by laying down his life for all who pass through it.

For he would rather die than to live in eternity without us. Emmanuel! God is with us! Let earth receive her King! He retired with the gift.

December 10, 2009

Litchfield Hills Luminaries

Charlie Kafferman, *"A Dear Man"*

An Appreciation by William O'Shaughnessy

In my business we "warehouse" obits ... so that when someone departs for another and, we are sure, a better world ... we are ready with the details, minutiae, and landmarks of a person's life. No such trove or repository exists for Charlie Kafferman, because everyone in Litchfield fully expected him to be around forever to feed us, to counsel us, and to entertain and anchor us with his wisdom of eighty-eight years.

But at 2:30 on the summer Saturday just past, the legendary Mr. Charles Kafferman (I know the word is overused, but he was that), proprietor of the West Street Grill, an iconic eatery that has existed for twenty-five years in his lovely Connecticut town, died in Danbury Hospital after ten days in the hospital's intensive care unit. The formal notices of his passing will mention the culprit as "congestive heart failure."

But earlier, and for many years, Charlie had battled lung cancer with visits to Memorial Sloan Kettering in the great City, so many that he was known among the doctors and nurses as "Lazarus Kafferman."

He is survived by his shy, modest, retiring life and business partner, James O'Shea, who knew his genius and goodness for forty-two years. They lived together in a Colonial-era house in the historic district of Litchfield that was once owned by J. P. Morgan.

By day and on most nights, Charlie and James repaired to their *labor of love* known by locals as "The Grill" and operated almost as a private club. But Charlie made *everyone* feel welcome ... from the landed gentry and hilltoppers of Litchfield and residents of Morris, Bantam, Woodridge Lake, Washington Depot, Bethlehem, New Preston, and even as far away as Newport ... to the newest arrivals in town for whom Kafferman was a generous, benevolent and knowledgeable counselor. He took great pleasure in personally welcoming these tentative young couples and providing them with his food *and* inexhaustible repository of wisdom and his love for the town and its colorful and influential inhabitants.

They loved his stories about Sinatra and Mia Farrow. "I was there the night they got engaged ... and I told Frank I knew her before he did!" (It's quite remarkable that Frank let him live!) One night at The Grill ... I asked Mia, who was with Philip Roth, if the story was true. She swore it was ... "but Frank did ask me where that guy lives! I wouldn't tell." Or the night at the Latin Quarter when he was mistaken for William B. Williams, the famous "Make Believe Ballroom" disc jockey. He also regaled listeners with the tale told by the great writer Philip Roth that when President Obama presented him with an award at the White House ... the president whispered, "Where's Charlie?" who, as a favor to his pal Roth, had picked up an earlier award for Roth from the governor of Connecticut. (Roth swore it was true!)

He could also discuss the rock groups U2, Mumford & Sons and The Rolling Stones with the millennials. And he once trooped all the way uptown to Harlem for a concert.

Day after day, in nice weather, Charlie would sit with his beloved Labrador, Cashel. As both were somewhat aging and together battling the diminishments, Cashel and Charlie had a special bond. Everyone would stop to pet Cashel and greet the restaurant proprietor, who one day told me, "Cashel and I are 'hookers.' We tell them 'The food is great ... go on in. You can pet him.'"

His warm, agreeable, and welcoming personality—as well as his canon of stories and jokes (many of which could not be told on the radio) helped transform The Grill from your usual run-of-the-mill "country restaurant" into a dazzling mecca of influence and celebrity.

Night after night actors, publishers, artists, newspaper and magazine editors, Wall Street types, merchant princes, famous authors, Broadway and television producers, food critics and wine aficionados, and colorful townie characters repaired to The Grill. Among them: Henry Kissinger ... William Styron ... Philip Roth ... Richard Widmark ... Mia Farrow ... Sheila Nevins and Sidney Koch ... Daniel Glass ... Milos Forman ... Judge Anne Dranginis and Judge Charlie Gill ... Arthur Hill Diedrick ... Tara Stacom Diedrick ... Rex Reed ... Debra and Declan Murphy ... Sirio Maccioni ... Bill Plunkett, Esq.

... Teno West ... Richard Gere ... Cathy and Greg Oneglia ... Renate and Tom McKnight ... Ellen and Ray Oneglia ... Rod Oneglia and Michael Quadland ... David Pecker ... Melissa and Paul Bennett ... Julian Niccolini ... Lauren and Armand Della Monica ... Danny Meyer ... Brooke Hayward ... Bob Summer ... Norman Drubner ... Nancy Kissinger ... Kim and Bobby D'Andrea ... Joe Cicio ... Lou Amendola ... Norman Sunshine ... Douglas Clement ... Jim Hoge ... William vanden Heuvel ... Gregorio Alvarez ... Ron Leal and Joseph Montebello ... Alan Shayne ... Daniel Day Lewis ... Andrew Thompson and Bradley Stephens ... Robin Johnson and his family ... Gina and Alexander Duckworth ... Ann Sutherland Fuchs ... Francine du Plessix Gray ... Margot Wick ... Wendy and Royal Victor IV a.k.a. "Mike" (I love the name!). But *everyone* was welcome *except* an occasional ill-educated *"gavone"* who insisted on wearing a baseball hat in the dining room! That would never do.

Charlie was a class act in every season. And there was a big, broad range to his life. His patron, admirer, and friend Daniel Glass, the music impresario and record producer, was also taken by the unique professional and personal relationship between Kafferman and his partner O'Shea. "It was a merger of two cultures: the *Irish* and the *Jewish*. They were a perfect team!" I myself saw this for many years as Charlie and James covered for each other. They protected and sustained each other. James was, shall we say, a little more "colorful," ahem, "outspoken" and, if you will, a little more "dynamic." But Charlie was always wonderful, calming, and reassuring. And it worked. *They* worked together.

James attracted and mentored many young, talented chefs while Charlie "dressed" the dining room of an evening ... moving people around the way Nelson Riddle arranged notes and making them feel important. But he was much more than a skillful "maître d'" or talented restaurateur.

He had an eye for the ladies, and he wasn't at all happy when I called him a "babe magnet." But he got a lot of kisses of an evening from rich widows and pretty young girls.

He could sense when people at his tables were hurting and their lives had turned sad and difficult. That was his genius. He just "knew." He would sit for hours trying to reconcile warring husbands and wives and help them sort out their marital problems. And he "adopted" their offspring and followed them and their exploits down through the years.

He'd often trot out one of his marvelous stories (or a risqué joke). Daniel Glass, the record producer, had a lovely line: "He gave us the nourishment of his own life before he gave up the nourishment of his food. His ability to deliver a punch line was flawless. I'd try to re-member them ... but they never worked for me." Glass, the discoverer of Mumford & Sons, also admired Charlie's attire and way of dressing ... "dapper, with such flair ... all casual elegance."

I've run on too long. But how do you distill a life of eighty-eight years that included his enthusiasm for Litchfield County ... Florida ... Ireland ... *and* the fashion world in Manhattan. He especially loved Ireland and took his last trip over there all alone at the age of eighty-eight, leaving James home to watch over things at The Grill. He also loved to head south in Ray and Greg Oneglia's jet, which had been acquired from Ted Turner.

Before becoming a celebrated restaurateur and country squire late in life, Charlie Kafferman had an earlier career in the world of merchandising and fashion. As a young man he teamed with John Pomerantz, the founder of Leslie Fay ... becoming one of the young-est vice presidents in the history of the famous conglomerate, which, to this day, still makes women's dresses and apparel. And Charlie then went on to own his own dress factories in this country and abroad, the products of which were featured at Macy's, Gimbels, JCPenney, Saks, Dillard's, Belk's, and I. Magnin.

He will be buried this week in a *Catholic* cemetery in his beloved Litchfield as a result of only the most recent gracious and thoughtful gesture of one absolutely unique Reverend Father Robert Tucker, the popular and charismatic Roman Catholic pastor for Litchfield and surrounding towns.

That black Lab named Cashel, *however*, is just moping around today, feeling "few" ... and missing his pal, "The Hooker."

So is most of the town Charlie so loved.

He was a dear man.

We thought he'd be around forever.

July 8, 2019

"Lacey"

A Remembrance by William O'Shaughnessy

(Litchfield, CT)—I've written of a marvelous cast of characters we've been privileged to encounter as community broadcasters. Among them were *politicians* like Nelson Rockefeller and Mario Cuomo of sainted memory and the latter's son and heir Andrew Mark Cuomo, Bobby Kennedy, John F. Kennedy Jr., George Latimer, Edwin Michaelian, Gerald Ford, Lyndon Johnson, Richard Nixon, Hugh Carey, Pat Moynihan, Henry Kissinger, and Jack Javits, as well as marvelous *entertainers* like Fred Astaire, Mabel Mercer, Hugh Shannon, Chet Baker, Louis Armstrong, Bobby Short, and the great Sinatra among them.

I've also admired *media* players and *journalists* who were much more graceful and articulate than yours truly . . . William S. Paley, Walter Thayer, Jock Whitney, Lance Morrow, Chris Ruddy, Mark Simone, Neal Travis, Jimmy Cannon, Phil Reisman, Philip Roth, Pete Hamill, Jimmy Breslin, Don West, Sol, Larry and Rob Taishoff.

I've tried to remember my *pals*: Jeff Bernbach, who is still with us, Joseph Migliucci, Sirio Maccioni, and the saintly Mario Cuomo. I once almost wrote about a horse, a quarterhorse, who, I think, loved me.

But I've never written about a *dog*.

Her name was Lacey. She was a cockapoo. And my *compadre* Gregorio and I loved her unreservedly. She was ten when her heart stopped beating over the weekend at 4:30 in the morning at an animal hospital in Newtown, CT after a central casting veterinary Chief Doctor Adam Porter, with help from a surgeon, Jason Headrick, and another amazing doctor, Tracy Zeldis, tried to save her from bleeding and a tumor. Her regular vets at Aspetuck, Dr. Michael Gorra and Dr. Trish Grinnell, will not be happy to hear of Lacey's passing as well.

Actually, we have two other *cockapoo* puppies (I hate the word "dog"). Their names are Coco and Jack and they have the same provenance as Lacey, having come from a litter of the legendary breeder Carol Bobrowsky of Mulberry Farm in the Hudson Valley.

Lacey was a daughter of Izzy and Kandi Kane. She was born on July 13, 2010. In the ten years we had her never once did she ever bark. Lacey was a hugger and a lover. I mean she wasn't a "roll over and pet me" girl like our Coco. But she was a lover, too, and had a great following among our friends, who were always taken with Lacey's civility and those big, gorgeous eyes.

She would sit on Gregorio's lap while I drove and loved to play with our niece Briana Alvarez and my grandchildren Lily, Izzy, Amelia, Flynn, and Tucker. She also had pals at the radio station: Irma, Maggie, Gregg, Cindy, Don, Judy, and Kevin. They recognized Lacey as a "real lady" and were friendly as all get out when she would come to visit.

Mario Cuomo once accused me of always trying to find something good or, as he put it, "sweet" in everyone I meet. Unfortunately, I sometimes fail to find that goodness. I often have the same reaction to *animals*, with all due respect, recognizing that all pets are beloved by their owners. The Carpenter's Son would not like this observation ... but I don't really like *all* people or even all *babies*. You can often imagine they'll grow up to resemble their parents. Maybe it's the same with our four-legged friends, some of which, it is said, actually begin to look like their owners.

I'm just trying to tell you how really extraordinary this little girl Lacey was, and I beg you to believe there *was* something special, something very special about her.

My friend Judy Fremont, a great woman of the theater and a radio legend, who is also a killer on the golf course, called Lacey "an elegant lady." Judy would know.

During her brief time among us, Lacey was also our "Weather Forecaster." Whenever a rough patch of weather started coming in from east or west, my girl would know and warn us of any approaching rough weather by shaking or shivering. She was our Flip Spiceland, Al Roker. and Joe Rao combined. (Whatever happened to Flip Spiceland?)

Lacey the puppy also loved the outdoors with its wonderful and fragrant whiffs and smells. And she loved the flowers that bloomed around her swimming pool every spring. And she would also carefully check the smells and fragrances of the emerging fresh summer vegetables and plants in her garden every year.

She loved her "sister" Coco, who *is* that "roll over and pet me"–type cockapoo who also loves me unreservedly. And who could not love our Jack Alvarez, who is the "guard dog" of the neighborhood and watches over the entire historic district of Litchfield. Jack weighs in at a mighty seventeen pounds. He is fearless and barks at every bird and rustle of wind just to let the wind and birdies know that he is The Boss of the 'hood. Coco and Jack are also beloved, irreplaceable characters in our lives.

And speaking of which, my wonderfully bright daughter Kate O'Shaughnessy, under whose West Coast roof resides a "Shirley" and a "Potter," two adorable mutts and real "colorful" types who were adopted without benefit of Carol Bobrosky's, shall we say, proper *lineage* or *breeding*, but adorable nonetheless. When my brilliant Kate heard we lost Lady Lacey last weekend, she said: "That's really sad, Daddy … she was the only one with all her marbles!"

I love the line. And I loved Lacey.

That's why I had to put down my pencil many, many times as I tried to get through these reminiscences of a little puppy I loved and miss so much.

As I read back over these notes … I'm thinking I may just keep them to myself and not let anyone peruse these overly sentimental meanderings and certainly not permit my distinguished publisher, Mr. Fred Nachbaur, or any of the brainy Jesuits at Fordham University Press in the City of New York to see them because, after all, she was … just a doggie … just a pet … just a puppy. Her name was Lacey.

That Fremont woman told me *all* doggies go to Heaven. Well, just to make sure … I also know a priest named Robert Tucker who is very beloved in these parts and was just made a big-time monsignor. I am going to ask the Reverend Monsignor Tucker to pray over Lacey. He knows that a somewhat "unusual" Italian named *Francis* from the hill town of Assisi became the greatest saint in the entire history

of the Roman Church and that he, this Francis, being somewhat unusual himself, talked to animals and the sun and the moon and fire,
even the wind. Tucker will understand all this.

I hope you will pray for our Lacey too.

Gregorio and I will have a talk with Coco and Jack about where
their sister went.

But I think they already know ...

She was a great puppy, a great lady.

July 13, 2010–May 8, 2020

Caryl Donnelly Plunkett

An Appreciation by William O'Shaughnessy

I once received by U.S. Postal Service a letter from a William Plunkett, Esquire. As I usually do not open letters from practitioners or solicitors of the law, I did not rush to retrieve said missive from Plunkett, Esquire. "You'd better open it," said Cindy Hall Gallagher, amanuensis without whom my life would resemble a seven-car pile-up.

Mercifully lacking any of the usual bad news conveyed by your typical lawyer's letter, inside was instead a very nice note from this Mr. Plunkett, Esquire, complimenting us on a tribute we had broadcast over the radio airwaves. He called it a "eulogy."

Now as I do not like to do eulogies or even think about them, I quickly deposited the compliment in our very thin "nice letters" file, which in bulk, depth, and volume, pales in comparison to our "not so nice letters" file, which after some fifty years is fairly bursting out of the file cabinets.

When he wrote his gracious note some years ago, I'm quite certain William Plunkett never anticipated that I would one day take pen in clumsy hand and sit over a pad with lines across it onto which I must now write words and later speak them into a radio microphone about the passing of one Caryl Donnelly Plunkett, who died earlier this week after some seventy years as the matriarch of a powerful and influential New York and Connecticut family. She was his wife, this Caryl Donnelly Plunkett.

All of this must be told on this particular radio station because Caryl and her husband, Bill Plunkett, barrister, lived together for many years in Tarrytown, in Sleepy Hollow country, where they were neighbors of the Rockefellers and patrons of Historic Hudson Valley and Phelps Hospital.

Our colleagues in the public press and especially our friends at *Page Six* always refer to Caryl Donnelly's surviving husband, Bill, as a "power broker" and "king-maker." On the morning after the worst night of his life, when Mario Cuomo lost to George Pataki, Mario Cuomo was on the phone saying, "Do you know the Plunketts?"

Plunkett, you see, took a law firm once called Plunkett & Jaffe and built it into a legal and lobbying powerhouse with lines into the Executive Mansion and the New York State legislature in Albany. This occurred when one of his junior partners, George Elmer Pataki, became governor and another partner—the estimable John Cahill—started thinking about running for attorney general. It was also at this time that a daughter of Caryl Donnelly and William Plunkett advised governors of Connecticut on judgeships. One of the firm's clients owns a big chunk of Ground Zero real estate, and their children are making their mark in law enforcement, real estate, and high finance. And a son-in-law who practically ran the Justice Department in Washington may one day be a governor of Connecticut. But this is about Caryl Donnelly Plunkett, who left us just before the current sad September weekend.

And if you lay the appellation "power broker" on her famous husband you have to also acknowledge that Miss Donnelly was very much The Power behind the kingmaker. They especially know of her standing and stature up in the Litchfield Hills of Connecticut where this amazing Caryl Plunkett was identified as one of the fabled Donnelly girls of Bantam Lake, where the Plunketts summered each year before life turned sad and difficult as she battled the cancer that took her a few days ago.

A man named Jim Lamond walked out of Murphy's Pharmacy this morning with his fancy dog and the daily newspapers with tears in his eyes after being told of Caryl Donnelly's passing. And Mark Murphy, an affable, gregarious Townie who, with his sister Marla runs this old-fashioned family drugstore, went suddenly silent. And Father Robert Tucker, the charismatic, most colorful pastor of Saint Anthony's, the Roman Catholic church in the little town, was on the phone requesting prayers for Mrs. Plunkett. In his most direct manner and completely typical way, the priest Tucker even directed an Irish broadcaster to weigh in with prayers.

"Look ... I'm desperate ... I've even got to ask *you*, O'Shaughnessy. This was a special person. Start praying." As Tucker is a "Three Hail Marys for a homicide" priest and known in these parts as "The *God-*

Father," I quickly mumbled some prayers, for all the good they will do.

Timothy Dolan, the Cardinal Archbishop of New York, will have more to say and do it much more artfully and gracefully than I am able at 1:30 Monday in the Cathedral of Saint Patrick in New York City.

It is almost certain he will speak of her influence "behind the scenes." I know preachers have spoken for years about women who were "powers behind the throne." They struggle to find a way to exalt and memorialize a woman's standing and stature in marriages and in our midst. They do this with many words and elegant paragraphs. I don't struggle with this refrain. I have just two words to sum up the category: Caryl Plunkett.

A woman of my acquaintance from another robust, well-founded Westchester family once expressed to Caryl Donnelly bewilderment that the Plunkett offspring got along in such harmonious fashion and without any rivalry among their siblings. As the woman was of a tribe of brawlers and intriguers given to constant internecine warfare among brothers and sisters, she was quite astonished by the reply, "Well ... *we* just wouldn't *allow* them *not* to get along," using the royal *we*, which meant "*I* just wouldn't permit it." Miss Donnelly was pretty clear about things.

Cardinal Dolan will also speak to those assembled of the clout of the Plunkett family and of Caryl's personal dynamism, energy, effervescence, and radiance. *Radiant* is a good word for her. And radiant she was in every season. And Timothy Dolan will then look out in the great cathedral on Fifth Avenue and acknowledge her generosity of purse *and* spirit and recite how much she did for Catholic charities, hospitals, religious orders, and high schools in his care and keeping. This will take some time.

One can expect His Eminence will also speak of Miss Donnelly-Plunkett's bravery and courage as she checked in and out of hospitals all up and down the East Coast as she refused to yield to the killer that pursued her for almost ten years. At the Sloan Kettering hospital, where they daily battle this lethal stuff, she was known as "Lazarus." The priest Dolan, who slipped into Sloan Kettering earlier this week without staff and miter or the trappings of his high Roman office to whisper prayers into Caryl Plunkett's ear, won't have to work too hard to get this particular dame into Heaven.

And then, on Tuesday, up in Litchfield, the aforementioned old country priest Robert Tucker will say final prayers over the woman as she is laid to rest.

She was a high church lady who presided over a family that rivaled the Maras and Rooneys, and she was a Dame of Malta, the fabled international Catholic charitable organization.

Mrs. Plunkett had homes in Westchester, Connecticut, the Carolinas, and Florida, and she was known on the Sleepy Hollow fairway overlooking the Hudson River. Such disparate types as Paul Tagliabue and Senator Lamar Alexander would take a Plunkett call in every season.

Caryl Donnelly Plunkett leaves two daughters, four sons, a whole posse of grandchildren. And that one husband.

The goodness and marvelous spirit of the woman will inspire them—and all of us—for a good long time.

I hate eulogies ....

September 11, 2015

Philip Roth

Out and About of an Evening by
William O'Shaughnessy

Philip Roth has died. He was eighty-five, tall, trim, an attractive man who carried broad shoulders and a smoldering genius for the English language. And in his eighty-five years he wrote some thirty-two books that caused him to be accused by the *New York Times* of being "a giant of American letters" and "a pre-eminent figure in 20th century literature."

Dwight Garner, the *Times* graceful book critic, who can bang words around pretty good himself, called Roth "*an archwizard whose best books eat into the mind like acid.*"

And Michael Chabon, the prolific American novelist and short story writer, said, "*He was a giant, an artist as versatile and virtuoso as Sinatra and graceful and fireballing as Koufax.*" Philip Roth would have liked that.

I bought and collected a few of his books, but I never read one of them. I much prefer nonfiction, and, as Roth himself once confessed, he did too.

I "*knew*" him mostly through our mutual patronage and affection for the West Street Grill, the estimable country restaurant on the Village Green in tony Litchfield, which has been lovingly operated for almost thirty years by two marvelous and dear souls, Charlie Kafferman and James O'Shea. Philip Roth got there long before I darkened the door of the eatery. For years he was a member-in-good-standing of "The Roundtable," a weekly private luncheon and lemon squeeze featuring the writers William Styron, John Updike, and Arthur Miller and the actor Richard Widmark.

In recent years Roth would dine at The Grill on Sunday nights with Mia Farrow, still a knockout at seventy-three. She would drive over from her Frog Hollow Farm in Bridgewater. And the great writer would journey down from his farmhouse in the woods of Warren, Connecticut.

And on one of these agreeable nights the proprietor Charlie Kafferman, as I was about to sit at table 21, steered me over to the adjacent table #22. My compadre Gregorio Alvarez and I were at table 21.

Here is a snippet of dialogue from that evening:

KAFFERMAN: *"Philip ... Bill writes books too."*

O'SHAUGHNESSY: *"Charlie, don't do this to me. I am not worthy to loose the strap of his sandal ...."*

ROTH: *"I know him, Charlie ... we talk baseball. You know Mia [Farrow]. We thought you were in radio. What kind of books do you write?"*

O'SHAUGHNESSY: *"Anthologies ... but my new one is about Mario Cuomo and our friendship ... I admired him."*

ROTH: *"Well ... so you do anthologies ... about whom? Who do you write about ... ?"*

O'SHAUGHNESSY: *"Oh, New York characters ... Toots Shor ... Nelson Rockefeller ... Sirio Maccioni ... John Lindsay ... Cardinal O'Connor ... characters ...."*

ROTH: *"Oh, I see ... you really write about all your friends!"* (laughter)

Here's another marvelous anecdote that comes out of our favorite restaurant in the Litchfield hills ....

The great writer couldn't count the number or frequency of the literary awards bestowed on him or the encomiums showered on the canon of his prolific works. So one day Roth called his friend Charlie to beg a favor. "Charlie ... I'm being given some big award up in Hartford by the governor and I just don't feel like schlepping up there. Could you 'represent' me and accept on my behalf ...?" So Kafferman and his partner, James O'Shea, journeyed to Hartford to accept the award, a two-foot-tall bronze with outstretched hands in a "winged victory" stance, from the governor's hands and lugged it back to The Grill, where it sits to this day.

But the story doesn't end there. A few weeks later Roth was summoned to Washington to be honored as "America's Greatest Living Novelist" by President Barack Obama.

When Mr. Roth came in for dinner the next week, his friends at the restaurant inquired how the presidential award ceremony went:

"*It went fine ... but when I went up to receive the award ... the president whispered, 'Where's Charlie'?' He was really disappointed when he saw me!*" (Roth swore it was a true story.)

Someone once said he could have been a stand-up comic. When he wasn't out and about of an evening making people laugh, Philip Milton Roth published almost ninety books, including Hispanic and foreign editions of his American classics, among which were *Goodbye, Columbus ... American Pastoral ... Portnoy's Complaint ... My Life as a Man*. And then in 2012 he closed down his computer and put a lid on his genius for all time to come.

"*I was by this time no longer in possession of the mental vitality or the physical fitness needed to mount and sustain a large creative attack of any duration.*" He actually put a Post-it note on his computer: "*The struggle with writing is done.*"

He also said: "*Old age isn't a battle, old age is a massacre.*"

He inveighed against the "diminishments" that assault us as we confront old age. It's a marvelous word often used by Mario Cuomo and Father Pierre Teilhard de Chardin, the brilliant Jesuit philosopher-paleontologist.

And,

"*When I write, I'm alone. It's filled with fear and loneliness and anxiety and I never needed religion to save me.*"

He was a Jew, to be sure. But he hated to be called a "Jewish writer." "*I am an American writer, if nothing else ....*" he once said. And like Mario Cuomo, he was denounced by his own. Mr. Cuomo was criticized and censured by auxiliary bishops. Roth was assailed by influential rabbis.

He was also a self-professed "atheist" who had a deep and abiding distrust of organized religion. But despite his strong feelings on the subject, he was a nice man in every season with an altogether attractive persona who in his eighty-five years entertained millions and made them *think* ... while causing some of us to laugh of an evening at his favorite watering hole.

He left us earlier this week with all those books I never read ... his great good nature ... and that marvelous sense of humor.

May 23, 2018

NOTE

Philip Roth was buried at Bard College in Annandale-on-the-Hudson on Memorial Day, May 28, 2018. Invitations to a reception at the residence of Leon Botstein, longtime president of Bard, went out a few days before the service on the college campus. Charles Kafferman and partner James O'Shea were of course invited. But as their country restaurant was fully booked for the holiday weekend, they had to reluctantly decline. When a torn and conflicted Kafferman told Mia Farrow of his anguish about the decision to stay at their post, she texted: *"Don't worry, Charlie. He won't be there either. And he'd much rather be at The Grill with you guys. Love, Mia."*

I was not worthy to loose the strap of his sandal.

Closing Thoughts

Another
"Thoughts and Prayers" Day

A WVOX Commentary by William O'Shaughnessy,
President and Editorial Director, Whitney Global Media

"Thoughts and prayers." We tote out the phrase and cling to it with a fierceness as we apply it to the victims after every tragedy, every shooting, every bombing. It has become banal, hoary, and hackneyed from overuse.

And so here we are again on a Monday, October 2, 2017, with another "thoughts and prayers" day, which comes at us from a glitzy, hedonist town out in the Nevada desert called Las Vegas, the Baghdad of North America.

It is a place where dentists, deputy sheriffs, plumbers, electrical contractors, doctors, judges, matrimonial lawyers, John Deere dealers, politicians, and even broadcasters and, ahem, gun manufacturers, go each year to get away from their wives. They call this annual rite a "convention," where they meet in high council for a few hours each day before succumbing to all the earthly pleasures of this remarkable city that grew up around a big, broad, sprawling boulevard they call "The Strip."

Slot machines line the concourse leading to and from jet planes parked on the tarmac. And a van advertising a shooting gallery for sawed-off automatic, repeating guns is parked even now outside the vast Las Vegas Convention Center to greet visitors to this lovely city, which once sent Harry Reid to run the entire Congress of the United States.

This time it was several of those automatic weapons that dispatched death and destruction from the 32nd-floor windows of the Mandalay Bay Hotel, spewing it among 22,000 helpless people there assembled for a concert. The said individual behind the weapons with a scrambled-egg mind didn't let up on the trigger as he murdered 59 and wounded almost 550 with one of his beautiful repeating guns that pumped murder into the desert night air.

And on our televisions once again there is praise for the first responders, the police, the doctors and nurses, and calls for an end to all this by banning instruments designed for killing.

They will blame this carnage on the faux and make-believe violence that plays nightly across television screens and in movie theaters. They will also target the politicians and especially President Donald John Trump, who is so hated by the Democrats and the Deep State establishment for trying to do the right thing by the nation he inherited from a well-intended, but ineffective, adjunct college law professor and Chicago community organizer.

This time it was a shooter. But it could have been a bomber or a glassy-eyed deranged driver behind the wheel of a huge careening truck mowing down innocents out for an evening stroll. Banning guns and weapons won't stop it. The guns are already out there ... under mattresses in house trailers and wrapped in towels in five-floor walk-ups in the Bronx, Harlem, and Chicago. And, implausibly, in luxury 32nd-floor hotel suites in Las Vegas. There will be rioting in the streets if we try to take them and damn near a civil war. These hidden guns are everywhere and await only a prompt and a caress from one of life's losers boiling with rage.

And those who want guns only in the hands of law enforcement officers forget it was a former NYPD cop who left his house trailer in New Jersey to murder federal Judge Richard Daronco as he tended a rose bush in his back yard on Monterey Avenue in Pelham here in Westchester just a few years ago. Judge Daronco's name is on our courthouse in White Plains as a reminder.

Call for gun control all you will. But the halls of Congress have no wisdom on the awful dilemma that resides so close to our home as well as in foreign capitals abroad.

And how about the vengeance known as capital punishment, the death penalty, which has never saved one life or prevented one murder? As Hugh Leo Carey and Mario Matthew Cuomo warned us: It diminishes us as a people and makes the state no better than the perpetrator, the killer.

"*60 Minutes*" had a stunning piece Sunday night about the cosmos and the intergalactic world trillions of miles out in space that made us feel small and insignificant, if not in awe of the Creator's magnificent handiwork, all this startling and breathtaking information coming to us courtesy of the revived Hubble Space Telescope.

But on this blood-drenched Monday you can just forget about those planets and stars that exist millions, nay trillions, of miles out in space. For here in this very country, the great United States of America, we are shooting the *bejesus* out of each other.

I wish we had a Mario Cuomo to explain this killing that comes so easily and so often to us and the rage behind it. The holy men from all walks and persuasions will try in the next several days. The Jesuits will advocate for reason while the Franciscans will come at you with love. And the rabbis will recommend that we rebuild the universe and remind us that we are all brothers and sisters. They will use words from the ancient Hebrew like *Tzedekah* and *Tikkun Olam*.

But I'm not sure "thoughts and prayers" work on this stuff. It may help with the fury and force of a hurricane or a tsunami. But not in the roiling, scrambled-egg mind of a madman bursting with loneliness, fury, and hatred.

For once I have no answer ....

October 2, 2017

Something to Believe In

The Broadcasters Foundation of America, Remarks of
William O'Shaughnessy, 2021–2022

I won't intrude for very long on your evening ....

Permit me, please, in the few moments during which I reside in your enlightened care and keeping ... a few thoughts about our tribe ... our profession ... (I wince when they refer to it as an "industry"— some southerners call it an in-*dust*-try) and just a few observations about our trials and tribulations.

I'm also most anxious to tell you about the wonderful work of a national charity—the Broadcasters Foundation of America.

We broadcasters and our colleagues don't have an easy time of it today as we battle the Internet with its constantly intrusive, so-called social media, a changing technical landscape, attacks on content, government control, federal and sometimes even local regulation, consolidation, shifting mores and societal unrest with its cultural upheavals, the changing national political winds, and, most trouble-some of all—the erosion of the precious First Amendment and at-tacks on free speech.

Yet in our best moments, we're still devoted to the people's busi-ness ... especially when we look upon the franchises that reside with us as more than purveyors of passing fancies or disseminators of distraction and entertainment ... instead viewing radio and televi-sion as platforms and forums for the expression of many different viewpoints.

Our profession brings a unique and almost sacred duty to amplify *Vox Populi*, the Voice of the People ... however strident, disagreeable, and sometimes raucous it may be. We were defined by E. B. White, who found that we are "more than a kitchen appliance."

That's what we are.

Platforms. Forums. To amplify the often sweet but sometimes dis-agreeable and unattractive voices in our communities.

That's our legacy ....

As envisioned and dreamed by William S. Paley ... David and Robert Sarnoff ... Leonard Goldenson ... Ward Quaal ... Rush Limbaugh ... William B. Williams ... Howard Stern ... Scott Shannon ... Chris Ruddy ... Edward R. Murrow ... Joe Amaturo ... Stan Hubbard ... Lowell Thomas ... Walter Cronkite ... Marty Pompadur ... Lowry Mays ... Martin Stone ... Lee de Forest ... Edwin Armstrong ... Dan Rather ... Phil Lombardo ... Ed McLaughlin ... Stu Olds ... Kerby Confer ... Rupert Murdoch ... Scott Herman ... Dan Mason ... Perry Sook ... Joseph Field ... George Beasley ... Richard Dimes Buckley ... Dick Robinson ... Jeff Smulyan ... Ralph Guild ... Mac Tichenor ... all of them pioneers and visionaries, and one of our founding fathers, H. V. Kaltenborn, who many years ago conjured up the Broadcast Pioneers. Legends and pioneers, every one of them. Assisted as well by those wise seers and keepers of our tribe: the essential Sol and Larry Taishoff ... Bob Bennett ... Harry Jessell ... my old friends John J. O'Connor and Jack Gould of the *Times*, Eric Rhoads, Deborah Parenti, Rob Dumke and Ed Ryan, Les Brown, Jay Mitchell and Jack O'Brian of the old *Journal-American* of sainted memory.

And we salute and remember those thousands of disc jockeys who each morning drag themselves into lonely studios to strap on their headphones by the cold light of early dawn in rural, remote studios to dispense vital community news and information.

And despite the hardships and roiling competitive weather, we enjoy all our privileges and prerogatives and our elevated status in our communities.

We are broadcasters.

Television and those who labor behind the camera and anchor remotes have been with us since 1930 ... but we've been at it since 1920, when KDKA took to the air in Pittsburgh.

We've been around for one hundred years, a century. We're centurions, you might say ... the airwaves' soldiers of truth, liberty, and *access* for all. And later we became centurions, too, like those in the Bible, bringers of good ... restorers of health.

Then, thank God, in our profession there appeared over the years a unique, national charity: the Broadcasters Foundation of America.

We take care of *our own*.

It is the latest, most glorious and stunning expression of our caring, concern, and innate generosity.

Previously if someone mentioned "broadcasters," the instant Pavlovian reaction was to summon up a hippy-dippy, finger-snapping, "Rodney Radio" disc jockey. Or a glib, smiling advertising salesman armed with ratings, cost per thousands, and ROI's. And our television brethren had their perpetually grinning game show hosts and impresarios broken up by occasional depictions of violence and degradation.

But...

But through it all we've always been looking for something or some*one* bigger than we are.

Something more beautiful than the marketplace and its competition.

Something that when we find it, we can say "This is *right* ...."

"This is *good*."

This is something I can *believe* in with passion.

Something we can throw our arms around and wrap our souls around.

This is something I can hold on to and glue myself to.

And when we've found it, we can say, "Eureka!"

Something larger than myself!

Something beautiful!

Something bigger and better than I am!

And no dispute. No equivocation about it.

That something is the Broadcasters Foundation of America ... and our Guardian Fund that might even seem a bit heroic for those in our *family* whose troubled lives are buoyed, however small or large the swell, by the munificence of the Foundation ... and by those *broadcasters* who dip into their own pockets year after year to help.

And so we are able to assist those lonely, hurting, almost forgotten, often desperate souls—all of them colleagues, from the past ... or right before us, in the present.

They are of us.

And ours.

Most of them, not at all famous or well known.

Many of them sidemen in orchestras long dispersed.

Backup players in supporting casts who work on the other side of the camera or microphone. Or in offices surrounded by the clatter of business machines.

But they too are ... broadcasters.

And they are *ours*.

Not all of them so blessed or successful as some like Rush, Oprah, or Imus.

Many are battling illnesses, struggling to breathe, attempting to walk across a room, go to the bathroom, to maintain their balance, unable to afford food, rent, or medicine to ward off their diminishments and constant pain.

Struggling to stay alive while fighting off the aftermath and debilitating, lingering thumbprints of a stroke or a slowly fading mind while dealing with a cancer or cardiac diagnosis that they must confront, many of them, alone.

All of it, as we have learned, often without government assistance of any kind.

They are out there. They exist. All across the country.

Members — past and present — of our own tribe, struggling to live, trying to just go on, dreaming of time with their grandchildren.

And waiting for another Spring. Longing for an eternal summer that shall never fade.

Many of them have also had to confront natural disasters which caused all their possessions, memories, and memorabilia to be swept away in raging floods, wildfires, devastating earthquakes ... and a cruel pandemic.

And then ...

Then comes the Broadcasters Foundation of America ... and the Guardian Fund. Like the cavalry ... like Gary Cooper or the Duke, John Wayne, appearing on the ridgeline atop a proud steed, white hat shining like a beacon of hope.

It is our Eureka moment!

Something good.

Something bigger than we are.

It is a noble work ... a glorious mission known to those many hundreds of dear and generous broadcasters who support the Foundation to take care of their own.

Eureka!

A final word as I mercifully yield.

Broadcasters have had a lot of gifted and lyrical commentators who have inspired us, like Lowell Thomas, Paul Harvey, Ed Murrow, Charles Osgood, Charles Kuralt, my friend Dan Rather, and H. V. Kaltenborn, our founder of the Broadcast Pioneers, which gave birth to our beloved Foundation. But I also often wish we had an E. B. White behind the microphone in our stable.

Mr. White, a print guy, wrote for the old United Press, *The New Yorker*, and some West Coast newspapers and even did several children's books, including *Charlotte's Web*. White, ever the craftsman, also edited and updated *The Elements of Style*, the essential handbook for writers of the English language.

E. B. White would have been greatly taken, I believe, with our work and would have found the mission of the Foundation is to our profession what the church spire is to the village—"the visible symbol of aspiration and faith, the white plume saying the way is *up*."

He also, I suggest, might admiringly observe that the Foundation is like poetry in that it compresses all life "into a small island and adds music" and the accompaniment of generous hearts that produce desperately needed philanthropy.

We are all too aware that our profession has changed in tempo and in temper ... but still remains viable and relevant for loving instincts and caring for one another.

We don't need a large intellect, moral urgency, or scholastic intensity to understand and subscribe to the unique work and mission of the Broadcasters Foundation of America.

It's all about generosity in our own profession (you'll notice I still refuse the word *industry*). Most of our colleagues have a becoming instinct for philanthropy, which had fallen out of fashion with some who fled from the lovely instinct to put something back in account for all the privileges and prerogatives that accrue to them as broadcasters.

Thank you for letting me rattle on ....

WO Responds to a Facebook Query
"WHO IS THE MOST FAMOUS PERSON YOU HAVE EVER SPOKEN TO?"

Mario Cuomo, Stan Musial, Nelson Rockefeller, William S. Paley, John Hay "Jock" Whitney, Daniel Patrick Moynihan, Bobby Kennedy, Jacob K. Javits, Jinx Falkenberg, Shipwreck Kelly, Jimmy Breslin, Philip Roth, Larry King, Richard Rodney Bennett, Walter Nelson Thayer, Gabby Hayes, Gerald Ford, Donald Trump, Tony Bennett, Francis Albert Sinatra, Henry Kissinger, Sirio Maccioni, Frank Gifford, William B. Williams, Jim Lowe, Cardinals Dolan and O'Connor and O'Brien and Egan, Tony Federici, Gianni Russo, Archbishop Henry Mansell, Monsignor Robert Tucker, Happy Rockefeller, Gregorio Alvarez, Wellington Mara, Rosemary Clooney, George Clooney, Mel Tormé, Matilda Raffa Cuomo, Andrew Mark Cuomo, Chris Cuomo, Maria Cuomo Cole, Kenneth Cole, Oscar de la Renta, Charlie Rose, Wendy Vanderbilt, Fred Astaire, John Van Buren Sullivan, Phil Lombardo, William "Billy" Bush, Cindy Adams, Dan Rather, Mark Simone, Ogden Rogers Reid, George Latimer, Edwin Gilbert Michaelian, Tim Russert, Tim Rooney, Murray Richman, Lionel Michael LeBron, Rush Hudson Limbaugh III, Andrea Bocelli, Alvin Richard Ruskin, Bill Bratton, Jeanine Pirro, Jonathan Bush, George H.W. Bush, Barbara Taylor Bradford, Emily Smith, Steve Cuozzo, Richard Neal Travis, Walter Cronkite, Brian Williams, Eric Shawn, Ernie Anastos, Dr. Mehmet Oz, Kevin Barry McGrath, Bill Clinton, Hillary Rodham Clinton, Michael J. Fox, Malcolm Wilson, Giorgio Chinaglia, Ossie Davis, Ruby Dee, Reverend Al Sharpton, Reverend W. Franklyn Richardson, Ralph Branca, John Branca, Deborah Norville, George Stephanopolous, Bill Butcher, Nancy Q. Keefe, Milton Hoffman, Sheila Nevins, Herman Geist, Barbara Walters, Scott Shannon, Gay Talese, Ken Auletta, Sam Roberts, "Punch" Sulzberger, John Sterling, Ward Quaal, Bob Grant, Page Morton Black, Lowry Mays, Stan Hubbard, Joe Amaturo, Doug Clement, Tracey O'Shaughnessy,

Tom Mullen, Joe Valeant, Mac Tichenor, A. J. Parkinson, Leonard Lauren, Jerry Lauren, Bill Modell, Shelby Modell, Bruce J. White, Fred Klestine, C. Glover Delaney, Harry Novik, Nick D'Arienzo, Leonard Riggio, Liz Smith, David Donovan, John Kelly, Fred Dicker, Alan Chartock, Bill Clark, Bill McElveen, Don Rickles, Roger Ailes, Sean Connery, Robert Merrill, Judge Judy Sheindlin, Sean Driscoll, Jackie Neary, Jack Welch, Whitney Moore Young, Joyce Hergenhan, Regis Philbin, Sol Taishoff, Larry Taishoff, Capt. Rob Taishoff, Polly Bergen, Martin Stone, Harry Thayer, Bernard Curry Jr., Jerry Speyer, Rob Speyer, Steve Roth, Arthur Hill Diedrick, Julian Niccolini, Alex Von Bidder, James Anthony O'Shea, Charlie Kafferman, James A. Farley, John Templeton, John F. Kennedy Jr., Gene McGrath, Dick Gregory, Perry Duryea, Nick Pileggi, David Patrick Columbia, Arrigo Cipriani, Bonifacio Brass, Adam Tihany, Natale Rusconi, James Sherwood, Frank Bowling, Pete Kreindler, Jerry Burns, Fred Nachbaur, Louis Armstrong, Sy Syms, Walter Isaacson, Walter Curley, Edward Elliot Elson, Charles Gargano, Walter Anderson, Bill Fanning, Ed Hughes, Brother Jack Driscoll, Angelo Martinelli, Phil Reisman, Jacques Lesourd, Mabel Mercer, Father Joe Cavoto OFM, Father Michael Carnevale OFM, Father Kevin Mackin OFM, George E. Pataki, John Cahill, Bill Mulrow, Steve Cohen, Michael DelGiudice, Msgr. Charles Kavanagh, Terry Golway, Bishop James McCarthy, Joe Spinelli, Peter Mintun, Judge Paul Crotty, Richard Berman, Milton Mollen, Jed Rakoff, Alan Scheinkman, Patrick Maines, Floyd Abrams, Bishop Emeritus Howard Hubbard, Robert J. Milano, Bill Eimicke, Carl T. Hayden, Msgr. Terry Attridge, Caryl Plunkett, William Plunkett, Ryan Plunkett, Kathleen O'Connor, Kevin O'Connor, Bob Abplanalp, Bob Giuffra, Evan Davis, Joe Percoco, Joseph Wood Canzeri, Brother Darby Ruane, Arthur "Jerry" Kremer, Daryl Sherman, Cartha "Deke" DeLoach, Brian Lamb, Robert Rosencrans, Marty Glickman, Charles Dolan, Lou Borrelli, Billy DeLuca, Frank Trotta, Nick Trotta, Dominic Procopio, Marsha Gordon, Kylie and Louis Cappelli, Joe Cohen, Allison Ake Fulton, Pat Adducci, Joe Napolitano, Mary Lou Whitney, Herb Schlosser, Tom Rogers, Jack O'Brian, Roy Cohn, General of the Armies Omar Bradley, General Alfred M. Gray, Jay Mitchell, Michael Dandry, Christopher Reeve, Jim Campbell, John

Ianuzzi, Richard Berlin, Honey Berlin, Joe Sitrick, Phil Gilbert Jr., Harold Seagal, John Donnelly, William Randolph Hearst Jr., Nelson Doubleday, Gavin K. McBain, Gardner "Mike" Cowles, Bucky Dent, Volney "Turkey" Righter, Lionel Van Deerlin, Joan Rivers ....

Funeral Mass for
William O'Shaughnessy

St. Anthony of Padua, Litchfield, Connecticut,
June 1, 2022

HON. ANDREW CUOMO

To the O'Shaughnessy family, Kate, David, Matthew, Bill's grandchildren, Tucker, Isabel, Flynn, Lily, and Amelia, we feel for you and your loss and we hope you find peace.

To Cindy Gallagher, who made all the good things happen. Thank you for what you did for Bill and for all of us who loved him.

I'm sure it will surprise no one here to know that Bill literally planned his own funeral—telling Cindy, Kate, and David exactly how to implement his vision.

He actually called me just the other day and asked if I would speak at the funeral. I said there was not going to be a funeral but was tempted to ask him what he would want me to say if indeed there was a funeral. I thought the better of it because I was afraid he would tell me to draft something and send it over for his review. Bill was a much better writer than I am.

They say great men often have complicated journeys in life, and that is true for Bill O'Shaughnessy.

Brother Bill, as my father and I called him, was from Elmira, New York; his mother was a prison guard and his father was for the most part absent. Bill truly came up the hard way. He had no advantages, no one to mentor him or help him up the ladder.

Bill graduated from Canisius High School but was never able to attend college—although you would never know it. And I suspect that is just the way Bill wanted it.

In some ways Bill traveled as far from Elmira as his talent and energy would take him, and in some ways he never left.

Bill was a New York icon. He reveled in New York City, its highlife, its glamour, its culture, its arts, its superlatives. Le Cirque and the "21" Club, the Waldorf, the Café at the Carlisle, the grand events, the eccentricities that make New York City glitter. He enjoyed it all and he fit right in; in fact, he was a natural.

Bill cut a stunning figure. His presence filled the room, and his mannerisms and eloquence were enthralling. Tall, debonaire, handsome, even dashing. Bill always looked like he stepped off the cover of a magazine. And of course, that incredible flowing white mane, which only seemed to get thicker and more luxuriant as he aged. The O'Shaughnessy Crown. It was intimidating. I am sure many men here had hair envy.

I once said to Bill that I didn't believe his hair was real. I said I thought it was an elaborate hair weave done at a fancy Manhattan boutique. Bill did not rise to the bait but was not to be outdone either. Bill simply smiled and said, "Impossible, my son, this could only be a gift from God."

Bill's lion-like mane was matched by a magnificent smile, broad and bright and ever present. I never asked but I think God also gifted Bill with more than the thirty-two teeth given the rest of us.

Bill was always dressed to impress and always elegant down to his famous magnificent loafers, often embroidered, rarely worn with socks. Many of us enjoyed teasing Bill about the socks, or lack thereof. Bill enjoyed the teasing. Bill knew he was making a statement. Yes, it was eccentric, and he knew it. I think it was a wink and a nod by Bill to let you know he did things a little differently. He was not bound by convention. He did things his way. He was one of one.

He was a character in the best sense of the word.

In a world that is programmed to ask why, Bill O'Shaughnessy asked why not.

Bill reached the top echelons of political power and was proud of it. His license plate was O. Not OH, just the letter O. He loved the bells and whistles and lights and sirens. He liked seeing people and he liked to be seen.

He called himself a Rockefeller Republican and enjoyed a close relationship with Nelson Rockefeller. He was friends with President Trump. And he truly enjoyed a special bond with my father.

A boy from Elmira and a boy from South Jamaica, who both made good.

My father and Bill shared a passion for the art of writing and the use of language. They enjoyed the craftsmanship and beauty of a piece well written. They would compare their work much as two painters would stand back and compare portraits. They had a mutual admiration club. Bill was a prolific writer with a natural talent. He wrote six books and was an expert on the First Amendment.

And in my father Bill appreciated the power of language not only as an art form but for its ability to move people, move people not only to emotion, but to action.

One of my last conversations with Bill was after the Buffalo and Texas shootings, and he was focused on writings and speeches that could motivate people to lobby for government action on the gun issue.

Bill's professional love, of course, was broadcasting. WVOX and WVIP are paragons of community broadcasting. Airwaves providing a forum for civic discourse. "Vox populi" ... the voice of the people. The essence of democracy. Bill knew Westchester, its towns and villages, struggles and opportunities, like no one else. He knew the personalities and the relationships. He also knew the gossip.

Bill was a true broadcasting talent. His sharp mind and resonant, melodic, accentuated voice were made for radio. Or maybe radio was made for Bill. His commentaries and editorials were always well reasoned and provocative.

And if by chance you missed the editorial on the radio show, Bill would make sure you were mailed a copy, or two, or three.

Bill was dedicated to broadcasting, serving as head of the New York State Broadcasters Association and working with professional associations all his life.

But most of all Bill just loved being on the radio. The radio station was the Town Hall and Bill was the mayor. Even more, the station was the theater, and he was the star performer. He loved the microphone and the microphone loved him.

David has now been managing the stations and carrying the legacy forward and doing a great job, making his father proud.

Yes, in many ways Bill traveled far from Elmira, but as the old saying may have been, you can take the boy out of Elmira but you can't take Elmira out of the boy.

As much as Bill enjoyed the city lights, he was still a small-town boy at heart. He saw himself living in a town celebrating the locals and the intimacy of a small community. He loved Litchfield, its history, charm, and people.

The struggle of Bill's early life never left him and drove a deep sense of compassion. Bill had achieved power and influence, but he was very aware of how different life can be. Bill always had a soft spot for the underdog, the little guy, the powerless and the voiceless. He was a champion for the left out and the left behind.

He would go to extraordinary lengths to help people. His philanthropy and charity were of the highest form: anonymous. Only now do we hear stories of the many people Bill helped. He would help gardeners with immigration issues, young people who needed help getting into college, low-income workers who needed help with medical bills, the Middle Eastern fruit vendor who was going to be deported after 9/11. He helped waiters find jobs when their restaurants closed.

At his core Bill was a gentle, charitable, loving soul.

He helped people down on their luck. He didn't judge. He was skeptical of judgment by others and even cynical about those who deemed themselves worthy of sitting in judgment. He believed that we are all flawed beings in need of forgiveness and redemption. He lived by the words of Matthew 7:1, "Judge not, lest ye be judged." And of John 8:7, "Let he without sin cast the first stone."

I watched his relationship with my mother and especially my sister Maria. They would talk frequently about family and friends, and who was struggling and whom they could help.

My father used to say that at the end of the day the measure of a life well spent is simple. Is the world a better place because of our time on this Earth? Bill challenged us to view life through a different lens and to appreciate a myriad of perspectives, loves, and lifestyles. Bill O'Shaughnessy made this place a better place, a sweeter, kinder, more generous, more accepting place, and he did it with a charm and a flair that leaves us all with a smile. That, my friends, is a life well lived. That is Bill O'Shaughnessy.

KATE O'SHAUGHNESSY NULTY

I just want to take this in for a moment because he would love every minute of this day ... and yesterday. He loved all of you so much. And I know how much you all loved him. I'm going to read a poem to you ... but before I do I just wanted to say that if you are a person who was a recipient of my father's goodness, kindness, help, or generosity, I hope in honor of his legacy that you will take that forward and help others. That is a gift that you can give to him and my family. In the last couple of months of his life when he had more time, we talked — almost every day — multiple times a day. I'm a social worker, and every day he would ask me, "How many people did you help today, Katie?" I would tell him five ... seven ... eight. He said to keep helping people. And that is what I would say to everyone here ... keep helping people.

This is a poem that Madeline Cuomo shared with me. Her father read it at his mother's funeral and it moved me very deeply so I wanted to share it with you. It's called *Gone from My Sight*.

I am standing upon the seashore.

A ship at my side spreads his white sails to the morning breeze and starts for the blue ocean.

He is an object of beauty and strength, and I stand and watch him until he hangs like a speck of white cloud just where the sea and sky come down to mingle with each other.

Then someone at my side says: "There he goes!"

Gone where? Gone from my sight — that is all.

He is just as large in mast and hull and spar as he was when he left my side, and just as able to bear his load of living freight to the place of destination.

His diminished size is in me, and not in him.

And just at that moment when someone at my side says: "There he goes!"

There are other eyes that are watching for him coming; and other voices ready to take up the glad shout: "Here he comes!"

MONSIGNOR ROBERT TUCKER

The word *imprint* means to leave a mark or an impression that will indeed make a difference. We come because, indeed, Bill O'Shaughnessy has left that mark in all of you, and in Gregorio, and in his sons and daughter, family and friends. And of those of you who aren't aware, if you look around, at least from this area, everybody who runs a restaurant and all the politicians are here too.

So the mark was left on all kinds of people. And we are very grateful to the people from WVOX and others who have given him so much support, love, and nurturing in the past months. You and his family have always been there. And that's the great gift of love. Death leaves a heartache that we can't heal ... but love gives memories that no one can ever steal. And those memories are what is important as you try to sit back—remember them ... share them and keep them going. Those are the ways that our hearts are so touched and it's not so much what type of man he was because indeed, yes, he was an author ... he was a radio broadcaster ... he was flamboyant. He always seemed to be oversized whenever you saw him ... between the white hair and the blue jacket, and I always wanted to steal the ring. That's the only thing I felt it would be great to own, that ring, because I don't know of any bishop or cardinal with a ring as big as that (Yankees World Series ring) and I thought it would be fun some Sunday at the door to get the whole damned town of Litchfield to bend down and kiss that ring! I always felt what a stunning, stunning thing it was and stood out so well. That was a mark of who he was in a sense.

The thing I was amazed at by reading the obituary ... he never told me this ... but of course he was older than I, but not by many years. We both carried the same name ... his mother was a Tucker. And he suffered with me as Tucker for over twenty years here. He never mentioned that and he never mentioned that Tucker was in the family.

That whole idea of quietly being who he was in love and generosity ... and a very vivid person. There was no hiding about him at all.

There wouldn't be a chance of this story being true concerning Bill O'Shaughnessy.... A priest was walking down the aisle. All of a sudden he realized he didn't have his little card. He couldn't remember the name or the sex of the person in the casket! So he said, "I'll ask the mortician." The mortician wasn't there; it was just a young pallbearer and he looked at the pallbearer and said, "Who is it?"; he said, "My cousin!" You're all rather slow, it must be the New Yorkers ... that doesn't help the priest in any way ... it's OK. The whole idea of anyone who knew Bill or anyone who loved and appreciated the great gift that he was ... he left that imprint. He was not only for all of us ... and such Irish charm, which could almost kill you at times.

We talked about that Irish charm ... and I always wanted to do something as a priest and never had enough courage, and finally after fifty some-odd years I had enough courage. In the last couple of weeks, I went to see Bill many times and heard his confession and anointed him and everything. He called and he said last week, "I'd like you to come by one more time." And I said, "I will," and I said, "You know ... Jesus was a much smarter man than most of us ... what did he do? He had the Last Supper." He said, "Yes," and I said to the family, "We're going to have a cocktail party at quarter of five! And we're going to have margaritas. Get him out of bed ... get him dressed and we'll have a Last Supper that he won't forget! And that you won't forget!" And indeed we did ... he got the Lord and the Last Supper right there in his own home.

That's what he would really like all of us to do. To be able to go forth from here—to love ... to celebrate ... not to worry about the name but to vividly give the best that we are. The smile, the generosity ... all that we've heard so far, and more importantly the Irish charm of giving one's best to everyone each day.

FATHER CHRISTOPHER MONTURO

Thirty-two years ago I met ... or got to know ... Bill O'Shaughnessy as an eighteen-year-old student at Iona College. In the course of my studies, one of my professors who is a communications professor said to me after class one day, "Chris ... you've got to get into broadcasting!" And I said never ... I said, "I have the worst voice in the world and I look horrible," and I said, "No way!" And she said, "No ... no ...

you must think about it. I have contacts at WVOX in New Rochelle and I have contacts at WABC and WCBS in New York—television and radio. Think about it." I never entertained it. And yet I saw Bill all the time on campus, he was always the man about town—the Georgie Jessel of toastmasters and always, always the life of every party.

And years later—six-and-a-half years ago—[I was] the guest on someone else's program at WVOX in New Rochelle and as I was leaving I saw Mr. O' sitting at the desk in the office there and I said, "Before I leave I better go in and say hello" ... he doesn't know me but I've known him all these years. And so I walked in and I said, "Hello, Mr. O'Shaughnessy" ... and he said, "Who is this handsome young priest?" And I immediately looked behind me to see if another priest had come in! And he laughed. And he said, "No ... you, who are you?" I told him who I was ... Father Chris Monturo ... and told him where I was the pastor at the time, and that began an hour-long conversation and we came to learn that we had so many of the same friends, so many of the same interests, and at the end of that hour he said to me, "Father Chris, I need you on the radio!" I said, "Well, what do you have in mind?" and he said, "No ... what do I have in mind, what do you have in mind?" I said, "Nothing!" And he said to Don Stevens ... "Come over here and find an hour that is agreeable for Father Chris so we can give him a program." And that began six-and-a-half years of a great friendship with Bill O'Shaughnessy.

In the course of those years, we had many, many wonderful conversations, and of course Bill loved to write in superlatives and many times he said to me ... "Why haven't they made you a bishop or even a cardinal yet?" I said, "Bill ... I'm having such a good time, please don't mess it up!" I said, "I love being a priest," but I'm sure that all of you, every one of us who are here, all feel the same way. He made me feel special. He made every one of us feel special. It's why we fill this church, and yesterday the funeral home was overflowing. It's why we share so many happy memories of him. Governor Cuomo and Monsignor Tucker have spoken so beautifully and so personally of him. And I'm happy to be able to say a few words today as well.

A few years ago I said to Bill one day after a broadcast ... I said, "I was given the greatest public speaking advice ever." He said, "What is that, Father Chris?" I was told to stand up straight so they could see you ... speak loud so they can hear you and speak briefly so they could love you!

So I'll end by simply saying, Bill after all these wonderful years, after so many you've helped, after so many charitable works and so much generosity to so many ... go now and amplify the voice of the angels in Heaven forever.

DON STEVENS

President and General Manager, WVOX Radio
WVOX Re-broadcast of Funeral Mass

The funeral Mass came to a close. We all disassembled out of the church onto the front lawn there of St. Anthony of Padua Church in Litchfield County and on what had been an overcast morning ... we looked up at the sky, and for a brief time the clouds seemed to part and the sun shone down on all of us and Mr. O'Shaughnessy.

We all then got into our cars and the motorcade went down the street past Mr. O'Shaughnessy's home in Litchfield, which he loved so much, and then we went to his final resting place at St. Anthony Cemetery, which has become the final resting place of so many friends of Mr. O'Shaughnessy's over the years as well. So he was with company.

I think for a lot of us ... that is where we tended to break down. Because we knew that was the last time we were going to see him and say goodbye to him.

After the cemetery, we all got into our cars and went to the Torrington Country Club, a place that Mr. O'Shaughnessy loved very much and he frequented many a weekend. And we went to bond with many of his Litchfield neighbors who loved him so much.

You see, he had the benefit of having so many people in his life. His broadcasting colleagues, his people here in New Rochelle, which he called home still, and then the last twenty years his community of Litchfield County in Connecticut and his neighbors there who embraced him as he embraced that community as well.

So we got to meet some of them, and a lot of them we knew but we got to bond with them again. And it was a lovely afternoon.

We had a delicious lunch. The menu, of course, was chosen by Mr. O'Shaughnessy. Would you expect anything else?

And at the end of the day, we got into our cars and we left. And so that comes to the end of one chapter and the beginning of another chapter. But we have to keep the legacy of Mr. O'Shaughnessy and we all need to do that. Not just the O'Shaughnessy family. Not just us here at wvox ... all of you listeners and callers. We have to honor the mission that Mr. O'Shaughnessy believed in so well, and that is defending the First Amendment and keeping free speech alive. wvox will continue. This was his baby. His beloved wvox. And his helping people. That is something we have to continue as well.

Last week the wonderful tribute that we did on Tuesday for six hours, where so many of you called in and shared your thoughts and people stopped by and it was so wonderful. I will remember that and the visitation at Lloyd Maxcy where a lot of you came to pay your last respects to Mr. O'Shaughnessy. Finally the funeral Mass. That beautiful funeral Mass on Wednesday at St. Anthony of Padua Church in Litchfield.

All such wonderful events. But the thing that I'm going to remember the most is that motorcade. Going back to that motorcade ... from here in New Rochelle all the way to Litchfield to the church. Closing down parts of the Hutchinson River Parkway ... I've never seen anything like it!

And I could only imagine the hundreds of people on the sidelines watching this motorcade go by from here to Connecticut bringing this remarkable man, this man who helped so many people ... this champion of free speech ... this radio legend, a radio mogul ... this boy from Elmira who lived in New Rochelle and called it his home and finally called his second home Litchfield, Connecticut.

I just wonder if they thought in their minds who is this guy? And if I were next to them, I would have turned to say, "Oh, that guy ... his name was Bill O'Shaughnessy, and he was a Townie!"

INDEX

Jobs, Steve, 165
Joel, Billy, 167
John Paul II, Pope, 218–19
Johnson, Lyndon, 54, 156, 247
Johnson, Robin, 245
Jordan, Vernon, 38
Joyce family, 111

Kafferman, Charlie, 191, 243–46, 255–56, 258, 270
Kaltenborn, H. V., 265, 268
Katz, David, 173
Kaufman, Elaine, 175
Kavanagh, Charles, 222, 270
Keating, Kenneth, 53
Keefe, Kevin, 159–60
Keefe, Nancy Q., xv, 159–63, 269
Keh, David, 169
Kelly, Dorothy Ann, 112
Kelly, John, xx, 270
Kelly, John S. "Shipwreck," xi, 156, 269
Kempton, Murray, 54
Kendall, Donald, 58–59, 74
Kendall, Irv, xv
Kendall, Irving, xv, 70–71
Kendig, David, 78
Ken from Pelham (caller), 78
Kennedy, John F., xi, xiii, 10, 19, 49–51, 58
Kennedy, John F., Jr., xi, 247, 270
Kennedy, Robert F., xi, 49, 51, 53, 247, 269
Kennedy, Rose, 128
Kenny, Ann, 36–37
Kern, Jerome, 225
Kerr, Walter, 157
Ketcham, Bill, 205
Kiernan, Doc, 112
Kilgannon, Corey, 180
Kilmer, Joyce, 235
King, Greg, 120
King, Guy, 171
King, Larry, 269
King, Martin Luther, Jr., 58, 149

Kissinger, Henry, xi, 6, 114, 244, 247, 269
Kissinger, Nancy, 245
Kissinger, Sam, 63, 112
Kitchen, Ruth, 52, 112
Kitt, Eartha, 153
Klein, Calvin, 137
Klestine, Fred, 171, 270
Kley, John, 97
Kluge, John, 111
Klugman, Arnie, 112
Koch, Connie, 221
Koch, Sidney, 244
Kornsweet, Jack, 112
Koufax, Sandy, 255
Kowalski, Laura O'Shaughnessy, xx
Kragle, Ralph, xx
Kreindler, Pete, 56, 270
Kremer, Arthur "Jerry," 270
Krim, Seymour, 54
Kuralt, Charles, 164, 268

Lacey (dog), 247–50
Lafayette, Reggie, 71
Laird, Melvin, 9
Lamb, Brian, 270
Lamond, Jim, 252
Landry, Jack, 175
Langan, Tom, 33, 97
Langone, Ken, 173
Lardner, Ring, 63, 81, 124
Larkin, Art, 74
LaSorsa, Frank, 71
Latimer, George, xv, 247, 269
Lauper, Cyndi, 172
Lauren, Jerry, 270
Lauren, Leonard, 270
Lawrence, Clare, xx
Lazzari, Franco, xx, 191
Leal, Ron, 245
Lebron, Michael "Lionel," 171, 269
Lee, Gypsy Rose, 153
Lee, Peggy, 153
Lefkowitz, Louis, 113, 115
Lehrman, Lewis, 78